Secularism, Gender and Middle East

The Egyptian Women's Movement

A considerable literature has been devoted to the study of activism amongst Islamist groups. By contrast, Nadje Al-Ali's book explores the anthropological and political significance of secular-oriented women's activism by focusing on the women's movement in modern Egypt. In so doing it challenges stereotypical images of Arab women as passive victims and demonstrates how they fight for their rights and confront conservative forces. The argument is constructed around interviews with some eighty women activists, who offer fascinating insights into the history of the women's movement in Egypt, the goals and priorities of different groups and individual activists, and how the Egyptian state and Islamist constituencies have impacted on women's activism generally. In this way, the author defines one of the central themes of the book, the reconceptualization of secularism in the Middle East and Muslim world. Another significant contribution of this book is its challenge of prevailing dichotomous constructions of 'the West' versus 'the East'. Here the author proposes to transcend notions of cultures being bounded entities and to acknowledge the entanglements and creative encounters between and within cultures. Throughout the book, the balance between the empirical and conceptual material is adeptly handled. The author frames her work in the context of current theoretical debates in Middle Eastern and post-colonial scholarship and, while some of the ideas are complex, her lucid and engaging style means they are always comprehensible. The book will therefore appeal to students, as well as to scholars in the field.

Nadje Al-Ali is a lecturer in social anthropology at the Institute of Arabic and Islamic Studies, University of Exeter.

Cambridge Middle East Studies 14

Editorial Board
Charles Tripp (general editor)
Julia A. Clancy-Smith   Israel Gershoni   Roger Owen
Judith E. Tucker   Yezid Sayigh

Cambridge Middle East Studies has been established to publish books on the nineteenth- and twentieth-century Middle East and North Africa. The aim of the series is to provide new and original interpretations of aspects of Middle Eastern societies and their histories. To achieve disciplinary diversity, books will be solicited from authors writing in a wide range of fields including history, sociology, anthropology, political science and political economy. The emphasis will be on producing books offering an original approach along theoretical and empirical lines. The series is intended for students and academics, but the more accessible and wide-ranging studies will also appeal to the interested general reader.
A list of books in the series can be found after the index.

Secularism, Gender and the State in the Middle East

The Egyptian Women's Movement

Nadje Al-Ali
University of Exeter

CAMBRIDGE
UNIVERSITY PRESS

PUBLISHED BY THE PRESS SYNDICATE OF THE UNIVERSITY OF CAMBRIDGE
The Pitt Building, Trumpington Street, Cambridge, United Kingdom

CAMBRIDGE UNIVERSITY PRESS
The Edinburgh Building, Cambridge CB2 2RU, UK   http://www.cup.cam.ac.uk
40 West 20th Street, New York, NY 10011-4211, USA   http://www.cup.org
10 Stamford Road, Oakleigh, Melbourne 3166, Australia
Ruiz de Alarcón 13, 28014 Madrid, Spain

First published 2000

Printed in the United Kingdom at the University Press, Cambridge

Typeface Plantin MT 10/13 pt   *System* QuarkXPress™   [SE]

A catalogue record for this book is available from the British Library

ISBN 0 521 78022 5 hardback
ISBN 0 521 78504 9 paperback

For my parents, Dagmar and Sadig Al-Ali

Contents

Acknowledgements

I would like to thank the many people who have helped me in different ways to write this book. I am grateful for the time, patience and trust of all the women I interviewed in Cairo. Without their help this book would not have been possible. I would especially like to thank Amal Abdel-Hadi, Shereen Abu El-Naga, Jihan Abou Zeid, Marie Assaad, Shahida El-Baz, Aida Seif El-Dawla, Aida Gindy, Hoda El-Sadda, Nadia Ramses Farah, Arab Lotfi, Hala Shukrallah and Marlyn Tadros for their encouragement, for sharing their knowledge, their friendship and support.

Several friends in Cairo provided constructive criticism, helpful comments and a support network while I was doing research. I owe a great deal to Yasser Alwan, Anita Fabos, Zein Abdeen Fuad, Barbara and Saad Eddin Ibrahim, Sherif Hetata, Manal Kamal, Cynthia Nelson, Hassan Saber and Moheb Zaki. I am thankful to Nadia Wassef, Aida Seif El-Dawla and Marlyn Tadros for helping me to obtain some 'last-minute' information through e-mail. Nadia was particularly helpful during the final phase of writing the book. I would like to thank MERC (the Middle East Research Centre) for funding my fieldwork in Cairo. I am also grateful to my colleague and friend Heba El-Kholy who shared my ups and downs during the past years in both Cairo and in London and helped me with her knowledge and insight.

In London I was sustained by several friends who reminded me that life consists of more than writing a PhD dissertation book. I am grateful to Amal Al-Mohanna, Tahrir Jasem, Ahmed Nahid, Maureen O'Farrell and Alida Petri. Despite the physical distance, my friend Nadia al-Bagdadi (living in Berlin and later Beirut) remained soul-mate and helped me through difficult times. My partner, Mark Douglas, made sure that the period of writing this book was not a lonely time but filled with happiness. He dealt with my occasional panic and distress with his admirable calmness, solved my various computer problems, cooked me wonderful meals, never showed signs of boredom when I told him about yet another chapter and remained patient, even at times when I was 'always busy writing'. I thank him a lot.

Cynthia Cockburn not only provided me with a wonderful new 'home', but she has also been incredibly supportive and encouraging. Cynthia has taught me a great deal about the ways feminism can actually make a difference in scholarship and in people's lives. I am very grateful for her friendship and thank her for the many helpful comments on my chapters. My thanks also to Nancy Lindisfarne at SOAS for her comments and advice.

I am greatly indebted to my supervisor, Deniz Kandiyoti, who has been a very inspiring, encouraging and generous mentor. She has read the manuscript with great care and her comments have been invaluable. I cannot thank her enough for her guidance and support.

I am grateful to the two anonymous readers from Cambridge University Press for their helpful comments and suggestions. I should also like to thank my copy-editor, Mary Starkey, for her thorough and extremely skilful work. My thanks also to Hoda Lutfi who shared her wonderful artwork with me and provided the cover.

Finally, I would like to express my gratitude to my parents, Dagmar and Sadig Al-Ali. They could not have been more understanding and supportive. This book is dedicated to them with lots of love and thankfulness.

Note on transliteration

Transliteration of Arabic words and phrases generally follows the system adopted by the *International Journal of Middle East Studies*. I have omitted diacritics except for the *hamza* and the *ʿayn*. In order to preserve the Egyptian pronunciation of Arabic and to follow colloquial language, I have replaced the classical *j* sound with *g*.

All Arabic words, except for proper names and standard English forms, are italicized.

Groups, networks and organizations

Independent women's organizations
- Markaz Dirasat Al-Mar'a Al-Gedida (New Woman's Research Centre)
- Rabtat Al-Mar'a Al-'Arabiyya (Alliance of Arab Women)
- Markaz Dirasat Al-Mar'a: Ma'an (Women's Study Centre: Together)
- Gam'at Bint Al-Ard (Daughter of the Land Group in Mansoura)

Development-oriented organizations
- Gama'at Nuhud wa Tanmeyyat Al-Mar'a (Association for the Development and Enhancement of Women (ADEW))
- Markaz Wasa'il Al-Ittissal Al-Mula'ama min agl Al-Tanmeyya (Appropriate Communications Techniques (ACT))

Professional organizations
- Lagnat Al-Mar'a fi Ittihad Al-Mohameen Al-'Arab (Women's Committee of the Arab Lawyers' Union)
- Gama'iyat Al-Katibat Al-Masriyat (Egyptian Women Writers Association)
- Dar Al-Mar'a Al-'Arabiyya Nour (Arab Women Publishing House Nour)
- Gama'iyat Al-Cinemai'yat (Egyptian Women in Film Society)

Human rights organizations
- Markaz Al-Mussa'ada Al-Qanuniyya li Huquq Al-Insan (Centre for Human Rights and Legal Aid (CHRLA))
- Markaz Al-Qahira li Dirasat Huquq Al-Insan (Cairo Institute for Human Rights Studies (CIHRS))
- Markaz Al-Dirasat wa Al-Ma'lumat Al-Qanuniyya li Huquq Al-Insan (Legal Rights and Research Centre (LRRC))

The names provided here do not present a comprehensive list of women's groups and organizations in Egypt. They refer to those groups that were part of the research on which this book is based.

Women's committees affiliated to political parties
- Ittihad Al-Nissa'i Al-Taqadummi (Union for Progressive Women (linked with socialist Tagammu party))
- Lagnat Al-Mar'a fil Hizb Al-Nasseri (Women's Secretariat of the Arab Democratic Nasserist party)

Networks based on specific issues
- FGM (Female Genital Mutilation) Task Force
- Women's Media Watch
- Women and Violence Network

Abbreviations

ACT	Appropriate Communications Techniques
ADEW	Association for the Development and Enhancement of Women
AUC	American University in Cairo
AWSA	Arab Women's Solidarity Association
CAPMAS	Central Agency for Population, Mobilization and Statistics
CEDAW	Convention on the Elimination of all Forms of Discrimination against Women
CHRLA	Centre for Human Rights and Legal Aid
CIAD	Canadian International Arab Development
CIHRS	Cairo Institute for Human Rights Studies
EFU	Egyptian Feminist Movement
FGM	female genital mutilation
GTZ	Gesellschaft für Technische Zusammenheit
ICPD	International Conference on Population and Development
IMF	International Monetary Fund
LCDA	local community development association
LRRC	Legal Rights and Research Centre
MERC	Middle East Research Centre
MERIP	*Middle East Report*
NCPD	National NGO Committee for Population and Development
NGO	non-governmental organization
NPT	nuclear non-proliferation treaty
PVO	private voluntary organization
SOAS	School of Oriental and African Studies
UNICEF	United Nations (International) Children's (Emergency) Fund
USAID	United States Agency for International Development
WAF	Women against Fundamentalism

·

Introduction

The contemporary situation of women in Egypt – who are at the centre of and are reacting to apparently contradictory discourses and interests – is emblematic of tensions and dilemmas characteristic of many post-colonial societies. Inherent in the power struggles and conflicts within these societies are fierce debates about modernization, its relation to westernization and contestations of 'authentic' national culture and traditions. Recent writings within the broad and diverse field of post-colonial studies have documented political contestations linked to processes of decolonization and state-building. They have particularly pointed to the emergence of powerful local elites which tend to reproduce unequal relationships between classes, gender and religious groups (Chatterjee, 1993; Hall, 1996a; hooks, 1990; Kandiyoti, 1991, 1995; Maiello, 1996; Prakash, 1995; Rattansi, 1997; Said, 1993; Spivak, 1988). Caught between the pursuit of modernization, attempts at liberalization, a pervasive nationalist rhetoric of 'authenticity' and ongoing imperialist encroachments, women are often the focus of conflicting and ambiguous interests.

In the Egyptian context, growing Islamist currents have further limited the discursive horizon of the debates and the choices available to women. This holds particularly true for those who are actively engaged in contesting existing gender relations and various forms of inequality and injustice within the hegemonic narrative of 'the Nation'. Egyptian women activists, whose efforts have been historically rooted in nationalism and the struggle against colonial powers, have inevitably run the risk of being stigmatized as anti-nationalist and anti-religious. They have increasingly been accused, particularly by Islamist movements and conservative nationalist forces, of collaborating with western imperialism by importing alien ideas and practices and disseminating them throughout society. These very intimidating weapons have given rise to a specifically Egyptian feminist phobia that has silenced many voices.

By focusing on one specific, yet heterogeneous, segment within post-colonial Egypt, namely secular women's activism, I hope to unravel many of the tensions and conflicts that mark the complex processes of decolonization and continue to affect contemporary political culture. Egyptian women's activism today is very much shaped by the fear of transgressing the norms and values deemed permissible within the national fabric. The question of identity is as central to their activism as concrete struggles over women's rights and aspirations. For secular women activists even more is at stake as their rejection of Islam as the only possible framework for political struggle and nation-building evokes suspicion and doubt about their place within the indigenous landscape of 'traditions' and 'authenticity'.

In this book I attempt to provide a detailed ethnographic account of the context, content and political significance of contemporary Egyptian women's activism. This is mainly achieved through my analysis of interviews with members of women's groups and individual activists. However, it is my argument throughout this work that women's activism cannot be analysed without contextualizing it in the wider political culture in which it takes place. Subsequently, I will explore a range of factors, such as the Egyptian state, Islamist constituencies and the political left, as well as international organizations and agendas which all, in one way or another, have an impact upon the forms, content and discourses of women's activism.

A critique of modernity in the Egyptian context will enable me to examine the traditional–modern and indigenous–western dichotomies which are not only conspicuous in academic writings about women in the Middle East, but also constitute forceful oppositions in the cultural, historical and political discourses within Egypt. In the context of scholarship dealing with Islamist movements, the categorization of 'modern' as opposed to 'traditional' has increasingly come under scrutiny. Despite Islamists' call to return to 'the glorious past', many writers have pointed to the 'modern' and 'modernizing' character of Islamist trends (Al-Azmeh, 1993; Ayubi, 1991; Esposito, 1992; Moghadam, 1993; Munson, 1988; Paidar, 1996; Sayyid, 1997; Zubaida, 1989, 1993). Not surprisingly, the rigid opposition between 'modern' and 'traditional' has proven to be more difficult to challenge with respect to women in the Middle East, but several recent writings reflect this endeavour (Abu-Lughod, 1995b, 1997, 1998b; Badran, 1995; Baron, 1994; Kandiyoti (ed.), 1996; Macleod, 1991; Moghadam, 1993; Nelson, 1996; Paidar, 1996). Perhaps even more difficult to unsettle is the categorization of 'western' versus 'indigenous', which even underlines some of the writings that self-consciously oppose the 'modern' versus 'traditional' dichotomy.

I perceive this book to be as much about unsettling a rigid East–West divide and its implications as it is about secular Egyptian women's activism and the political culture it is embedded in. I shall therefore take issue with essentializing and homogenizing constructions of 'difference' between cultures, which as Partha Chatterjee (1993) so lucidly put it, actually reproduces those perceptions and representations which were originally created by the colonizers. At the same time, I hope to offer a detailed and in-depth ethnographic account of a movement that has often been analysed and categorized in a rather removed and homogenizing manner.

Finally, the book presents an attempt to contribute to the contemporary Egyptian women's movement by providing an in-depth account of the broad range of secular women's activism. My ambition has been to produce a perspective, however partial and limited, which may be used as a resource by Egyptian women activists. My very position as a researcher might have facilitated the acquisition of insight into a broader range of activities and attitudes which may be concealed from someone totally involved in the activities in question. The tension between researcher and activist was never totally resolved in the course of my research, however, and I continued to struggle with its implication in the process of writing up my findings.

Conceptual considerations

While being aware of debates about whether the often disparate forms of action of contemporary Egyptian women activists could be subsumed under the label 'movement', I espouse the view that there are different forms of women's movements. Some movements are certainly more easily identifiable as collective action than others; however, agreeing with Molyneux's analysis (1998: 223), I would argue that the relatively large number of women's groups and networks, as well as individual activists in Egypt, amount to a women's movement.

As for the questions of what constitutes a 'group', my starting-point would be Dawn Chatty's definition of a group being constituted by a collection of individuals who interact with each other on a regular basis, and 'thereby shaping the identities each form of themselves and of others in the group' (Chatty & Rabo, 1997: 8). For the purpose of my study, I will modify the criterion of regular interaction between members, as membership and activism of Egyptian women activists can be sporadic and irregular, yet they may still form a group. Chatty distinguishes between primary groups, such as families, where there generally exists face-to-face interaction between all members, and secondary groups where 'most members are linked to each other through more complex organizational relationships' (ibid.: 9). Furthermore, she distinguishes between informal and formal groups, the latter being perceived to be more stable over time with more stated rules. However, Chatty points to the fluctuation between the two categories that concurs with my own research findings. Throughout this book I am using 'organization' and 'group' (as in formal group) interchangeably. A 'network', on the other hand, refers to a more or less loose association of formal and informal groups and possibly individual activists linked together on the basis of common objectives. Networks are generally established in order to tackle very specific campaigns or tasks, as, for example, the female genital mutilation task force in Egypt.

From the outset there was a filter through which I selected organizations, groups, networks and individuals, since I had decided to focus on secular women activists. It was not my intention, however, to suggest that all women activists have to be secular or that Islamists could not be women activists. Rather, my decision was based on several reasons which I will elaborate in greater detail in the course of this work. Aside from the fact that I had been involved with a secular group prior to my research, I had noticed the tendency to overlook secular constituencies in much of the recent scholarship dealing with Egypt where the emphasis was on Islamist tendencies and activism. Moreover, if dealt with at all, secular constituencies, such as secular women activists, tend to be homogenized and presented in an undifferentiated manner, almost as a residual category: those who are *not* Islamist.

As one of my aims in this book is to problematize the notion of 'secular', I will only provide a very preliminary working definition at this point: 'secular' refers to the acceptance of the separation between religion and politics, but does not necessarily denote anti-religious or anti-Islamic positions. Furthermore, I suggest that secular women activists do not endorse *shari'a* (Islamic law) as the main or sole source of legislation; but they also refer to civil law and human rights conventions, as stipulated by the United Nations, as frames of reference for their struggle.

My use of the term 'women's activism' rather than 'feminism' is related to the fact that many of the women I interviewed reject the label 'feminist' for pragmatic and ideological reasons. The English term 'feminist' evokes antagonism and animosity, and sometimes even anxiety, among a great number of women activists, who seem to have internalized the way feminists are being portrayed in prevailing Egyptian discourses: men-hating, aggressive, possibly lesbian (but most likely to be obsessed with sex), and certainly westernized women.[1] The reluctance of many Egyptian women

---

[1] Paradoxically, western feminists often have to face very similar stereotyping and hostility within their own societies. Consequently, many women shy away from using the label 'feminist', even if they are engaged in various forms of political struggle for women's

to identify themselves with feminism is not only related to its negative image in society, but is also linked to the conviction that it detracts from such 'larger issues' as imperialism, class struggle and Zionism (Al-Ali, 1997).

The women I interviewed generally distinguished between *al-haraka al-nissa'iyya* (the women's movement) and *al-haraka al-nassa'wiyya* (the feminist movement), the latter being a recently coined term. The majority of women activists perceive this newly invented concept of *nassa'wiyya* (feminism) as only being concerned with *abawiyah* (patriarchy),[2] but not including analyses or critiques of economic and political inequalities. In contrast to 'the feminist movement', they argue, 'the women's movement' entails the concern with national independence, class struggle, and other social and political issues. A small yet growing number of women reject the way the term *al-haraka al-nassa'wiyya* (the feminist movement) is generally represented and understood. They consider themselves self-proclaimed feminists, or *nassa'wiyat*, and cautiously stress that their feminism does include the struggle against all forms of social injustice. They are *not*, they also emphasize, men-haters. Yet another group of women describe themselves as *nassa'wiyat Marxiyat* (Marxist feminists), emphasizing that they are Marxists fighting patriarchy, as opposed to feminists fighting class inequality.

Within these very broad labels, there exist obvious resonances with western feminist categories which correspond to the divergences between women who emphasize 'equality' (liberal feminists), those who stress 'difference' (radical feminists) and those whose concern extends to women's exploitation in the broader sphere of politics and economics (socialist feminists). A rigid separation of the three categories of liberal, radical and socialist feminism has been hard to sustain in the West and is even more problematic in Egypt. The terms are not, however, devoid of meaning in either place, deriving as they do from similar broad dimensions of oppression to which women have attested in many societies.

The struggle to remove obstacles to equality – women's *rights* activism – manifests itself in various campaigns to change existing laws that reflect and reproduce gender inequality. It also aims to improve women's access to education and paid labour, and increase political participation. The 'women's rights' approach constitutes the main form of engagement

rights, against socially defined roles for women, against sexual and economic exploitation and so forth (Kaplan, 1992: 21–2).

[2] I have adopted Heidi Hartman's definition of patriarchy as 'a set of social relations which has a material base and in which there are hierarchical relations between men, and solidarity among them, which enable them to control women. Patriarchy is thus the system of male oppression of women' (1979: 232). It is important to stress, however, that forms of patriarchy vary historically and cross-culturally.

among contemporary Egyptian women activists, since concerns with legislation and equal access to education etc. are also part of the agenda of socialist-oriented activists. However, socialist activists differ from their liberal counterparts in that they reject the idea that reforms will bring about women's equality; instead they perceive women's exploitation as part of structural inequalities which are rooted in class divisions, capitalism and imperialism.

As for the western category of 'radical feminism', which broadly encompasses opposing patriarchy, emphasizing differences between women and men, and focusing on sexuality as a site for women's oppression and liberation, it has not found great resonance among Egyptian women activists. Even the few activists who have addressed the culturally sensitive issue of sexuality cannot be characterized as separatist and do reveal a concern with women's exploitation in other spheres. Several of the liberal and socialist-oriented activists have increased their concern with sexuality, but none has made it her focus. Ironically, however, a number of women who altogether reject the label 'feminist' for being too narrow and separatist increasingly seek the company of other women in their social worlds and frequently express their grievances and frustrations with 'men', thereby quite often inadvertently essentializing differences.

Aside from a few groups, which can be placed on either side of the spectrum in terms of emphasis on equality in the liberal tradition and a concern with political economy as part of the socialist orientations, these strands do not present clearly bounded categories. I could detect a great deal of overlap and flux among and within various groups, which also applies to the specific forms of engagement within women's activism. I will therefore document the heterogeneity of women's activism by exploring the attitudes and positions of group members and individual activists with respect to specific issues and debates that have meaning in contemporary Egyptian society, rather than along the western feminist categorization of liberal versus socialist.

The very term 'activism' glosses over a variety of involvements and activities, which, if considered in isolation, are not all forms of 'political activism': charity and welfare, research, advocacy, consciousness-raising, lobbying and development. What justifies the label 'women's activism' for a broad range of engagements is the fluid nature of this field in which certain activities, not strictly defined as activism, such as research, for example, might develop into more political engagements, such as advocacy or lobbying. Moreover, groups and individuals, at any given point of time, might be involved in different kinds of activities, some not strictly 'activist' and others more so. Thus for the lack of a better label, I will use the term 'women's activism' throughout this book to refer to the broad and fluid range of activities and involvements in the women's movement. Throughout this book, 'women activists' specifically alludes to women involved in *qadiyyat al-mar'a* (women's issues) and the Egyptian women's movement.[3]

Typology of women's activism

A useful analytical categorization of women's activism is furnished by the tripartite model deployed by Maxine Molyneux in her analysis of women's movements historically and cross-culturally (1998). She suggests three ideal types corresponding to their respective organizational principles and conceptions of authority: groups may be (1) independent, (2) associational and (3) directed. '*Independent* organizations' are characterized by 'independent actions, where women organize on the basis of self-activity, set their own goals and decide their own forms of organization and forms of struggle' (ibid.: 226). Molyneux emphasizes that autonomous female collective action is not necessarily feminist in the sense of presenting 'real gender interests', but could also perform self-help activities of various kinds, pursue goals not directly related to gender issues, or even abrogate women's rights. For the purpose of my research, I will narrow down her categorization to those independent women's groups that are expressive of any of the broad feminist approaches outlined above.

Sometimes independent women's groups choose to form alliances with other political organizations while maintaining their own goals and institutional autonomy. This second type of women's organization, characterized by '*associational* linkages', calls for the constant negotiation of power and authority and could present a model for democratic politics. An acknowledgement of diverse and sometimes conflicting interests, a sense of trust and established procedures of accountability are key to avoid the co-option of women's organizations' agendas by their associational partners (ibid.: 228).

Molyneux contrasts these two types with her third category, '*directed* mobilisations', in which 'the authority and initiative clearly comes from outside and stands above the collectivity itself. The women's organization or movement is therefore subject to a higher (institutional) authority, and is typically under the control of political organizations and/or governments' (ibid.: 229). In the case of these women's groups, the directing authority characteristically uses gender issues, if addressed at all, as

---

[3] Some of the women I interviewed referred to themselves as *munashattat* (activists).

means to achieve other goals. Historically and cross-culturally, three different types of directed mobilization emerged: (a) women are mobilized to help achieve a general goal, such as overthrowing the government, or bringing a party to power; (b) a general commitment to advance women's interest but within the general commitment to social change, such as expressed in modernizing nationalisms and socialist movements; (c) women are mobilized for causes which may abrogate rights they already have in the name of collective, national or religious struggle (ibid.: 228–31). While all three different sub-categories of directed mobilization may be found in the course of the history of the Egyptian women's movement, I will confine myself to the second type of directed mobilization in which general goals of social change include the support of women's rights, but no independent organization or alternative definition of women's rights is permitted.

It is obvious that the various 'ideal types' suggested by Molyneux only present heuristic categories and do not necessarily occur in reality in this 'pure form'. Often, women's organizations fluctuate in their level of autonomy or dependence, depending on several factors such as the nature of the state (or other forms of authorities, such as political parties and their policies) and their access to political and economic resources. And here I believe we also need to differentiate a more recent phenomenon that has arisen due to development of international authorities such as UN organizations and international funding agencies. These have given rise to semi-independent/semi-directed mobilization which, while it remains largely autonomous from state authority and political groupings within the state, is nonetheless heavily shaped by international intervention.

The ethnographic field

Prior to the actual research for this book, which took place in 1995–6 over a period of fourteen months, I had lived, studied and worked in Cairo for about six years. During that time the city had become much more than the mere site for fieldwork, as I had established many friendships over the years and had become rather involved in Cairo's dazzling social life. When I returned to Cairo in September 1995 there was a sense of 'coming home' and a comforting familiarity after having spent a year in 'strange' London. I knew where I was going to live, with whom, where to shop, how to find my way around the city without getting lost (most of the time that is). In brief, all the practical arrangements, which tend to take up lots of time and effort in the initial phases of fieldwork, were already sorted out. After intense socializing with friends and acquaintances, catching up with the latest gossip and telling them about my life in London, I could plunge myself into work.

Because of my prior involvement in women's activism in Egypt I was already aware of a number of key figures and groups. However, I spent the first weeks trying to map out a 'field' by speaking to numerous people – scholars, funding agencies and women activists – about their perception of which groups and which individuals were significant in the contemporary women's movement. In the course of these discussions it soon became obvious to me that the contemporary scene of women's activism is extremely varied in terms of activities and institutional frameworks: NGOs with clear structures and decision-making bodies exist side by side with more loosely organized groups; *ad hoc* networks mobilizing around specific issues or tasks are formed and dissolved by activists who are often simultaneously involved in other groups or activities; several women's committees exist which are attached to political parties, professional organizations and human rights centres; and a number of individual women intellectuals work independently through their specific professions or are loosely affiliated with specific groups and might co-operate on specific projects.

Reverting to the first of Molyneux's three categories, varying political orientations can be found among independent women's organizations, such as Markaz Dirasat Al-Marʾa Al-Gedida (the New Woman's Research Centre), Rabtat Al-Marʾa Al-ʿArabiyya (the Alliance of Arab Women), Markaz Dirasat Al-Marʾa: Maʿan (the Women's Study Centre: Together) and Gamaʿat Bint Al-Ard (Daughter of the Land Group). The Alliance of Arab Women, whose members are mainly professional upper-middle-class women in their fifties and sixties, exists on the most liberal end of the broad spectrum of feminist approaches, endorsing both welfare work and women's rights activism. The Alliance[4] is officially registered as an NGO with the Ministry of Social Affairs, the implications of which I will discuss in chapters 2 and 5. Others, such as Maʿan, Al-Marʾa Al-Gedida and Bint Al-Ard, have circumvented the strict regulatory codes linked to the ministry by registering as non-profit companies or research centres.

All three groups initially grew out of previous political activism: members of Bint Al-Ard were initially mobilized around the Israeli invasion of Lebanon (1982), while the founding members of Al-Marʾa Al-Gedida and Maʿan had been involved in socialist politics during the student movement in the 1970s. Despite Bint Al-Ard's concern with issues related to economic exploitation, imperialism and religious

---

[4] I will occasionally employ the abbreviations of group names which are commonly used in Egypt.

sectarianism, the group can be placed closer to a liberal women's rights activism than either Al-Mar'a Al-Gedida or Maʿan. The latter represents the most empathic group in terms of socialist ideology and approach as its older founding members and the younger generation within the group emphasize issues pertaining to political economy, considering themselves *nassa'wiyat Marxiyat* (Marxist feminists).

The group Al-Mar'a Al-Gedida is frequently referred to as the most radical feminist group in contemporary Egypt, which, as I explained earlier, carries the negative connotation of being westernized and merely focusing on the issue of patriarchy. It is certainly true that members reject the subordination of *qadiyyat al-mar'a* (women's issues) to issues related to economic exploitation and national independence and also endorse the recently coined term *al-haraka al-nassa'wiyya* (the feminist movement). They do, nevertheless, include those issues associated with socialist and nationalist agendas in their analyses and activities. Although the group has taken on board the culturally sensitive issue of sexuality (in relation to debates about female genital mutilation and violence against women), they are not separatists between men and women, nor, as I will show throughout this book, are they blindly following western agendas.

In addition to these independent groups, which are, to different degrees, involved in advocacy, research and grassroots projects, there are service-oriented NGOs with a special focus on the role of women in both development and underdevelopment. These NGOs, such as Gamaʿat Nuhud wa Tanmeyyat Al-Mar'a (the Association for the Development and Enhancement of Women, known as ADEW) and Markaz Wasa'il Al-Ittissal Al-Mula'ama min agl Al-Tanmeyya (Appropriate Communications Techniques, known as ACT), combine concrete development projects with political campaigns. Members of these NGOs vary in terms of their specific analyses of gender inequalities in a way that liberal and socialist-oriented approaches exist simultaneously.

Under Molyneux's second category, '*associational*' activism, can be subsumed those groups and activists who are either affiliated with political parties, professional organizations or human rights organizations. As for professional organizations, although some might themselves be independent, the goals and interests related to their professional umbrella might override the specific aims related to women's activism. Some members of the Lagnat Al-Mar'a fi Ittihad Al-Mohameen Al-ʿArab (Women's Committee of the Arab Lawyers' Union), Gama'iyat Al-Katibat Al-Masriyat (the Egyptian Women Writers' Association), Dar Al-Mar'a Al-ʿArabiyya Nour (the Arab Women Publishing House Nour), and Gama'iyat Al-Cinemai'yat (the Egyptian Women in Film Society) have been most outspoken and active concerning the plight of women.

The specific approaches of individual members within these professional organizations vary considerably, and can therefore not easily be categorized. Furthermore, women activists working within the framework of human rights organizations such as Markaz Al-Dirasat wa Al-Ma'lumat Al-Qanuniyya li Huquq Al-Insan (the Legal Rights and Research Centre – LRRC), Markaz Al-Qahira li Dirasat Huquq Al-Insan (the Cairo Institute for Human Rights Studies – CIHRS) and Markaz Al-Mussa'ada Al-Qanuniyya li Huquq Al-Insan (the Centre for Human Rights and Legal Aid – CHRLA) can be subsumed under the label of associational activism, since the general framework of their activism belongs to human rights agendas and frameworks. All of the women affiliated with human rights organizations are involved in reformist women's rights activism; however, many are simultaneously involved with other women's groups or networks and their specific analysis of gender inequalities is diverse.

Women's committees affiliated to political parties, such as the Ittihad Al-Nissa'i Al-Taqadummi (the Union for Progressive Women), which is affiliated to the socialist Tagammu party, and Lagnat Al-Mar'a fil Hizb Al-Nasseri (the Women's Secretariat of the Arab Democratic Nasserist party), represent associational women's organizations whose members are, to different extents, involved in women's activism beyond party politics. The level to which their activism is actually '*directed*' by party politics seems to vary, which indicates that the analytical categories used only present ideal types and actually fluctuate and change over a period of time. Although members of the Union for Progressive Women emphasize structural inequalities due to class divisions and capitalist relations, their activities fall mainly between welfare work and women's rights activism. These forms of activism can also be attributed to members of the Women's Secretariat of the Arab Democratic Nasserist party, who put special emphasis on national independence and the threat of imperialism.

In addition to members of the various groups mentioned above, I also included some women intellectuals who do not belong to any organization or committee, but work individually through their professions as lawyers, journalists, writers, social and development workers, and only occasionally link up with particular *ad hoc* working groups for a specific project, such as the Female Genital Mutilation Task Force, the Women's Media Watch, or co-ordination committees for international conferences.

Aside from relative levels of independence and freedom of action, Egyptian women's groups vary with respect to their membership size, their access to women at the grassroots and their national and international affiliations. The terrain of political engagement ranges from social and development work, to consciousness-raising through seminars, conferences and discussion groups, research activities, advocacy, campaigning and the publishing of pamphlets, magazines and books. Within the groups, individual members differ in terms of their personal and political motivations for activism, their ideological backgrounds and orientations, their proclaimed aims and their actual engagement in activities.

As heterogeneous as the groups and their individual members might be, they are united by their middle-class backgrounds and their commitment to retain and expand their civic rights and equality before the law. They share a secular orientation and a concern about growing Islamist militancy, but their actual positions vis-à-vis the various Islamist tendencies and discourses are variable as much as their specific understandings and interpretations of secularism.

Negotiating multiple allegiances

The 'pursuit of the other' (Visweswaran, 1994: 20) has been increasingly problematized by post-colonial critics and feminist anthropologists, who have addressed power relations between researcher and informant as well as the issue of representation (Hale, 1991; Harding, 1987; Mohanty, 1988; Patai, 1991; Reinharz, 1992; Visweswaran, 1994). A new kind of feminist scholarship related to the 'wind of cultural decolonization' (Morsy, Nelson, Saad & Sholkamy, 1991) has taken different directions. One manifestation of this approach to research is marked by the various ways in which female ethnographers confront their specific social location in terms of class, colour, religion etc. Many anthropologists have pointed out that fieldwork is situated between autobiography and anthropology (Okely & Callaway (eds.), 1992) and that it connects a personal experience with a general field of knowledge. Fieldwork is not the unmediated world of 'others', but the 'world between ourselves and the others' (Hastrup, 1992). The concept of 'intersubjectivity' – the relationship between the researcher and the research community, the politico-cultural worlds to which each belong, and the ultimate purpose of the research project (Sayigh, 1996: 2) – is addressed by many feminist researchers. I will postpone the discussion of my own positionality to chapter 1; at this point, I would like to highlight some of the problems and tensions that emerged throughout my fieldwork.

Despite numerous challenges to the strict separation between researcher and activist in feminist scholarship (Huizer, 1986; Mohanty, 1988; Reinharz, 1992; Visweswaran, 1994), I occasionally did experience tension due to my multiple involvement with my respondents. One source of tension was related to the fact that my status as researcher allowed me to move and talk to diverse women activists (diverse in terms of group and political affiliations, interpretations of what women's activism actually means, as well as differences with regard to personality, lifestyles, support networks etc., which could translate at times into competition, rivalry or even hostility). The knowledge I acquired in the course of my research about the activities and opinions about 'the other women' was occasionally sought out, and often made me feel uncomfortable. I felt torn between my wish to engage in a more reciprocal relationship where I was not the only one asking questions and a fear that I could too easily slip into an act of indiscretion.

The concern with non-hierarchical and transparent research relationships, apparent in much of the writings on feminist methodology and epistemology, is based on a proposed 'feminist ethic of commitment and egalitarianism in contrast with the scientific ethic of detachment and role differentiation between researcher and subject' (Reinharz, 1992: 27). Ann Oakley, for instance, contrasted objective 'scientific' research with feminist research that requires openness, engagement and the development of a potentially long-lasting relationship (1981: 30–61). This dichotomous perception of 'objective' and 'feminist' research has been challenged over the past years, at the same time as feminist researchers have embraced diverse methodologies and research methods. However, the goal of engaging in feminist research that would entail a subversion of strictly bounded categories between researcher and informant underlined my own methodology.

Throughout my research I was trying to find ways actually to be of help, to be a resource and not just to obtain information. This worked in limited instances, mainly with those whom I got to know best and interviewed several times. With most women activists I found myself in the classic interviewer–respondent situation. Aside from the women whose life-stories I recorded, the most reciprocal relationship came about with one particular organization, Markaz Dirasat Al-Mar'a Al-Gedida (the New Woman's Research Centre), for which I prepared four seminars presenting different approaches to gender in the social sciences. This was one of the few moments where I felt that feminist theory and activism merged and that I could really contribute something concrete while doing research. It is probably not a coincidence that I got to know many of the members of this particular group on a personal and social basis.

Becoming friends was both the most pleasurable as well as problematic aspect of my research. While the label 'western' was used on certain occasions to discredit my views, it also opened up a sense of trust and confidence in other situations. I felt this most strongly when talking to some of the women whose life-histories I recorded and with whom I developed friendships. Several times I felt quite surprised, after having discussed a particular problem or crisis, to find out that my friend had not discussed it with anyone else before. I shared my own problems and troubles with those friends, often quite intimate ones, which certainly increased the sense of trust. Many of these friendships have certainly added to 'my world' and support network in Cairo and continue to do so from a distance as well.

Friendships with women activists from different groups required lots of diplomacy and sensitivity and were often met with a great deal of suspicion. I only realized how delicate this situation was when one activist told me that some people thought I was opportunistic as I was maintaining friendship with everyone just for the sake of my research. At that point I was slightly taken aback, understanding that this was the way this particular activist, and perhaps many more, actually thought about me, but I soon realized that the specific context of women's activism, that is the deep divisions and the personalized nature of many conflicts, could only make my behaviour seem suspicious.

The research process

In the course of my fourteen months of research in Cairo – the main centre for women's activism in Egypt – I interviewed about eighty women, most of whom are members of at least one group or network, but a few are working without a specific organizational affiliation. The interviews, which ranged from loosely structured to informal unstructured conversations and discussions, took place in the various 'headquarters' of the different groups, but also in cafés and restaurants, in the homes of women activists and in my apartment. About half of the interviews were carried out in the course of one meeting only. The actual length of these meetings varied greatly (between one and four hours), depending on several factors, such as my respondents' interest in my project, our respective time-schedules and whether a mutual rapport developed. Where rapport did develop, and if it was coupled with an interest in my research, this usually led to at least one more if not numerous other interviews and discussions, at times developing into more sustained social relations rather than one-off research encounters. This was especially the case with the ten women whose life-stories I recorded.

Most of my interviews and recording of life-stories were carried out in English, but some were conducted in Arabic and were later translated into English by a research assistant.[5] I did, however, tend to speak Arabic

[5] In the course of my research I employed several research assistants who were mainly responsible for transcribing tapes and translating written materials.

to the women activists I had not met before, introducing myself and explaining my research project. Many women appreciated that I made the effort rather than assumed that everyone would speak English. Those who were not fluent continued in Arabic, but most switched to English at some point during the research. My Arabic, however inadequate, was instrumental in convincing many women actually to spend time with me (Al-Ali & El-Kholy, 1999).

In conjunction with the very enjoyable time spent recording life-stories and engaging in interviews and discussions, I spent a considerable amount of time in various offices, centres and conference halls, listening to discussions, debates and seminars in informal and formal settings. It was in these situations that I mainly confined myself to being a mere observer and listener, trying hard to follow all that was said in Arabic, occasionally asking my neighbour about a word or two which I did not pick up. On those occasions when debates or seminars seemed to go on forever, I quite frequently lost my ability to follow the course of arguments and had to resort to my tape recorder to make sure that nothing important was lost.

Most of the numerous talks, debates and conferences I attended as well as the interviews I carried out were tape-recorded, unless this was specifically objected to. In those rare cases, I either took notes during the interview or as soon as possible after it. The tapes were subsequently transcribed. If the original interview or talk took place in Arabic, my research assistant transcribed and translated it for me. Throughout this book I am trying to maintain the original 'flavour' and tone of the interview when quoting women activists.[6] In order to protect the anonymity of my respondents I have decided to use pseudonyms. I do, however, mention the names of activists when citing their written work rather than quoting them from my interviews. Aside from protecting the anonymity of my respondents, especially those who shared their life-stories with me, the use of pseudonyms also facilitates the very difficult task of choosing whom to quote and whom not to. It allows me to select a specific quotation with respect to its significance and content rather than worry about the etiquette of including or excluding certain of my respondents.

When I presented my first paper based on my fieldwork in a seminar at the American University in Cairo, I had not been prepared for some of the reactions of my informants who came to hear my talk. Most women present expressed their support and agreed to my main arguments and analysis. Some, however, were obviously upset, but did not explain the reasons clearly. Only later did I realize that I had to free myself from the

---

[6] I have edited only in those cases where the original quote would have been too difficult to understand due to grammar or syntax mistakes.

drive to do justice to everyone, as this can never be achieved. But what I also learned is that some of the activists had a strong interest in their voices being heard and expressed discontent with the fact that I quoted someone else instead of them, even if they had spent a lot of time with me speaking about exactly the same subject matter. I had taken care to show my paper to the women whom I quoted and I had asked for their permission, but I had not considered the reaction of women I left out. After this incident I experienced what I had already known theoretically: the very process of selection, that is deciding whom to quote, what exactly and how much, is rather problematic as it involves editing out other voices. As many women activists I interviewed spent lots of time, thought and energy discussing various issues with me, there is not only a sense of responsibility on my behalf, but also a level of expectation on the part of the women I interviewed.

Active readership

Throughout my research and the early stage of 'writing-up' I had to ask myself whether my prior experiences with Egyptian women's activism made me initially less able to see the new, the 'strange' and the contradictory, and led me simply to reflect the familiar. When I presented my first paper in Cairo, I was indeed accused by some activists who had attended my talk of having 'gone native'. This was based on the sense that my paper betrayed a blurred perspective between my own personal point of view and those of the women I had interviewed. It was shown up as an example of not being able to take the necessary distance by a researcher, who had spent too much time in the researched community. As the Egyptian activist Heba El-Kholy argues in a joint paper with me (1999) the problem was not my lack of 'distance' or 'strangeness', but it was related to a much broader problem of 'studying up'. El-Kholy associates this issue with the problem of gaining and maintaining access, and the knowledge that what you have written will be read, and perhaps contradicted, by your informants.

In the paper, in which El-Kholy and I problematize notions of being an 'insider' or 'outsider' when doing research, I agree with El-Kholy's assessment to a large extent. The sense of knowing (and even fearing at times) that what you write will be read by your respondents is of critical importance. My 'blind spots' were also, and to an extent still are, related to the wish to do justice to everyone and please everybody. Such a project is bound to fail, yet very difficult to resist when knowing that the women activists I interviewed will not only read my work, but also challenge it (ibid. 1999:27)

The issue of 'audience' or, to be more precise, 'readership' has generally been ignored in discussions about ethnographic writing and reflexivity (Clifford & Marcus (eds.), 1986; Geertz, 1988; Strathern, 1976). However, El-Kholy and I agree that the issue of audiences, that is whom you are writing for and the risks involved in revealing your opinions and analysis, has to be acknowledged as a factor influencing both the research and the writing process. A significant issue, as El-Kholy and I argue, relates to the future relationships of the researcher to her or his research community. This is because for anthropologists who are planning to continue living in the same context as those they researched, whether or not they are 'native', the risks are quite different from those for researchers who return to a home far away from the research community.

For this particular work I am aware of at least three different audiences, that is scholars of the Middle East based in western institutions, Egyptian scholars and Egyptian women activists. While the thought of critical scholars does evoke tension, this does not compare to the anxiety I feel with respect to the women I interviewed and whose voices I am trying to present – a process involving selection, editing, analysis, interpretation and also revealing my own voice.

Organization of the book

The relevance of post-colonial and post-orientalist scholarship, which inform my own research, will be explored in chapter 1, where I tackle attempts to move beyond orientalism. The issue of essentialist representations leads me to a discussion of constructions of the 'West' in the Egyptian context, which I will then link to a presentation of the way in which my own 'hyphenated identity' influenced my research and the relationship to my informants. Problematizing the notion of 'identity' entails a consideration of the variety of discourses and positions on Egyptian national identity, and involves the question about links and tensions between nationalism and feminism. I will end chapter 1 with an analysis of constructions of the 'West' among Egyptian women activists.

I will contextualize the contemporary women's movement in chapter 2 by sketching out the history of the Egyptian women's movement as seen through the eyes of the women I interviewed. This is paralleled by an analysis of the changing relationship between the Egyptian state (from Nasser to Mubarak) and the women's movement. Here I will explore the role of the state and pursue the question of whether the state supports or hinders women's activism.

The analysis of the broader historical and political context in which women's activism takes place is followed by a presentation of individual trajectories in chapter 3. The life-stories of ten activists reveal conjunctures between personal motivations and experiences and historical developments that shape the content and form of activism they become engaged in.

In chapter 4 I shall take issue with the notion of secularism, a concept largely misunderstood and abused in the context of the Middle East and the Muslim world, but, also, as I will argue, in the European and North American context. My analysis of these misconceptions will be followed by a brief outline of discussions about secularism in the Egyptian context. I will then reveal how Egyptian women activists interpret secularism and how their understandings can contribute to largely male-centred accounts of secularism.

Questions about the form and content of contemporary women's activism will be explored in greater detail in chapter 5. In this chapter I present both the stated goals and priorities of women activists – what they say – and their actual practice – what they do. I will describe several projects in greater detail while trying to outline the general range of activities.

That debates and conflicts within the women's movement have to be contextualized within Egypt's broader political culture constitutes my main argument in chapter 6. Taking one specific case study of one group as a starting-point, I shall examine some of the main points of contention and conflict among women activists and show how they relate to political culture in general. Finally, I will conclude this book by drawing out some of the main issues and findings that crystallized in the course of this research.

1 Up against conceptual frameworks: post-orientalism, occidentalism and presentations of the self

As I think about the question of how post-colonial scholarship has influenced more recent works about the 'East', and also ponder on the gains and pitfalls of post-orientalist scholarship, I come across Edward Said's reassuring words in his introduction to *Culture and Imperialism* (1993): 'Gone are the binary oppositions dear to the nationalist and imperialist enterprise'(p. xxviii). This, no doubt, constitutes a radical shift from his earlier account of history and representation (*Orientalism*, 1978), in which Said stressed that relations between the 'West' and the 'non-West' have been continuously characterized by conflict, divisiveness and dichotomies as the inevitable consequence of and reaction to colonialism. A sense of relief, almost comfort, arises: are we living in new times in which processes of decolonization within formerly colonized as well as colonizing countries allow reconciliation, liberation and the necessary steps to go beyond essentialisms, hierarchies and binary oppositions?

The feeling of relief vanishes when I put down my books and papers on 'post-colonialism' – all full of promising notions of 'breaking down boundaries', 'hybridity', 'plural identities' and 'cultural interdependencies'. Reading the newspapers or watching television, I feel confronted with a very different language and reality: the ongoing battle of strength between the United States and Iraq (or rather Saddam Hussein, if we want to believe various spokespeople), Nato airstrikes in Yugoslavia, Serb aggression in Kosovo, and the ongoing oppression and humiliation of Palestinians in Israel. The list goes on with incidents of imperialist interference, ethnic violence, nationalist bigotry and religious fundamentalism, which not only give rise to a rhetoric of 'us' versus 'them' and a new system of hierarchies, but also show the dangerous and often bloody aspect of imperialism, and resistances to it, in our contemporary 'post-colonial' times.

Undeniably, the period of direct colonial occupation and rule by imperial powers has passed, but we are still left with processes and practices of domination as well as economic exploitation, all signifying present-day imperialism, sometimes called 'neo-colonialism'. Despite – or rather because of – this realization, I found a source of inspiration (as so many other 'younger scholars in and from the colonies as well as younger metropolitan researchers', as Rattansi (1997) puts it) in post-colonial scholarship, especially in the works of Edward Said, Gayatri Spivak, Stuart Hall and Lila Abu-Lughod. What then is the significance of the concept of 'post-colonialism' in our analyses of contemporary power relations, cultural representations and politics and global capitalism?

The post-colonial turn

Like the concept 'post-modern', the post-colonial denotes a sense of 'new times' as well as particular theoretical approaches and analyses. Post-colonial scholarship, like post-modernism, often transcends traditional disciplinary boundaries and displays an 'eclectic mix of post-structuralism, psychoanalysis, feminism, Marxism and postmodernism itself' (Rattansi, 1997: 481). A survey of the literature debating the content, methodology and politics of the 'post-colonial' reveals that the term has been variously applied to very different kinds of historical moments, geographical regions, cultural identities, political affiliations, predicaments and reading practices (Moore-Gilbert, 1997: 11).

A lack of clear-cut definition about what is 'post-colonial' and the blurring of boundaries between colonized and colonizer have often lent themselves to the criticism that the concept and its underlying analyses tend to be theoretically and politically ambiguous (Shohat, 1992). Another objection is related to its perceived linearity, as the word 'post' suggests a 'past', that is the final closure of a historical period (McClintock, 1992; Shohat, 1992). Other critics attack post-colonial scholars for their complicity with western 'high theory' and their embeddedness in western academic institutions, their fashionable use of trendy jargon and their remoteness from the struggles and material realities in the 'Third World' (Ahmad, 1992; Dirlik, 1992). The criticism of the widespread use of post-structuralism goes beyond the notion of trendiness and marketability; it is also argued that post-colonial discourse is a 'culturalism' (Dirlik, 1992: 347), which seriously neglects the role of global capitalism in the structuring of the modern world (Ahmad, 1992; Dirlik, 1992).

Taking all these criticisms seriously and acknowledging problematic areas, several scholars, who are either self-consciously post-colonialists or, at the very least, sympathetic, have managed to counter many of the most common and severe criticisms. Stuart Hall (1996a), for instance, stresses that the post-colonial period is characterized by a general process of decolonization among both the formerly colonized and the colonizers, which is not to suggest that it marks an 'epochal stage' that reverses old power relations once and for all. Post-colonial times are characterized by a series of transitions, a multiplicity of processes and developments towards decolonization and the de-centring of the 'West', but also, as many post-colonial critics point out, the emergence of powerful local elites and 'neo-colonial' dependency on the developed capitalist world (Hall, 1996a; Rattansi, 1997; Said, 1993).

Rather than downplaying the destructive role of the colonizers and neo-colonial powers, post-colonial scholarship intends to subvert the old colonizing–colonized binary and the clearly demarcated inside–outside of the colonial system by directing attention to 'the many ways in which colonization was never simply external to the societies of the imperial metropolis' (Hall, 1996a: 246). Effects of this inscription and 'transculturation' have resulted in hybridity among cultures, which were never as self-contained, authentic and 'pure' as they were characteristically portrayed by imperial powers in the past and nowadays by nationalist and fundamentalist movements in the previously colonized world.

But, for the time being, as Hall warns us:

We have to keep these two ends of the chain in play at the same time – overdetermination and difference, condensation and dissemination – if we are not to fall into a playful deconstructionism, the fantasy of a powerless *utopia* of difference. It is only too tempting to fall into the trap of assuming that, because essentialism has been deconstructed *theoretically*, therefore it has been displaced *politically*. (ibid.: 249)

Post-colonialism, then, does not have to be politically ambiguous, but it takes the complexity and ambiguity of politics into account. According to Hall, 'political positionalities are not fixed and do not repeat themselves from one historical situation to the next or from one theatre of antagonism to another'(ibid.: 244). Taking issue with Ella Shohat's criticism of the 'depoliticizing implications' of the post-colonialist project to subvert clear-cut politics of binary oppositions, Hall quotes her own words as backing up his argument:

The last three decades in the 'Third World' have offered a number of very complex and politically ambiguous developments . . . [including] the realization that the wretched of the earth are not unanimously revolutionary . . . and [that] despite the broad patterns of geo-political hegemony, power relations in the Third World are also dispersed and contradictory. (Shohat quoted in ibid.: 245)

Inherent in post-colonial politics is the questioning of the Enlightenment project and the de-centring of the 'West'. What cannot be stressed enough is that post-colonialism does not present a totalizing perspective on the formation and dynamics of historical moments and the contemporary world. Material relations and global capitalism should, ideally, figure as much as literary productions and cultural representations. Some of the shortcomings of post-colonial scholarship might be explained by the fact that, despite its claim to interdisciplinary practice, much of post-colonial scholarship is practised by literary critics who do not sufficiently engage with other disciplines such as sociology, anthropology, economics and political science. Or to put it in a different way: many anthropologists, sociologists, economists and political scientists have not yet taken on board the theoretical, methodological and political stipulations generated by post-colonial scholarship.

Beyond *Orientalism*

Some treatises about post-colonial scholarship suggest that it is something that begins with Edward Said's classic study and critique of orientalism – the knowledge production about the 'East' and its underlying power relations and politics. But as Said himself points out in his more recent work, the resistance to colonial systems of representation and the attempt to decolonize history and culture started long before *Orientalism* (1978), and is most explicit in Frantz Fanon's *Black Skin, White Mask* (1952) and *The Wretched of the Earth* (1961). Nevertheless, the influence and importance of *Orientalism* is evident in that it has extensively and passionately been cited, (mis)quoted, applied, evaluated, criticized, developed and subverted. Instead of belabouring *Orientalism* yet again, I would like to argue that Said's own intellectual and theoretical shift apparent in *Culture and Imperialism* (1993), which indicates the move away from essentializing differences between the 'East' and the 'West' and thereby refusing the hierarchical binary positions upon which imperialism depended, has not been sufficiently taken on board and acknowledged by either his critics or his supporters.

Certainly, Said's attempt to articulate a politics of liberation on the basis of 'contrapuntual ensembles' or cultural hybridity as an alternative to chauvinistic and exclusionary nationalist politics easily lends itself to the criticism of being vague and naive (Rattansi, 1997: 497). The danger of interpreting cultural hybridity as fuzzy multiplicity is not unique to Said's work, but inherent in many post-colonial and post-modern writings. However vague the actual politics suggested by Said are, he provides a useful and creative framework in which a liberation politics can be further developed. Moreover, as a theoretical and methodological approach, *Culture and Imperialism* offers a way out of the impasse of essentialism and reductionism that Said criticized in *Orientalism*, yet had reproduced to some extent himself.

Inside the Middle East,[1] as well as among scholars working on the region, orientalism, understood as the practice of homogenizing and essentializing differences, is well and alive, albeit better disguised than in the past and often undercover. Post-orientalist scholarship, with its underlying aspiration of breaking away from discourses and methods that constructed a timeless essence, either with reference to exotic strangeness or framed in terms of mono-causal explanations (mainly pertaining to Islam), has still a long way to go before transcending its legacy.

Within the wide variety of scholarship that self-consciously considers itself post-orientalist, some works, more successfully than others, expose and undermine the monolithic and hegemonic discourses underlying earlier codifications and misrepresentations of 'the Orient'. While the process of deconstructing the notion of the 'East' has been a central motif in recent analyses of historians, literary critics, sociologists and anthropologists, this process has generally not included the 'West' within the field called 'Middle East Studies'. Reifications of the 'West' and an East–West dichotomy are, arguably, much more naturalized and unchallenged in studies relating to the various Arab countries of West Asia and North Africa than in other area studies, such as South Asia, for example.

There are many reasons for the fact that post-orientalist scholarship in general has been more successful in displacing the 'East' than the 'West', ranging from an absence of problematization of the 'West' by scholars and institutions too busy problematizing 'others' to geo-political pressures and factors, such as the establishment of the state of Israel. One very important factor is post-orientalism's rootedness in post-structuralist scholarship, namely the influence of Foucault transmitted via Said. What has made the West more monolithic is the vantage point of a critique of Enlightenment. It is not the West in its variety of discourses and ideologies or its daily manifestation that has been under the microscope, but rather the project of modernity and the philosophy of Enlightenment. In this process, modernity as a project becomes conflated with 'western thought'.

---

[1] In referring to the 'Middle East' I am following the designation given by Eickelman (1989). There are several problems with this terminology as it homogenizes the variety of peoples, experiences and cultures in the region. Politically, the term has become particularly problematic in the light of recent developments, e.g. the so-called peace process and discussions about a 'Middle East market', including Israel. While the designation 'Middle East' has not been coined by people living in the region and represents a nomenclature of European historical experience, it has been adopted in translation (*al-sharq al-awsat*). The term 'the Arab world' does not present an adequate alternative as it equally simplifies and generalizes. Moreover, the designation 'Arab' marginalizes the existence of non-Arab ethnic groups in the region.

In Egypt, as in many other parts of the formerly colonized world, the awareness of orientalism, the way Egypt has been studied, (mis)represented and, in the perception of many, ridiculed, evoked several reactions. On one level it led to a more systematic knowledge production about the 'West', on another level, but intrinsically linked to the previous one, the call for 'the indigenization of social science' emerged.

The move to decolonize anthropology and engage in post-orientalist scholarship induced more and more 'indigenous' scholars to do 'home-work', or 'anthropology in reverse' (Visweswaran, 1994: 102). While 'home-work' is still viewed with suspicion by the mainstream canon, it is becoming increasingly clear that the profound insights, language skills and motivations of many indigenous anthropologists subvert some of the cultural stereotypes, generalizations and misconceptions perpetuated by earlier conventional scholarship.

This is not to suggest that an 'indigenous scholar' is able to engage in intimate and in-depth research by the sheer attribute of being a 'local'. Many 'native' anthropologists are extremely far removed from the communities they set out to study in their home countries, either by class or religious affiliations, educational background or particular sub-cultural connection. Then there are many 'native' scholars who engage in positivistic research, trying to quantify, categorize and scientifically prove their previously well-thought-out presuppositions. However, I argue that those researchers who self-reflectively and critically engage in research at home have greater potential for 'close', in-depth and also 'liberating' research than their 'foreign' colleagues. This might be due to some previous involvement out of which the research topic grew, e.g. development work and women's activism. This practical involvement might be entangled with an emotional involvement, a deep urge to 'do something for one's country', a sense of responsibility that might transcend the compassion of a non-native researcher. Another reason for increased potential is language skill which allows the 'native' anthropologist to hear nuances and connotations that often remain blind spots to the researcher struggling with language.[2]

Unfortunately, many scholars, whether 'western', 'indigenous' or 'hyphenated', who are engaged in critiques of orientalism are often locked in the dichotomies they try to deconstruct and therefore reproduce certain binary oppositions (see, for example, Abdel-Kader, 1987; L. Ahmed, 1992; Badran, 1991, 1993, 1995; Kabbani, 1986; Zuhur, 1992).

---

[2] The works of Hania Sholkamy (1996, forthcoming), Iman Bibars (forthcoming), Heba El-Kholy (1997, 1998) and Reem Saad (1988, 1997, 1998) are examples of the kind of sensitive in-depth research which does not only require a total grip on colloquial Egyptian dialect, but also a previous insight into policy making as well as the make-up of the community they chose to study.

Whether in terms of 'traditional versus modern', 'secular versus religious' or 'East versus West', in one way or another, these works 'keep our gaze fixed upon the effects of the discursive hegemony of the West' (Kandiyoti, 1996: 16). The extreme manifestation of this impasse, however, is revealed in the emergence of a new and now quite fashionable 'school of thought'. This trend is characterized by the portrayal of Islamists as the only alternative force to increasing western encroachment, a stress on heterogeneity among Islamists (while homogenizing secular constituencies) and the condemnation of feminist critiques of Islamists' conceptions of womanhood as ethnocentric.

Without minimizing the significance of the rising tide of Islamism, I believe that scholars themselves have been actively, if unwittingly, engaged in muting those groups and individuals who have opposed or reacted against Islamism. Not only have issues such as Islamic revival and militancy been at the forefront of research dealing with Egyptian women, but their struggles, experiences and identities have also often been explained with reference to a framework that operates with simplistic dichotomies: the Islamist, traditional and authentic on the one hand and modernist, progressive and western on the other. While more recent literature has emphasized that Islamism is a modern movement, it still largely homogenizes and dichotomizes 'religion' versus 'secularism' and 'indigenous' versus 'western'.[3]

What generally needs to be dismantled more systematically is the notion of a monolithic West and the homogeneous category of westerners. In the context of 'Middle East' scholarship, only very few works (Abu-Lughod (ed.), 1998; Kandiyoti, 1996; R. Lewis, 1996; Mitchell & Abu-Lughod, 1993; Nelson, 1996; Zubaida, 1994) display a concern with this project showing the variety and contradictory discourses emanating from the 'West', as well as the complex and multi-faceted encounters and struggles, but also co-operations and friendships between various heterogeneous constituencies from both 'sides'. By highlighting divided loyalties, interests and contradictions – on the level of both discourses and practices – of secular-oriented women activists in Egypt, I hope that my work will contribute to unsettling and challenging the East–West essentialism as well as its underlying relationships. This does not detract from the awareness that Egypt, like many other formerly colonized countries, continues to be subjected in various ways to imperialist politics[4] which

---

[3] Veiling, in these works, is often described as a phenomenon of upward social mobility with regard to education, work and public activities (Ahmed, 1992; El-Guindy, 1981; Karam, 1998; Macleod, 1991; Moghadam, 1993; Zuhur, 1992).

[4] For a detailed account of how American and international funding agencies portray and influence Egypt's economy, general policies as well as people's lives, see Mitchell (1991).

manifest themselves in the daily lives of people across class, gender, religious affiliation and place of residence. This does not prevent me from appreciating and even employing particular 'essentialisms' in specific contexts for strategic political purposes.

Occidentalism: the other side of the coin?

Achilles is replaced by Batman, the virgin and the child by Madonna, Michelangelo by Michael Jackson and even nation-states by the new international order.
Surely a new *ijtihad* is sorely needed.[5]

Reifications of the 'West' persist in scholarship dealing with Egypt, contributing to the consolidation of occidentalism as an increasingly powerful tool in contemporary Egyptian political culture.[6] Occidentalism, like orientalism, is part of a political ploy: it uses available cultural categories to gain symbolic advantages for 'the self' and to handicap 'the other'. It is shaped by political contingencies in the search for power and influence. However, it would be misleading to portray occidentalism as the counterpart of orientalism. Rather, I would characterize occidentalism in contemporary Egypt as a critique of modernity which is deeply aware of and reacting against orientalism. Historically, the so-called 'West' has been more powerful – and hence more able – to construct and impose images of alien societies (Carrier (ed.), 1995). Up to the present, unequal distributions of political and economic power characterize orientalism and occidentalism as two similar yet distinct processes.

Contemporary constructions of an imperialist, corrupting, decadent and alienating West take place in a variety of contexts: in leftist-nationalist as well as Islamist fora, such as newspapers, books, seminars, discussions in universities, in public meetings of intellectuals and artists etc. How far these public discourses are being reproduced at the micro level of interpersonal communication needs to be carefully analysed, but it can be said

---

[5] Dr Abdel Wahab El-Messiry (1996) 'Secularism and *ijtihad*', in *Al-Waha* (Oasis), 4th issue. Magazine by the 'Arab Cultural Association' (platform of Islamist students at the American University in Cairo). *Ijtihad* usually refers to the reinterpretation of the *Sunnah,* in which the prophet Muhammad demonstrates how to carry out the more general instructions of the Qur'an. In the context of the article the author uses *ijtihad* to mean a redefinition of secularism.

[6] The debates about the 'West', its promise of modernism and threat of imperialism, and the more recent articulations of what the 'West' is all about, are not peculiar to Egypt, but can be found in variations all over the Middle East in particular and the post-colonial world in general (Bhaba, 1994; Bouatta & Cherifati-Merabtine, 1994; Chatterjee, 1986; Nederveen & Parekh, 1995; Papanek, 1994; Spivak, 1988; Tavakoli-Targhi, 1994). However, this work concentrates specifically on the Egyptian context and the following discussion will reflect this focus.

with certainty that arguments about western conspiracies against Muslims, the failings and decay of western civilization and the threat of western cultural imperialism ring a bell among many Egyptians.[7] Historically, intellectuals and reformers in nineteenth- and early-twentieth-century Egypt shared the modernist enthusiasm for enlightenment, technological progress, positivism and an all-encompassing truth. Many Egyptian intellectuals articulated a vision of the *ancien régime* as arbitrary and controlled by faith. Their alternative project entailed an elimination of traditions and 'backwardness'.[8] Islam was being reinterpreted and reformed to prove its compatibility with progress and rationality by modernists such as Muhammad Abduh and Qasim Amin, to name just two. Meanwhile, secular modernists challenged Islam as the basis for political and social organization, associated Egypt's advancement with the efficacy of European culture and civilization, and particularly promoted scientific thinking as the key to progress.

The question arises as to why European thinkers have been credited for being self-critical in their attempts to overcome arbitrary and theological regimes, while Egyptians are easily discredited by notions of 'aping the West' – not only by European and North American scholars, but also by Egyptian intellectuals today. Can we speak about a more global and universal change of *Weltanschauung* in light of European hegemony and colonial oppression? Perhaps the relation between Egyptian modernizers[9] and European thinkers was not as linear as supposed. There could have been a convergence between disillusionment with the *ancien régime* and self-criticism on the one hand, and the encounter and engagement with the European Enlightenment on the other. One must speculate that Egyptian intellectuals were selective in their appropriations and repudiations of European ideas about a modern nation state, just as Islamists and conservative nationalist forces have been with regard to the notions of traditions, authenticity and foreign imposition (Abu-Lughod, 1998b).

---

[7] The current regime has been ambiguous concerning its rhetoric on the West. It rarely engages in outright attacks on the 'West' as such. Egyptian–American relations have been critically re-evaluated by various writers across the broad spectrum of the Egyptian press.

[8] During the reign of Muhammad Ali (1805–48), European education became a model to reform the Egyptian school system. Intellectuals such as Shaykh Rifaʿi Al-Tahtawi (1801–71) and Ali Pasha Mubarak (1824–93) aimed at transmitting knowledge from Europe in the service of the state under Muhammad Ali and his successors (Vatikiotis, 1991: 121).

[9] The most famous Egyptian modernist secularists are Salama Musa (1887–1958), Ahmad Lutfi Al-Sayyid (1872–1963), Muhammad Hussain Haykal (1888–1956) and Taha Hussain (1889–1973). Within the generation of modernist secularists, many were of either Lebanese Christian origin, e.g. Yaʿqub Sarruf (1852–1957) or Syrian Christian background, e.g. Shibli Shumayyil (1860–1917). Socialist ideas were introduced from the 1920s (Hourani, 1991; Vatikiotis, 1991).

As Chatterjee (1993) has forcefully argued in the case of Indian nationalism, nationalist elites employed the notion of 'colonial difference' in various ways. 'Colonial difference' – the representation of the 'other' as 'radically different, and hence incorrigibly inferior' (ibid.: 33) – had earlier been deployed by the British as a way to justify their policies of colonization. In post-colonial India nationalist elites attempted to erase notions of 'colonial difference' in the 'outer' or material domain of the state, the economy, law and administration, thereby making claim to 'universality of modern regimes of power' (ibid.: 26). However, within the 'inner' aspects of culture, language, religion and family life, the notion of an essential difference between the culture of the colonizer and the newly emerged nation state was emphasized (ibid.). Parallels can be found in Egypt where nationalist elites promoted credentials of modernity with regard to economic, political and social arenas related to the so-called public sphere. As I will show in greater detail in the following chapter, women were granted the right to vote, the right to education and work and were included in the processes of reform and modernization in post-colonial Egypt. Concerning women's roles and rights within the home and the family, the supposedly 'inner' aspects of a society, the notion of 'essential difference' to the colonizing culture and more broadly speaking the 'West' has been upheld and even magnified.

One significant and widespread flaw, which has only very recently been addressed, has been the conflation of Enlightenment and its appraisal of rationality, liberalism and democracy with European thought. Whether in Egypt, Britain or the United States, many intellectuals deal with Enlightenment and liberal egalitarianism as if it they were inherent characteristics of the 'West'. Ignored are the series of fierce historical struggles, such as the French Revolution, in which the outcomes were far from obvious (Zubaida, 1994: 7). As Sami Zubaida very lucidly put it, the props of liberal democracy are far from being inherent, and that 'in many parts of the "West", notably Spain, these struggles had failed until recently. We should also keep in mind the breakdown of rights and doctrines in much of Western Europe under Nazism and fascism' (ibid.). This historical view can be extended to present-day Europe and the United States where corporatism, sectarian strife, racism, neo-Nazism and religious fundamentalisms have been on the rise.

At present, years of colonial oppression, the ongoing experience of imperialist politics in post-colonial Egypt, disillusionment with a version of modernity that did not deliver its promises of linear progress, emancipation and affluence for all – linked to Egypt's internal social, political and economic crises – have contributed to a growing condemnation of 'the West'. It is not only Islamists and conservative nationalists who are at the forefront of slandering the 'West', but leftist opposition forces also engage in anti-western campaigns.[10] While constructions of the 'West' are used as a way to create an 'authentic' Egyptian identity, they are deeply informed by the way the 'East' has been misrepresented and stereotyped. Attacks on the West vary from outright polemics about sexual promiscuity and general decadence to more sophisticated cultural and political critiques.

Missing in the often very valid criticisms of atrocities carried out in the name of 'progress', e.g. World War II, Hiroshima, the destruction of the environment, the Gulf war etc., is any kind of acknowledgement that similar critiques and accusations have been made from within what is portrayed as a homogeneous and all-powerful West. Notwithstanding some Egyptian intellectuals' claim to originality, many of the critiques of modernity – ideas of scientific positivism, linear progress, hegemonic discourses and imperialist politics – have been put forward by writers, researchers and political activists in Europe and in the United States.[11] No allowances are made for the existence of contradictory discourses, opposition forces, power struggles or even self-criticisms internal to the 'West'.

However, generalizations put forward in certain contexts, e.g. public seminars or political meetings, discussions in cafés or friends' houses, do not necessarily reflect the complex and differentiated ways the 'West' enters into daily lives of a heterogeneous group of people – contemporary Egyptians.[12] What is prevailing on the level of discourses looks much more complex on the level of practices. Parallel to the negative imagery connected with western culture, politics and lifestyles, there exist various forms of glorification of the 'West'. In some instances, such as the praise for scientific thinking as being characteristic of the 'West', one can detect

---

[10] Many of the fiercest and most impassioned critics of the 'West', read here as the project of modernity and its glorification of 'progress', are a number of former Marxist intellectuals (many of them educated in Britain or America) who either turned Islamist or became sympathetic to Islamist activism and discourses. As Marxists their struggle was specifically directed towards western capitalism; now their attacks are much more broad and generalized.

[11] This is far from suggesting that critiques of modernity originated in the 'West' and similar arguments within Egypt are imitated. However, the mostly male intellectuals I am referring to work within or are in regular contact with the American University in Cairo, make public claims to their knowledge of and insights into 'western thought', yet deny the similarity of their arguments with particular strands of post-modern and feminist thinking. Feminist critiques of social inequalities and hegemonic modernist discourses are often dismissed as 'men-hating women wanting to rule the world'.

[12] Lila Abu-Lughod's work on Egyptian soap operas (1995a, 1997) and Walter Armbrust's work on popular culture in Egypt (1996) give evidence to the differences between the elite, middle-class and low-income cultures. Moreover, Abu-Lughod's articles reflect the gap between rural and urban culture.

remnants of earlier modernist stipulations. I came across this notion in various contexts, e.g. conversations with Egyptians who have studied abroad, parents who send their children to the German high school or women activists commending more scientific approaches to their policy-oriented research projects. Much more than the spirit of positivism is alive in the halls of Egyptian academic and research institutions which generally favour quantitative and statistical 'sound research' to qualitative 'gobbledegook'.

An elite and nationalist modernity, idealizing enlightenment and progress, has also been detected by Lila Abu-Lughod in her analyses of the intent, content and public reception of American and Egyptian soap operas (1995a, 1997). It is not merely American serials such as the popular *The Bold and the Beautiful* that reveal a tremendous gap between the lifestyles and the concerns of its characters and the people who watch it. Often, Egyptian soap operas hardly relate to the lives of their audiences. Aside from those serials merely produced for entertainment, Egyptian soap operas are often intended to convey social messages. A concerned group of culture-industry professionals, as Abu-Lughod states, perceives certain parts of the population, women and rural people, for instance, as being in need of enlightenment: 'Appropriating and inflecting Western discourses on development they construct themselves as guides to modernity and assume responsibility of producing, through their television programmes, the virtuous modern citizen' (1995a: 191).

Consumption, one aspect of this post-colonial modernity – especially consumption by Egyptian youths – has increasingly been dominated by western products (fashion, electrical appliances, music etc.). To be 'chic' means to aspire to the latest 'western fashion' – a phenomenon which is not limited to upper-class Egyptians, but is also widespread among the impoverished middle classes. Break-dancing in front of Al-Azhar mosque, McDonald's and a whole other range of fast food spin-offs, video arcades and discotheques have become part of the Cairo scene. While western goods are only affordable to the upper middle class and upper classes, modified versions of *Bitza* and *Hamborga* have gained mass appeal.[13] In the words of Bryan Turner, 'the corruption of pristine faith is going to be brought about by Tina Turner and Coca-Cola and not by rational arguments and rational inspection of presuppositions and the understanding of western secularism' (Turner, 1994: 10).

The ambiguities of western style consumption in material life and

[13] In one incident a few years ago, 150 teenagers were arrested on the charge of belonging to a 'satanic cult' which was identified with devil worship and digging out skulls from the cemetery, as well as heavy-metal music, pre-marital sex, drugs and hanging out at McDonald's.

culture are uncovered in Walter Armbrust's fascinating account of mass culture and modernism in Egypt. What can be, in certain contexts and by certain people, labelled as *shik 'awi* (very chic) could also have negative connotations designating inauthenticity and *noveau riche* (Armbrust, 1996: 26–7). However, he also shows how historically Egyptian modernity has embraced western technology, scientific methods and consumption products on the one side, and 'Egyptian authenticity', that is continuity with the past, on the other. In recent years this complex constellation of Egyptian modernity has become more polarized and problematic in the light of a decrease in social mobility, increased economic hardships and underemployment. Education, supposedly bridging the gap 'between official media theory of what modernity should be and social practice' (ibid.: 133), has lost its value considerably in terms of guaranteeing a comfortable 'modern' life. Yet education is still widely perceived to be 'the only way out'. In contrast to riches obtained by *bita al-infitah* (those of the open door policies) or *nouveaux riches*, education is seen to allow for morally sound and authentic social climbing.

It becomes obvious that anti-westernism and anti-imperialism are related to discourses about Egypt's past. The Nasserist undertones and anti-imperialist slogans of newspaper headlines reveal a certain nostalgia for 'Egypt's glorious days' associated with the Nasser period (1952–70). A similar nostalgia has been detected by Abu-Lughod with regard to television serials, which 'invoke the period of socialist ideals and nationalist vision through charged symbols of the Nasirist era, like the great singer Umm Kulthum or the Aswan High Dam' (1993b: 29). The Sadat period (1970–81), which many Egyptians today remember for its economic policies which boosted mass consumption as well as for Camp David and the sense of capitulation, is often evoked negatively, especially in the light of more recent geo-political developments.

Disappointment with the 'peace process', generally perceived by Egyptian intellectuals to have worked at the expense of Palestinians and Arabs, has revived anti-Israeli sentiments. Recently, debates on the 'Middle East Market' and the 'nuclear non-proliferation treaty' (NPT) further increased the rejection of the 'naturalization' process with Israel initiated by Sadat. Israel's strong link with the 'West', politically with the United States in particular, but culturally with Europe and 'western civilization', expands the ground for anti-western discourses. Jewish regional ties and common historical and cultural backgrounds are rarely being acknowledged in a context where Israeli culture is homogenized as Zionist and western.

In post-colonial Egypt anti-western discourses are mainly directed towards the United States and rarely address British colonialism. An

American imperialist presence has been experienced through its financial and political support of Israel. Anti-western feelings, then, are deeply caught up with Zionism. On an economic level, Egypt's dependence on the United States[14] and the various impacts of structural adjustment policies, such as the marked decline in government investment in the public sector, price increases and high interest rates, also contribute to the sense of prolonged imperialist presence and interference.

Geo-political factors might explain the pervasiveness and intensity of anti-western feelings, but internal political struggles and competitions over economic resources also need to be taken into account. As with orientalism, occidentalism's homogenizing thrust and its dichotomies cannot be explained in terms of simple misapprehensions or failures of understanding: they are put to use by Islamist and leftist–nationalist constituencies to gain symbolic advantage over adversaries within the Egyptian political landscape.

Without doubt, however, the particular reasons and context for Egyptian occidentalism can also be framed within a wider tendency found in many parts of the previously colonized world and also those countries subject to ongoing imperialist influence and expansion. Nationalist movements – whether during and after the fight for independence or in the process of decolonization – often homogenize and isolate their own and other populations and celebrate their 'authentic' identity in the name of nationalism. Blaming the West for most evils in the world is generally paralleled by a passionate and uncritical embracing of one's own primordial group without paying too much attention to the social, cultural, economic and political realities inside one's nation.[15] But to accept this 'nativism', as Edward Said argues, 'is to accept the consequence of imperialism, the racial, religious, and political divisions imposed by imperialism itself' (1993: 276).

The dangers of chauvinism and xenophobia as an aspect of nationalist consciousness were recognized by Frantz Fanon. In his view, nationalist independence will remain rigid and trapped in old injustices, and will create new hierarchies and systems of oppression as long as it will not also involve a transformation of social consciousness. '*Liberation*, and not nationalist independence, is the new alternative' (Fanon, quoted in Said, 1993: 277). Social movements that address social injustices and orthodoxies, such as political authoritarianism, class oppression and patriarchy, have to resist a new powerful nationalist bourgeoisie. After independence, according to Said, among the various social movements

[14] Egypt is the single largest recipient of American aid after Israel.
[15] The Iranian Jalal Ali Ahmad's *Occidentosis: A Plague from the West* (1978) is an often quoted example for nativism that engages in blank condemnations of the 'West'.

resisting old orthodoxies, feminism became one of the main liberationist tendencies in the Third World (ibid.: 263), thereby posing a threat to the status quo.

It comes as no surprise then that the strategy of gaining symbolic power by essentializing the 'West' and its corruption is regularly utilized when talking about women and feminism. Portrayals of loose western women as well as man-hating feminists are linked to prescribing moral codes, especially concerning the roles, rights and duties of women and gender relations in Egypt. Much has been written on the notion of women as 'bearers of authentic culture' and I will only briefly address this already well-documented point later in this chapter.[16] I will explore in more detail the questions of how negative constructions of the West are mobilized to discredit Egyptian women activists and how Egyptian women activists in turn use constructions of the West to legitimize their struggles.

It is my contention that contemporary secular-oriented women activists have, by and large, internalized the parameters within which permissible discourses are formulated. But what do the various women activists actually say about the 'West'? Moreover, later in this chapter and throughout this work, I will try to show that there are some women who go beyond the rhetoric of 'us versus them' and try to position themselves in value systems and political struggles that are not necessarily framed by the 'West' as 'the other'.

Egypt's gateway: dislocation of us versus them

Stereotypical representations create boundaries and make firm and separate what is in fact fluid and much closer to the norm than the dominant value system cares to admit. Many definitions of the 'West', and categories such as 'western feminism' are similar to the process, that, in Said's words almost two decades ago, seeks 'to intensify its own sense of itself by dramatizing the distance and difference between what is closer to it and what is far away' (Said, 1978: 55). The 'reality' of the West is invented anew every time it is deployed for this or that purpose. However, orientalism and occidentalism do not constitute two symmetrically opposed phenomena; rather they represent two historically specific processes based on very different power relationships. Moreover, occidentalism reveals a much greater degree of contradiction between prevailing discourses and social practices than orientalism. The earlier conceptions of the 'West' as delivering progress and modernity have largely been replaced by

---

[16] For a detailed discussions on the issue of women as 'cultural bearers' of the 'authentic nation' see Moghadam (ed.) (1994a); Yuval-Davis (1997); and Yuval-Davis & Anthias (eds.) (1989).

conceptions of the West as polluting and corrupting, but, in certain circles and in specific contexts, being 'western' opens up many doors. Let me try to illustrate this point with a little anecdote.

Throughout my seven-year stay in Egypt I occasionally travelled to visit my parents in Germany or friends elsewhere. I cannot recall one arrival back to Cairo that did not make me feel anxious and insecure, stirring up my conscience into wondering whether I had 'done something wrong'. Of course, I knew that being singled out from the other passengers, mainly Germans – who all proceeded through passport control without any delay – was just a formality, a simple process of checking 'my files' in the computers. Of course, I knew that this was due to my Arab name, a name that evokes suspicion among 'fellow Arabs'.

Usually the conversation at the passport control took the following course: first, I would be greeted in English with 'hello' (and often a smile). After a good look at my passport (turning the pages back and forth to look for the last entry and departure stamps) I regularly would be asked: 'bitkalami 'arabi?' (do you speak Arabic?) or 'aslan eeh?' (what is your origin?) The further tone of the conversation often depended on my answer to these questions. Several friends had advised me to pretend not to speak any Arabic, as 'you are always treated better at any Arab border if you are a foreigner'. I soon learned that the situation was much more complicated than my friends had imagined: it was a classic case of catch-22. If I answered in the negative to the question whether I spoke Arabic, some security personnel (who are always men) would react with a smile and try to figure out, in a more or less cordial way, how I came to my name. However, there were others who reacted to my negation with even greater suspicion and continued to insist that I must speak Arabic, because of my name. On good days I would play the game well and not reveal that I understood his questions; on bad days I would either 'give up' voluntarily and reveal my language skills, however imperfect, or due to tiredness and lack of concentration betray myself sooner or later.

At other times I refused to hide either my language skills or my father's origin and answered back in Arabic. This also evoked very different reactions, varying from praise of my command of the language (thereby often revealing a sense of amusement) to piercing and often hostile questioning. Whatever the scenario, the outcome was always similar: my passport would be taken and I would be motioned to step aside and wait, sometimes for just a few minutes, sometimes for over an hour. Most of the time I managed to calm myself down and feel less annoyed by thinking about the waiting time and humiliation many other people, especially Palestinians, have to endure. In comparison to them I could really consider myself lucky, as I was never actually kept waiting for many hours, nor was I ever prevented from entering Egypt.

Matters were further complicated by the fact that I not only carry an Arab name, but that I am also the daughter of a man who is originally from Iraq. The particular reactions to my 'Iraqi background' varied according to the political situation and Egypt's relationship with Iraq.[17] My worst re-entry ever into Egypt took place a month after Iraq's invasion of Kuwait. As I had visited my family in Baghdad in July 1990 and was stuck in Iraq for a couple of weeks after the invasion, my passport had arrival and departure stamps from Iraq, covering the period during which the invasion of Kuwait took place (2 August 1990). This time I was not merely asked to wait but was interrogated for some hours about my visit to Iraq. My student visa and ID card from the American University in Cairo certainly helped to diffuse some of the tension and suspicion. When I was finally allowed to go through, picked up my luggage and happily hugged some Egyptian friends who had patiently waited for me, I soon felt much more stress than under interrogation at the airport. My friend Mona told me to be silent about my Iraqi background, because everyone was very upset with Iraqis for what they had done to Kuwait; not that I had previously gone around Cairo waving a sign saying 'I am Iraqi', but the thought of having to conceal my Iraqi connection was highly distressing and frightening. This particular experience was certainly unique in the degree of suspicion with which I was viewed and the intensity of the situation. Most other times it became more of a routine, one of those unpleasant things one has to go through.

If I have spent a considerable amount of time writing about Cairo airport, it is because I see the airport, its organization, rules and regulations as a metaphor for some of the contradictions of post-colonial Egypt. Whatever claims are made to 'authenticity', however fiercely the 'West' is attacked for corrupting and damaging the country, however passionately 'Arab brotherhood' is being evoked, the gateway to Egypt is far more open to Europeans and North Americans than to either Egypt's African neighbours or Arab sisters and brothers.

Visitors from the 'West' are usually tourists who bring jobs and spend money. Both the government and the manifold segments of the Egyptian tourist industry encourage and actively seek floods of western tourists to boost the economy. Attacks on tourists by Islamist militants in recent

---

[17] Throughout my years of travelling, I also detected divergences from official government positions to Iraq among the airport personnel. Especially since Iraq was bombed during the Gulf war, the security person checking my passport has expressed his grief and anger about what is happening to the Iraqi people, despite the Egyptian military involvement in the war on the side of 'the allies'.

years have been so effective precisely because they are not merely expressions of hostile attitudes towards corrupting and sinful infidels, but they also hit the state at one of its most vulnerable spots, one crucial to survival.

It is not only 'western' tourists who are privileged when entering the country, but also businesspeople, development workers, UN officials, embassy personnel and even moneyless foreign students. As for foreign researchers, it has been increasingly difficult to obtain official research permits in Egypt. This has resulted in many researchers simply avoiding applying for one. Paradoxically, while the official research permit poses an obstacle, once it has been obtained (or circumvented) most European or North American researchers have relatively easy access to Egyptian top-notch intellectuals, artists and political figures, while Egyptian researchers would have to use *wasta* (connections) or affiliate themselves with western researchers. In recent years, however, there has been a shift in attitude towards western researchers and journalists, especially among NGO workers, women's and human rights activists and the political opposition, who increasingly perceive foreign researchers and journalists as politically naive and exploitative.

Presentations of self

Another reason for narrating my airport anecdote is that it alludes to some of the difficulties inherent in 'shuttling between two or more worlds' (Visweswaran, 1994: 119). Negotiating my identities during the airport proceedings involved a mixture of arbitrariness and strategizing. The 'rite of passage' at Cairo airport is emblematic of the ambiguities, dislocations and states of liminality inherent in identity constructions and representations of self. On rare occasions I actually felt strongly about a particular part of my identity; during the Gulf war, for example, I actually *felt* Iraqi. Most of the time though, while finding my way out of the airport, I *performed* being German or Iraqi. This manoeuvring continued throughout my research and I will explore issues of 'hyphenation' and 'positionality' as they crystallized throughout my research.

Throughout my actual 'fieldwork', in which I was to explore the different layers and elements of Egyptian women activists' identities, I realized that the only 'identity' that was really being discussed as such was mine. Sometimes I felt uncomfortable with the way some women identified me as Iraqi and therefore 'good' and trustworthy, just because of my name, 'blood' and my father's original nationality. It often reminded me of the situations and contexts when I was treated badly, also just because of my Arab name. One of the Nasserite women, who on several occasions cursed western conspiracies and western researchers implicated in them, put it most bluntly when I asked her why she talked to me: '*But you are Iraqi. I would not have talked to you if you had been just a westerner!*'

My airport anecdote has already given some indication as to how politicized identity constructions might be. The significance of 'Iraqiness' and 'Germanness' varied greatly between Cairo airport and the context of my actual research. Among most Egyptian women activists, as well as among leftists and Islamists, Iraq has become the epitome of resistance to imperialist violence and injustice. Others see Iraqis as among the most recent and acute victims of both their own government and American hegemony. At times the specific attribution of 'being Iraqi' was replaced by a more generalized perception of me as 'Arab'. '*You are one of us*', on rare occasions, could even mean 'Egyptian', but here it was not an attribute related to my 'background' as much as a designation based on my involvement in the Egyptian women's rights struggle. While I often felt uneasy and irritated by perceptions of who I am based on primordial elements of blood and heritage, I very much cherished the moments in which I became an 'honorary Egyptian'.

In specific situations, such as discussions about western feminisms, my education at the American University in Cairo and my upbringing in Germany, as well as during debates about homosexuality and relationships in general, the adjective 'western' was often ascribed to me. At times I actually experienced a sense of essential difference in attitude and outlook which I attributed to my 'socialization' in Germany. At other times I felt that the attribute 'western' was used as an easy device to discredit my opinion which happened to be different. 'Germanness' rarely figured in these ascriptions (except in the context of mocking my concern with punctuality and being organized), and when it was used, it had more positive connotations than the generalized term 'western'.

Due to my name and my father's origin, most of the Egyptians I met in the course of my stay assumed that I was a Muslim. However, my religious identity (having a Muslim Shi'a father and a Catholic mother) was never discussed among the secular women I interviewed. In the context of my research, ethnicity and my political outlook were perceived as more significant than my religious affiliation.

Parallel to, but not always in harmony with, the various ascriptions of my 'identity', I frequently sensed the 'hyphen', between Iraqi-German or Arab-Western. Hyphenated identities enact an often violent struggle between two or more worlds. Nasser Hussein's description of post-colonial identities certainly rings a bell: 'Hyphens are radically ambivalent signifiers, for they simultaneously connect and set apart; they simultaneously represent both belonging and not belonging. What is even more curious about a hyphenated pair of words is that meaning cannot reside in one word or the other, but can only be understood in movement' (1990: 10).

The attempt to negotiate the terms between shifting alliances results in the feeling of being 'born over and over again as a hyphen rather than a fixed entity' (Trinh, 1991: 159). Being an Iraqi-German doing research in the Arab world suggests more than an accidental academic trajectory, since the very subject matter of my book is related to this 'hybrid subject position' (Visweswaran, 1994). Moreover, the tension between my roles as researcher and woman activist in Egypt further increased the sense of uneasy travelling between 'speaking for' and 'speaking from' (Abu-Lughod, 1991: 143).

The issue of 'hybridity' is problematized by Rosemary Sayigh who questions the effects of prolonged exposure to a specific culture: 'While culturally enriching, hybridity perhaps induces a half-conscious adoption of the research community's ethos; and this, while enhancing rapport, may block off certain questions and inquiries' (1996: 146). In my view, it is not only important to acknowledge our 'positionality', that is the different components of our identities, presuppositions and political orientations that we bring from our home(s), but as Lindisfarne (1997) and Sayigh (1996) point out, we must also recognize that our research community will have an impact on the ways we see and think about the world. Lindisfarne, for example, explains how her fieldwork in Syria shaped her 'political voice' and identity (Lindisfarne 1997), which in many ways parallels my experiences in Cairo.

My political commitment to feminism and my attempts to counter dehumanizing depictions of 'Arabs' and 'Muslims' in the western media developed and grew while living and doing research in Cairo. Only later, during my recent fieldwork, did I also become sensitive to sweeping generalizations concerning the 'West', which have now also become part of my research agenda. My work helped me to understand some of the complexities and problems involved in women's activism in Egypt – some of which had been unknown to me at the time of my own initial involvement a couple of years ago. The material bases for many of the seemingly ideological struggles, the personalized nature of conflicts among the various groups and the impact of the international community were not obvious to me at first. It also prompted me to rethink 'secularism', a concept I had clearly defined for myself before my actual research.[18]

While gaining insights, awareness, and often empathy, I started to examine my own positionality more critically. My encounters and inter-

[18] In chapter 4 I will specifically take issue with the notion of 'secularism' and 'secular-oriented women activists'.

actions with women activists, as well as my Egyptian friends and acquaintances during the year of 'fieldwork', relieved me from my previous impetus constantly to demonstrate my 'Arabness' or rather 'non-Westernness', and, paradoxically, evoked a reconciliation with my own 'political voice'. Hybridity, as I described earlier, was often more than a sheer catchword. However, I also recognized that my own identity and political voice are not directly linked up with a hyphenated position. Without wishing to fall back into the traps of universalism or naive humanism, I endorse a set of values related to human rights, women's equality, freedom of expression and social justice, which I refuse to abandon for the sake of 'authenticity'. In my view, there is nothing inherently 'western' or 'Arab' about any of these values.

Recovering (from) identity

As I have already referred to the magic word 'identity', I would like briefly to examine its significance for my work. Prior to starting my research among Egyptian women activists in Cairo, I concentrated on the concept of 'identity' as key to my project. Based on my observations during my period of studying and working in Egypt, my experiences whilst being involved in one women's organization, as well as my readings, I assumed that women's activism was characterized by a struggle for both gender and national identity. One of my main aims was to understand the complex relations between women's liberation and the post-colonial struggle for independence in contemporary Egypt.

My theoretical encounters and struggles with identity left me with some vague notions of what identity was not (something stable, rigid and essential) and what it could be (changing, shifting and fragmented). This made sense to me personally, but did not seem to fit in with fierce struggles of people fighting for their 'identity' and 'authenticity'. When I actually started my 'fieldwork', this vague, puzzling, almost inexplicable concept 'identity' blocked my sight. It was in my mind all the time, but did not allow me actually to see and listen. Only when I had the courage to brush it aside and bracket my carefully researched concept could I actually start to grasp the issues, tendencies, problems and debates. Later on I understood that everything, in one way or another, can be linked back to 'identity': the life-histories of women whose personal lives are so often caught up in political changes, debates on what feminism means, struggles over priorities and issues among women activists (such as literacy, health care, awareness of legal rights, protection against violence at home), alliances and rivalries with national and international groups and organizations, debates on religion and secularism as well as friendships, lifestyles and so forth. I did not get any of this information and insight as long as I asked questions with 'identity' as a grid which effectively worked more like a blindfold.

There are many dangers of a broad concept such as identity as it could be and is easily (ab)used for reification, essentializing and exclusion. Nevertheless, it continues to act as a key idiom in cultural and political movements and a central heuristic tool in the social sciences. Although identity has been questioned, problematized and deconstructed, it has not been replaced by a new concept. Instead, identity has been thought about at the limit, 'operating "under erasure" in the interval between reversal and emergence; an idea which cannot be thought in the old way, but without which certain questions cannot be thought at all' (Hall, 1996b: 2). In other words, identity has to be read against the grain. With this recognition, I accept Stuart Hall's conceptualization of it as fluid, always in process, changing and transforming, lodged in contingency, subject to radical historicization, and multiply constructed across different, often intersecting and antagonistic, discourses, practices and positions (ibid.: 2–4).

Discussions of 'Egyptian identity' abound with essentialisms as I shall demonstrate in the following section of this chapter. I will briefly review discussions on nationalism and national identity in general and Egypt in particular and show the variety of discourses and positions on that issue.

Nationalisms and national identities in Egypt

Most of the 'classics' on the literature of nationalism deal with it as a kind of monolithic or universal phenomenon (B. Anderson, 1983; Gellner, 1983b; Kedourie, 1960; Kohn, 1955; A. Smith, 1971, 1976). The notion of 'nationalism' in the singular has been challenged from many positions, especially in the field of post-colonial studies (Bhaba, 1990; Chatterjee, 1989; Radhakrishnan, 1992; Sedgwick, 1992). 'Nationalisms' are political projects that make claims to territory or the separate political representation of an ethnic or religious group.

While nationalist movements have often been associated with the struggle for autonomy by ethnic groups, nationalist projects often articulate the interests of oppressed classes against colonialism and imperialism. It is therefore difficult to see them as emanating from an ethnic essence or always the outcome of ethnic processes. Moreover, as Sami Zubaida has argued, socio-economic and political processes linked to long histories of centralized governments created the sense of 'national unity' and ethnic homogeneity (Zubaida, 1989; referred to in Yuval-Davis, 1997: 16). However, as Nira Yuval-Davis points out, 'there is an inherent connection between the ethnic and national projects'. They might be different in scale but both present Andersonian 'imagined communities' (1997: 16).

Different nationalisms might even coexist in one country or shift during the history of nationalist struggle. Egypt is a case in point. A complicated choreography around the terms Muslim, Arab and Egyptian as bearers of 'authentic identity' and national belonging has marked Egypt's history. It is possible to identify three different conceptions for social solidarity: territorial nationalism, based on land (*watan*) and a sense of uniqueness because of geographical and historical unity; a linguistic–ethnic nationalism derived from the sharing of a common language and/or ethnicity with the 'Arab nation' (*qawm*); and the sense of religious belonging in which one's religious community (*umma*) is perceived to be the object of ultimate loyalty (Jankowski, 1986a: 193).[19] The latter basis for solidarity, that is the belonging to the *umma*, poses a contradiction as it conventionally implies a multi-national and multi-ethnic community opposed to the concept of *qawm* and nationalism. However, there has been an increasing Islamist trend in Egypt which frames religious belonging with nationalist discourse, striving for an Islamic state.

Reorientation towards the Arab world during Nasser's regime – and the resulting sense of Arab identification that developed – did not challenge the deeper sentiment of Egyptian identity felt by many articulate Egyptians (Jankowski, 1997). Arab identity did not replace Egyptian identity but acted as a supplement. 'Such as other supplements it had a heavily-instrumental aspect: the promotion of Egyptian self-defense or aggrandizement, economic advantage, cultural leadership' (Jankowski, 1986a: 201).

Pan-Arab nationalism decreased steadily under Sadat and Mubarak. However, the growing passion for pan-Islamism and the expansion of the *umma* (community of believers) beyond national boundaries is often linked to an identification with the Arab Muslim world. While pan-Islamism certainly represents the most noticeable and outspoken element of collective solidarity in Egypt today, I believe that the majority of

---

[19] Although intellectuals such as Mustapha Kamil and Ahmad Lutfi Al-Sayyid promoted devotion to the geographically defined Egyptian *watan*, traditional sentiments of belonging to one's religious community or kinship group, village or quarter prevailed among most Egyptians around the turn of the century. Nevertheless, Egyptian territorial nationalism became the most prevailing sentiment among Egyptian intellectuals and in public opinion after World War I. The beginning of the 1930s witnessed another shift as increasing numbers of Egyptians developed an increased sense of national identity with the surrounding Arab world, which laid the basis for the ascendancy of Arab nationalism in Egypt under Nasser (Jankowski, 1986a: 197; 1997).

the population expresses its nationalist sentiments in terms of Egypt's geographical entity and its civilizational achievements.

Like nationalisms, national identities are not fixed entities; not only can they shift in the history of a nation but their constructions also vary among different groups within the nation. In Egypt there has been a continuous oscillation between secular and religious underpinnings of national identity, in addition to the unresolved question of where Egypt belongs culturally and politically (*intima' misr*). As Beth Baron points out, the British tried to deny Egyptian nationality when Lord Cromer, British agent and consul general, wrote in 1890 that 'there is no such thing as an Egyptian nationality'. Egyptians themselves, however, could 'always resort to a multi-layered past and choose between Pharaonic, Coptic, Islamic, or Arab origins and symbols (or some combination thereof) to construct their "Egyptianness"' (Baron, 1993: 244). The national independence movement in the period before 1923 (Egypt's independence) attempted to create a secular national identity with the slogans *al-din lillah wa'l-watan liljami* (religion belongs to God and the nation to all), and *al-wataniyya dinuna* (nationalism is our religion), thereby linking the principle of nationality and citizenship (*muwatana*) irrespective of religious belief (Vatikiotis, 1983: 254).

However, certain strands in society, especially the Muslim Brotherhood, diverged in their ideas from the construction of a secular national identity and political community. For them, Egyptian national identity could not be separated from Islam. The proponents of the religious political community insisted on the application of the *shari'a*, thus begging the question of the rights and duties of non-Muslims in this Islamic polity (ibid.: 256–7).

The military regime that came to power in 1952 ended the debate over the nature of the national community by suppressing both secularists and Islamic nationalists. However, the 'Arab identity' that was decreed in the 1956 constitution under Nasser had started to emerge in the 1930s. During the government of Sadat, however, emphasis shifted away from identification with the Arabic *qawm* to the Egyptian *watan*, especially after his separate peace accords with Israel. Sadat is seen as having aggravated the controversy between secular and religious national identity by his deliberate manipulation of religion for his own political gains (Philipp, 1988).

The most prominent writers to deal with the question of Egyptian national identity – Ahmad Lutfi Al-Sayyid, Taha Husayn, Subhi Wahida, Husein Mu'nis, Mirrit Butrus Ghali, Gamal Hamdan, Tariq Al-Bishri and Milad Hanna – have emphasized different aspects of Egypt's history to construct its origins and identity. Hamdan, for example, stresses historical continuity with the Pharaonic past as well as Egypt's 'unique geography' as being essential to the revival of an Egyptian national consciousness that had been overwhelmed by wider identities, such as those of Islam or Arabism. He defines Egyptian national identity in the context of the juxtaposition between wider religious ideological and secular national trends which 'together with the civilizational–cultural interaction of Muslims and Copts in Egypt . . . generated the historical, intellectual, social and psychological climate for the crystallization of the national idea of the Egyptian political community' (1980: 44).

Muslim–Coptic relations, and in particular the question of whether religion should play any role in the definition of the Egyptian nation state (and if so, what role should be assigned to the Coptic minority), have been at the centre of many debates around the issue of national identity in Egypt (Philipp, 1988). Among the various positions on this issue, the argument has been put forward that religiosity – not one religion or the other in particular – is part of the Egyptian national identity. This response is indicated in Al-Bishri's (1980) attack on western secularism as irrelevant to the Egyptian national experience. In recent years, in light of growing Islamist activism, widespread economic discontent, the perception of western cultural and political infiltration, increased Muslim–Coptic sectarian strife and regional politics (especially the Gulf war, Palestinian–Israeli politics and the debate on a Middle East market), the issue of Egypt's cultural and political identity has been revived.

Political scientist and human rights activist Ahmed Abdallah and professor of engineering and leftist Tagammu leader Milad Hanna both argue strongly for 'compounded identities'. The latter, a spokesperson for the Coptic community and strong defender of national unity, had been accused by Sadat of stimulating sectarian strife and was imprisoned for several years. In his book *The Seven Pillars of Egyptian Identity* (1989), Hanna depicts Egyptian identity as constituted of four layers of civilization: the Pharaonic, the Graeco-Roman, the Coptic and the Islamic. These four historical 'pillars' are implanted in three geographical ones: the Arab world, the Mediterranean and Africa. In his account, these seven pillars, which are part of every Egyptian in different forms and with varying degrees, make up the sum of Egyptian national identity.

Ahmed Abdallah (1994) considers the debate on national identity within the framework of the perceived threat of absorption into broader entities: medieval Islamic, modern Arab and recent Middle Eastern. While depicting Egyptianness as a compound of Pharaonism, Coptism, pan-Arabism and pan-Islamism, Abdallah argues that the quarrel over national identity only flares up in times of crisis and socio-political struggle. Recently, the growth of extremism has threatened the notion of compounded identity by the search for an exclusive one. Furthermore, the suggested notion of 'Middle Easternism' as a framework for identity in the aftermath of the second Gulf war and the recent Arab–Israeli accords elicited a strong defence of Arabism among Egyptian intellectuals. He also mentions the various pressures under which national identity is debated and constructed:

> The first pressure relates to universalism/globalism, from gunboats and bombers (like the ones that destroyed Baghdad) to American soap operas. They are much nearer to home than they used to be, hence their influence on local interactions ... The second pressure comes from the younger generation of Egyptians, whose acute day to day problems seem to have led to the loss of ideals; the vast majority are alienated, the committed minority resorts to militant Islamism. (*Al-Ahram Weekly*, 1994)

What needs to be emphasized is that the debates and struggles over national identity do not only take place in magazines, newspapers, books and discussions among intellectuals. This is an ongoing and burning issue that is constructed, asserted and fought over in the daily lives of Egyptians today. Choices are not only being made concerning political and religious orientation, but also with regard to lifestyle, dress-code and social relations. For an outsider these choices often seem paradoxical (wearing a *higab* and Levi's jeans, for instance), but as the boundaries between 'inside' and 'outside' have become more and more blurred, it requires careful observation and sensitivity to become aware of the complexities and different layers involved in definitions of 'Egyptianness'.

Nationalism, gender and feminist politics

The link between nationalism and feminism has been increasingly discussed in different historical and cultural contexts (Kandiyoti, 1991; Moghadam (ed.), 1994a; Mohanty et al., 1991; Parker et al. (eds.), 1992; Yuval-Davis, 1997; Yuval-Davis & Anthias (eds.), 1989). Common to the various analyses is the centrality assigned to the role of women in nationalist projects. Yuval-Davis and Anthias identify five major ways in which women have tended to participate in ethnic and national processes and in relation to state practices: (a) as biological reproducers of members of ethnic collectivities; (b) as reproducers of the boundaries of ethnic/ national groups; (c) as participating centrally in the ideological reproduction of the collectivity and as transmitters of its culture; (d) as symbols in the ideological discourses used in ethnic/national differences; and (e) as participants in national, economic, political and military struggles (1989: 7).

The various roles differ in significance according to particular social and political conditions and might shift in the course of a woman's lifetime. Moreover, it is important to keep in mind that there is no unitary category of women (or men) that can be unproblematically conceived as the focus of ethnic, national or state policies and discourses: 'Differential positionings in ethnic, racial, class, age, ability, sexual and other social divisions interface with gender divisions, so that although women usually are constructed and treated by various agencies as different to men, "women" as well as "men" do not constitute homogenous categories as either social agents or social objects' (Yuval-Davis, 1997: 116). It is also important to stress the ambivalence of women's position within the national collectivity. Women are assigned the role of bearers of cultural values, carriers of traditions, and symbols of the community,[20] but are 'often excluded from the collective "we" of the body politic, and retain an object rather than a subject position' (ibid.: 47).

The ambivalence and differentiation of women's positions in the national collectivity can also be detected in Egypt. During the struggle for independence, gender played an important role in forging a sense of cohesion and bonding. Representing the nation as a woman, Baron argues, was not only meant to induce notions of honour and the sense that the nation had to be supported, protected and defended by its male citizens (Baron, 1993: 246–7; 1997: 121): 'By depicting the nation as a woman, nationalists hoped to stimulate love for the nation and draw male youth to the cause . . . The man was the actor, the speaker, the lover; the woman was acted upon, the listener, the beloved' (Baron, 1997: 121). Yet women were often not 'imagined' as part of the nation. Rather, they were used as subjects and symbols around which to rally male support (Baron, 1993: 245).

In present day Egypt, nationalist rhetoric often makes 'woman' the pure and ahistorical signifier of 'interiority' by mobilizing the inner/outer distinction against the 'otherness' of the West. According to Chatterjee (1989), the ideology of nationalist politics in its very specificity acts as the normative mode of the political as such, and 'the imagined community' of nationalism is authorized as the most authentic unit or form of collectivity. Consequently the women's question is constrained to take on a nationalist expression as a prerequisite for being considered political. As R. Radhakrishnan argues: 'Faced with its own repression, the women's

[20] Women are not only given the duty to teach and transfer the authentic cultural and ideological traditions of the nation, but very often they constitute its actual symbolic figuration. Nationalist discourses and representations recurrently depict the homeland as a female body whose violation by foreigners requires its male citizens to rush to her defence. Men defend her as they would defend 'the mother who lost her sons in battle', their lover, their 'women and children', or their honour (Yuval-Davis & Anthias, 1989: 10).

question seems forced whether to seek its own separatist political autonomy or to envision other ways of constituting a relational-integrative politics without at the same time resorting to another kind of totalizing
umbrella' (1992: 78). My own experience with women activists in Egypt
today parallels Chatterjee's and Radhakrishnan's works about the Indian
women's movement and I will illustrate this point further in this book.

Feminist projects in anti-colonial struggles have often been sacrificed
to the cause of national liberation and, in the aftermath of independence,
women have been relegated to their former 'domestic' roles. However,
there were points of convergence between nationalist and feminist struggles, especially when the nation was envisioned as 'modern'. Issues of
suffrage, women's welfare and reproductive rights also challenged the
inequalities concealed in the vision of a 'common' nationhood (Parker et
al. (eds.), 1992: 7).

It is difficult to say in advance whether or how different feminisms must
negotiate through or around national political discourses. Kumari
Jayawardena (1986) attempted to show how feminism and nationalism in
Asia were linked in the nineteenth and early twentieth centuries. In her
account, the movement towards women's emancipation took place
against a background of nationalist struggles aimed at achieving political
independence, asserting national identity and modernizing the society.
Referring to different countries (e.g. Turkey, Egypt and Afghanistan),
Jayawardena argues that feminism and nationalism used to be comple-
mentary, compatible and solidaristic.

However, Beth Baron (1993) convincingly shows how in Egypt at the
beginning of the century the relation between feminism and nationalism
was much more tense and conflict-ridden than that described by
Jayawardena. She depicts some of the leading rituals of the independence
movement, such as funeral processions and demonstrations, as mainly
'male experiences' (ibid.: 248). I agree with her contention that 'in spite
of the rhetoric of the "woman question" and women's participation in the
nationalist movement, reforms on many of those issues important to
women's advocates proved hard to pass once the nationalists came to
control the state' (ibid.: 252). Baron shows how this seeming paradox of
women's mobilization in the national struggle and their failure to realize
their own agendas with independence may be better understood if one
considers the 'gendering of nationalism'. The vocabulary and signs
employed to spread nationalism strengthened certain deeply embedded
beliefs about gender, reinforcing ideals of sexual purity, morality and
motherhood (ibid.).

Egyptian women activists: the quest for authenticity

Egyptian feminists, whose activism has been historically rooted in nationalism, have always run the risk of being stigmatized as anti-religious and anti-nationalist. In recent years, women activists have been increasingly accused – particularly by Islamists and conservatives, but also by leftist–nationalist voices – of collaborating with 'western imperialism' by importing alien ideas and practices and propagating them throughout society. In the light of these very intimidating charges it is not surprising that many women activists internalized these accusations, and themselves equate feminism with a western concept, alien and alienating to their social, cultural and political context.

As already mentioned in the introduction, the unwillingness of many Egyptian women to identify themselves as feminist is not only related to the negative image of feminism in society, but is also linked to the conviction that it detracts from such 'larger issues' as imperialism, class struggle and Zionism (Al-Ali, 1997). In this view, feminism is seen to divide women and men in their common struggle against these forces. Nevertheless, many women activists in Egypt are engaged in producing knowledge about and attitudes towards 'feminism' that diverge from the idea of it as another form of western infiltration.

The actual Arabic terminology used when the women's activism is addressed varies according to ideological outlook and political affiliation. All terms seem to be loaded with a 'heavy baggage', as the women's and human rights activist Mona T. shows by expressing the difficulty of choosing the 'right' words:

There exist different words for feminism in Egypt. This is problematic. Tahrir al-mar'a [women's liberation] has a horrible connotation to many people. They associate it with promiscuity: she has to go out until midnight to be a free woman. The term was used in the past . . . Al-haraka al-nassa'wiyya [the feminist movement] is very elitist. Very few people would understand it. It is only used with educated leftist people . . . Whether nissa'iyya or nassa'wiyya [women's or feminist]: even the haraka puts people on guard: 'Eh, da, sitat fi haraka?' [what's that, women in the movement?] It tends to be exclusive. Men get very offended. Normally I use qadiyyat al-mar'a [women's issues]. But all of these terms have horrible connotations. If you say qadiyyat al-mar'a, of course you get all kinds of comments. If you use wada' al-mar'a [situation or status of women] you are actually just making people feel safe. This is the status of women and it has a less threatening connotation. Wada' al-mar'a is also more narrowly defined. It mainly addresses women's legal rights.

Unfortunately, this particular quotation reflects a very sad reality: women activists constantly have to be on the defensive against a vast number of charges ranging from being 'loose women' to aping the 'West'. The attempt to legitimize and justify their outlooks and activism is at the centre of many debates and can be detected in the various trends of women's activism. Stressing the close link between the beginning of the women's movement and 'the nationalist view', many activists allude to an attitude, in which *tahrir al-mar'a* (women's liberation) is part of anti-colonial and anti-imperialist struggle. This perspective can be traced back to what has been called the 'national liberation discourse', in which women are dealt with as 'part of the struggle for economic and political decolonization' (Hatem, 1993: 42).

While early feminists (such as Huda Sha'rawi, for example) struggled with 'a West' perceived to be outside the Egyptian nation (British colonialism), contemporary struggles with *al-hagma al-thaqafiyya* (the cultural offensive) and *imberiliyya* (imperialism) are of a far more complex nature. When asked about the actual meaning of imperialism, women activists affiliated with leftist organizations often allude to American policies which are seen to lead to both Egypt's dependence and the expansion of capitalism. Many women mentioned the IMF and USAID, as well as multi-national companies and enforced privatization policies. Zionism and normalization of relations with Israel are also seen as part of 'imperialist hegemony'. For many activists the coincidence between the abandonment of 'state feminism'[21] and the Camp David accords during the Sadat period created a conjuncture in which imperialism had a direct bearing on peoples' lives.

Several women referred to 'western culture' and its attempt to undermine local cultures as posing a threat to Egypt. Mass consumption, disrespect for the family, promiscuity, the AIDS epidemic and drug addiction are presented as the characteristics of 'western civilization'. It became obvious to me that, in this context, discussions about the 'West' often revealed a malaise about social classes within Egyptian society. Some consider the *nouveaux riches* and 'westernized Egyptians' *khawagat* (foreigners) just like the tourists who roam the country.

In response to my question of what is unique about Egyptian culture, the late writer and activist Latifa Zayyad said: '*There are so many things that are unique about Egyptian culture. The answer to your question is: what is so beautiful about American culture that you want to make it the only culture? Racism? Loneliness? Absence of human relations? Technology?*'

Other women were more cautious with their generalizations about the 'West' and differentiated between government politics and people. Many women stressed that they refer to the United States and not Europe when

---

[21] I shall discuss Nasser's 'state feminism' and the impact of Sadat's *infitah* on the women's movement in chapter 2.

talking about imperialism. I rarely heard women activists referring to British, French or German imperialist policies or cultural impositions. In particular European countries such as The Netherlands or Norway, countries that have increasingly become involved in Egypt's NGO movement, are generally seen as more trustworthy than the USA. Most anti-imperialist sentiments are articulated within the framework of Egypt's economic dependence on the United States.

The range of interpretations and meanings attributed to the 'West' coincides with different perceptions of 'feminism'. Some reject it outright on the basis that *'when you use the word feminist most people think about the western interpretation, and that is very dangerous. A western feminist is someone who is opposed to men, someone who is very strong and who wants women to dominate the whole world and have the upper hand on men.'* The conflation of feminism with a particular radical strand is a phenomenon not unique to Egypt, but also very common in Europe and the United States, as Susan Faludi's *Backlash* (1992) illustrates only too well. Stereotypes of man-hating feminists ravaging everything in their way and being obsessed with lesbianism exist all over the world.

In some arguments, however, the struggle against women's oppression is separated from its association with the 'West'. Leila K., a young activist in her thirties, argues passionately:

Why when we talk about the patriarchal dimension should we be accused of imitating the West? As if rebellion, freedom, dignity and awareness are privileges that Arab women cannot have, and if they do, then they are imitating the West. I have got as much brains as 500 western women. I can reach conclusions better than the West. Why these complexes? I am daily oppressed by class relations as well as by patriarchy. I do not need an American woman to tell me this. The patriarchal dimension is felt here more intensely, because in the West they separated the state from religion. In our societies it is more obvious, because of our religion, traditions and customs.

Other women activists stress that feminism has different faces and allows for different approaches. Egyptian approaches, in these arguments, are frequently juxtaposed to 'western approaches':

I think there are lots of contradictions here in our country. We live them every day. On the one hand, there is a very conservative culture – you know – there are certain habits, customs that have been going on for years and years; and on the other hand, there is the western approach to things. And perhaps we do not perceive things the same way as westerners, but we definitely see when traditions and customs affect us negatively. Often this results in a confrontation with our culture, especially concerning sensitive issues. So FGM [female genital mutilation] is one of them . . . the legal situation of women is another issue . . . abortion is one of them too. These are all confrontations. There are certain facts our culture is imposing on us. But we see that they are wrong things which need to be corrected. Not all women who try to correct what is wrong approach it from a western perspective though. (Deena M.)

In line with this view, attempts are made to prove the 'authenticity' of Egyptian women's activism by either pointing to its history which is linked to nationalist struggle or by identifying certain groups and activists as deviant because of their 'western orientation'. Few activists break out of the 'authentic versus western' dichotomies and reifications. Nadia M., who has been active in the women's movement since the 1950s, told me:

I work on women's issues, because I happened to be the fourth girl in the family and I was unwanted. Since I was a little girl I always felt the oppression. I felt very vulnerable. My real experience with oppression started from there. But I got an idea about feminism through my contacts with western feminists. One thing we have in common is that we women have always been defined by men. I still get very angry if anyone tries to define me. A sense of identity is very important for any human being. I am struggling so that women define themselves. Gender oppression is as bad as racial oppression, if not worse. Of course, I can dialogue with western feminists. Anyhow, it is not very clear what is western feminism. It is certainly not one thing. In 1975 I attended the women's conference in Mexico. There were lots of radical feminists who would not even listen to the Mariachi, because they were all men. Since then they have mellowed a lot. And there are many different trends.

This voice represents an exception among the women activists I have interviewed. Nevertheless, I have sensed that the more recent experiences related to international conferences (International Conference on Population and Development in Cairo, 1994; and the International Women's Forum in Beijing, 1995) had an impact on many women activists in that encounters with feminists from all over the world, in some cases, led to an increased awareness that, world-wide, there exist many different movements with distinct approaches and agendas. Some women revealed to me their surprise that, despite all the differences, similarities and solidarities can be found across cultural borders.

I will return to discuss the various positions on international conferences and organizations and their impact on local agendas in greater detail in chapter 6. In the following chapter, where I will inquire into the historical context of Egyptian women's activism, I will explore some of the ways in which international conferences have influenced the contemporary women's movement.

2   Contextualizing the Egyptian women's movement

The airport anecdote of my previous chapter is of broader relevance to my research: rather than merely being a metaphor for contradictions in post-colonial Egypt and states of liminality inherent in identity constructions, the airport is also the gatekeeper of the nation state. Procedures of regulating arrivals and departures, visa requirements and stamped passports, scrutinizing and questioning by airport officials and computerized personal files are all manifestations of government regulations and state power. But how do women activists in Egypt 'travel' within and through 'networks of contested power relations' (Rai & Lievesley, 1996: 1), usually referred to as 'the state'? To what extent have women's groups and organizations maintained their independence from the state? And, conversely: to what extent did the Egyptian state (and various constituencies within it) manage to co-opt the women's movement?

These questions need to be tackled historically since the role of the Egyptian state and its relationship to women's activism has varied a great deal during the periods of Nasser, Sadat and Mubarak. In this chapter I would like to explore the relationship between changing state policies and women's activism. I will focus particularly on the way women activists today interpret various historical phases and transformations of the women's movement in relation to the state. Rather than attempting to rehearse and document the history of the Egyptian women's movement, a task already carried out by several scholars (Ahmed, 1992; Al-Sabaki, 1987; Badran, 1988, 1991, 1993, 1995; Hatem, 1986, 1992; Khalifa, 1973; Nelson, 1986, 1996; Philipp, 1978), I will concentrate on presenting its construction by contemporary activists whose interpretation of the past also reveals their own understandings of the present.

Aside from historical transformations, the state, at any given point in time, does not constitute a homogeneous entity. Moreover, we find variations in what is understood by 'the women's movement' both in relation to the past and the present time. In the first part of this chapter I shall briefly discuss analytic approaches to the state. I will then examine constructions by Egyptian women activists of the women's movement from

51

its early days at the turn of the century to its evolution under Nasser, Sadat and Mubarak, thereby giving an indication of contemporary activists' relation to this history.

Women and state policies

Until very recently, feminist scholarship on gender in the Middle East and South Asia was myopic concerning the role of the state and remained trapped in ahistorical and essentialized accounts of 'Muslim women' (Kandiyoti (ed.), 1991: 1). The lack of concern with the state in earlier scholarship has been paralleled by homogenizing and generalizing definitions of the state in the context of the Middle East by a number of political scientists and sociologists (Al-Naquib, 1991; H. Amin, 1978; L. Anderson, 1986, 1987; Badie, 1986; Gellner, 1991/1994; Khuri, 1980; Pipes, 1983; Vatikiotis, 1983; Zureik, 1981).

Sami Zubaida's work (1989, 1993), in contrast, does not only address characteristics of 'the nation state in the Middle East', but also looks at the specificities of various states within the region. His project is based on the conviction that specific histories can be written in terms of general socio-economic processes in relation to particular given configurations and conjunctures (1993: 121–82). Zubaida forcefully challenges essentialized assumptions of some western scholars as well as Islamist constituencies concerning the contrast between western and Islamic states by rejecting the view of historical continuities and inevitabilities. Instead, he offers a detailed analysis of specific historical, social and political developments, their various manifestations and variations, the content of specific 'political fields' and contestations within them.

Recent literature by feminist scholars considers historical transformations of states, contestations of state power, nation-building and changing state projects as critical factors in the analyses of women's position and gender issues in a more differentiated manner (Afshar, 1985; Badran, 1993; Hatem, 1993; Kandiyoti (ed.), 1991, 1995; Karam, 1998; Moghadam (ed.), 1994a; Yuval-Davis, 1991, 1997). Increasingly, the notion of the state as constituting one homogeneous force against which other social forces such as Islamists, communists or feminists struggle has been replaced with conceptualizations of heterogeneous institutional arenas with different power relations and offering different possibilities of contestation.

The thorough genealogy of western feminist approaches to the state provided by Pringle and Watson (1992) sheds light on the shifts in and diversity of feminist approaches. Arguing from a post-structuralist vantage point, Pringle and Watson challenge recent socialist and feminist work which recognizes the varieties, diversities and contradictions of 'the state' by altogether rejecting the assumption of the state as structurally given: 'rather than an object or an actor it denotes a series of arenas or a plurality of discursive forums' (p. 63). The rejection of the idea of a unitary state led to a focus on social policies and institutional arenas, such as the law, as well as discourses (Connell, 1990; Yuval-Davis, 1997). However, the theoretical acknowledgement of differences and specificity by Pringle and Watson is mainly based on European and North American experiences and does not include a consideration of nation-building and state formations in previously colonized states.

A post-colonial critique of western feminist approaches to the state is offered by Shirin Rai (1996). She points out that both Marxist and post-structuralist approaches are rooted in the specific circumstances and material conditions of various women's movements. Feminist scholars living in welfare states, such as Australia and Scandinavia, were much more inclined to treat the state as a potential provider that could accommodate women's interests than feminists in countries with a strong tradition of class-based political action, such as Britain (p. 6). She further argues that the specific experiences of 'Third World'[1] women are linked to the historical context of colonial interventions and post-colonial nation-building and have direct bearing on women's positions and women's activism.

The post-colonial state in Egypt was shaped by nationalism and nation-building, regionalism (pan-Arabism and pan-Islamism), contestations over legitimacy and interest-based and populist corporatism (Ayubi, 1991). More recently the focus shifted to discussions about civil society and democratization (Al-Sayyid, 1993; S. Ibrahim, 1995; S. Ibrahim (ed.), 1993; Norton (ed.), 1995; Zaki, 1995). In these works special attention has been given to Islamist organizations and their role in Egypt's 'civil society' associations (Kepel, 1985; Marty & Appleby (eds.), 1991; Stowasser (ed.), 1987; Zaki, 1995; Zubaida, 1992). Zaki, for example, contrasts the general weakness and political ineffectiveness that he attributes to the overwhelming majority of associations to the overall strength of Islamic associations.[2] This tendency has been analysed by Zubaida, who argued that Islamic associations have benefited from preferential

---

[1] Rai, like many other post-colonial critics, uses the 'Third World' as a term of 'political opposition, as well as being indicative of the colonial experience of these states' (Rai & Lievesley, 1996: 2).

[2] Islamic private voluntary associations run major schools, hospitals and charitable organizations. Mosque-associated organizations provide social services such as nurseries, medical clinics and educational centres. The dense network of Islamic organizations and associations has replaced the state in many of its social welfare services (Zaki, 1995: 63).

treatment with regard to authorization and funding by government officials (Zubaida, 1992).

Some of the characteristics of Egypt and other post-colonial states reflect attributes associated with 'weak' states, such as huge and 'flabby' bureaucracies, infrastructural weaknesses to implement policies, a high degree of corporatism and corruption (Rai, 1996: 28–30). However, the distinction between 'strong' and 'weak' states, as initially put forward by 'developmental model' theorist Gunnar Myrdal (1968) and later developed by Joel Migdal (1988), glosses over the patriarchal power of any state formation (Rai, 1996: 30). It also overlooks the complexities of power struggles, sites of contestation, negotiation and potential influence that characterize the relation between the state and the women's movement.

A useful conceptualization has been put forward by Robert Connell, who defines the state as embodying 'gender regimes' and points to the various ways in which the state is implicated in gender relations. As he put it, the state is 'constituted within gender relations as the central institutionalization of gendered power. Conversely, gender dynamics are a major force constructing the state, both in the historical creation of state structures and in contemporary politics' (1990: 519). The state's power to regulate and shape gender relations can work towards the consolidation of existing gender relations, but it also has the potential to unsettle the existing gender order through reforms (ibid.: 529–31).

The ambiguities inherent in state policies have significant implications for feminist politics which has to work both against and through the state, depending on the specific nature of the state and its policies. Connell specifically addresses the liberal state within industrial–capitalist economies; yet his analysis of the ambiguity inherent in the state's construction of gender relations is even more relevant to post-colonial states. Contradictions, as Kandiyoti argues, emerge in nationalist projects which simultaneously reflect portrayals of women as 'victims of social backwardness, icons of modernity or privileged bearers of cultural authenticity' (1991: 431). In other words, tensions between civic forms of nationalism (which describe women as modern citizens who share rights and responsibilities in the process of nation-building) and cultural forms of nationalism (which depict women as the symbols and safeguards of 'uncontaminated' culture) characterize post-colonial state formations. Nationalism under Nasser, for example, included women as modern actors in the general scheme of redistribution, modernization and national development. The state under Nasser did not, however, challenge existing gender relations within the family, nor did it allow independent women's organizations to articulate their own agendas. Within the parameters of nationalist projects in post-colonial states, resistance to western cultural imperialism became equated with the preservation of existing gender relations, which consequently meant the perpetuation of patriarchal control (ibid.: 442).

The fractured nature of the Egyptian post-colonial state, its changing policies under different regimes, its internal divisions and its links to international constituencies account for women activists' shifting relations to the state. Women are affected in different ways: they are recipients of state policies (which could be either supportive or oppressive) and also try to influence state policies. In this process of mobilization at the level of the state, women activists become part of Egypt's civil society.

While I agree with Moheb Zaki (1995) that feminist activists represent only a small segment within civil society, his cursory examination of women's groups and their effectiveness reflects the general trend of ignoring women's organizations. This treatment is not unsurprising in the light of general conceptions of civil society and their philosophical underpinnings. The tendency to disregard women's roles and contributions is based on the assumed split between public and private domains which are also gendered (Joseph, 1993; Pateman, 1989). As Suad Joseph points out, 'civil society is already identified or defined in a site from which women are thought to be excluded – the public domain. And it is characterized by sets of associations that are linked with male activity' (Joseph, 1993: 24); hence women's activism is mainly overlooked.

Throughout this chapter I shall explore women activists' participation and particular positions in civil society. I will also try to show how different groups within the women's movement use different strategies towards the state and have different relations with it. This set of issues leads me to a categorization of women's organizations with respect to their recognition of 'authority' and their organizational forms.

The past in the present: constructions of the history of the Egyptian women's movement

Rather than attempting either to reconstruct or reinterpret the history of the Egyptian women's movement, I attempt to interweave women activists' interpretations of the history of the Egyptian women's movement with its accounts in existing literature. Particular emphasis is placed on the major debates and areas of controversy among both scholars and activists.

The idea of approaching history through its interpretation by the women I interviewed evolved in the course of my research. It was interesting for me to see how much perceptions of the history of the women's movement differed from one activist to the other. It became obvious that particular interpretations of the historical contents and developments of the movement were related to each activist's own particular 'formative experiences' (which I will examine more closely in the following chapter). But it was also often used to either legitimize their own agendas or discredit those of others.

A consideration of history does not only enlarge an understanding of the current movement, it is actually impossible to grasp its demands, conflicts and identities without considering its history – a history which does not only relate to the attempt to create new gender discourses and awaken feminist consciousness (Nelson, 1998: 92), but is also closely linked with nationalist, anti-colonial struggles and projects of modernization.

Beginnings

Many studies dealing with the Egyptian women's movement begin their analysis with women's participation in the 1919 nationalist revolution and the subsequent rise of feminist activism associated with Huda Sha'rawi (Ahmed, 1982; Al-Sabaki, 1987; Ghoussoub, 1985; Hatem, 1986; Khalifa, 1973; Philipp, 1978). The development of the intellectual and ideological foundations of the early struggle for women's rights is often attributed to male modernist reformers such as Muhammad Abduh, Gamal Al-Din Al-Afghani and, most prominent among them, Qasim Amin (Cole, 1981; Haddad, 1984; Marsot, 1978; Tignor, 1966). More recent works emphasize that women's participation in the 1919 nation-wide marches, strikes and protests against the British colonizers was a continuation and extension of the activities of women in previous decades (Ahmed, 1992; Badran, 1995; Baron, 1994).

Qasim Amin, an Egyptian lawyer and jurist who devoted two books to the issue of women's liberation, *Tahrir al-Mar'a* (The Emancipation of Women, 1899) and *Al-Mar'a Al-Jedida* (The New Woman, 1900), has frequently been identified as the first Egyptian and Arab feminist (Cole, 1981; Haddad, 1984; Nelson, 1996). The contemporary group Al-Mar'a Al-Gedida (the New Woman) took its name from Qasim Amin's famous book.[3] Not all members were in favour of this name when a vote was taken in 1986, but all accepted the significance of this book, which symbolized a new beginning for Egyptian women. Some founding members recapitulated that the notion of Qasim Amin marking the beginning of

[3] The founding members were not aware of the philanthropic group Gama'iyat Al-Mar'a Al-Gedida, established by upper-class and some middle-class women in 1919 after the first nationalist demonstrations (see Badran,1995: 51)

the Egyptian women's movement '*constituted a piece of recognized information and shared knowledge when we first started to meet*'. However, very early
on, '*during our first meetings, during which we studied our history, we realized
and established that the movement took up with women's action and organizations, as well as with women writers and poets, like Malak Hifni Nasif*'.

Leila Ahmed (1992) and Beth Baron (1994), who have re-examined
Amin's writings, show that many of those women who were active in the
cause of women's emancipation were pushed to the background or have
been left out of the historical archives altogether. Baron's work, in particular, sheds light on the intellectual and creative output and diversity of
women journalists and writers at the turn of the century. Baron very
strongly argues against the 'pattern of stressing male thinkers at the
expense of female ones' (1994: 4). She quotes Leila Ahmed who con-
cluded that Qasim Amin was not 'the father of feminism', as so many
claim, but rather 'the son of Cromer[4] and colonialism'. Ahmed suggests
that many of Amin's ideas actually reproduced colonial thinking about
women's status in Muslim society and contends that his book, *Tahrir Al-
Mar'a*, 'merely called for the substitution of Islamic-style male dominance by Western-style male dominance' (Ahmed, 1992: 162–3, quoted
in Baron, 1994: 5).

The debate over the intellectual origins of the Egyptian women's movement has not only occupied the minds of scholars, but also constitutes an
ongoing controversy among some contemporary Egyptian women activists. Many activists stress the important role of male reformers in
pushing education – the first step to liberation. As Amal K., a scholar and
activist in her sixties, put it:

*There is a long history of feminism, but the word 'feminism' does not exist in Arabic. It
was always called* tahrir al-mar'a, *that is, the liberation of women. This has been a very
different kind of feminism than the western one. The bit that comes from the West is that
at the time of the Arab renaissance, in the nineteenth century, a movement of translation
started with the shaykhs who went to France.[5] These shaykhs learned the language and
they read a lot. The idea of women being free started from there. During the movement of
independence, the idea of a free country and a free society was linked to western ideas.
The shaykhs saw educated women in France and they started to realize that we lost something on the way. An educated woman can educate the children, so the future men will be
more educated. An educated woman makes a better mother and wife. This is what the
reformers like Muhammad Abduh and Qasim Amin realized. The other thing that*

---

[4] British consul general in Egypt.
[5] The first shaykh to accompany the first substantial mission sent by Muhammad Ali to
study in France was Rifa'i Al-Tahtawi. Although sent as an imam and not a student he
acquired fluent French and read widely on a number of issues, such as philosophy,
history and geography. The impact of French Enlightenment thinking can be traced to
his subsequent own writings (Hourani, 1983: 65–83).

influenced them was the relation between the sexes. People were talking to each other in France. All this pushed the issue of education for girls. Once a woman starts to read, she starts to question. Women began to object to the fact that they could not go outside to breathe fresh air. The first roots of emancipation of the Egyptian woman was education. Some of the women started to write under a pen name.

The discussion about antecedents of the historical women's movement entails several questions which are significant for self-definitions and struggles for legitimacy among present-day activists. Most women activists today are not very much concerned with the question of whether the intellectual origins of the Egyptian women's movement have to be traced back to male reformers or women journalists.[6] What is much more at stake today is the issue of whether the intellectual roots have to be traced back to 'western' or 'indigenous' sources. The charge of emulating 'western thought' and thereby betraying 'authentic culture' has constituted a continuous challenge to Egyptian feminists. From its very beginnings until the present day various constituencies opposed to the struggle for women's rights (Islamists as well as nationalist-leftists) have engaged in an evaluation of women activists with regard to their level of 'authenticity' or 'westernness'.

Some scholars (Ahmed, 1992; Baron, 1994) have used similar categories to those used by Islamists and conservative forces within Egypt to analyse the women's movement. Leila Ahmed contends that

critical tensions also emerged within feminist discourse; of the two divergent strains of feminism, one became the dominant voice of feminism in Egypt and in the Arab Middle East for most of the century, and the second remained an alternative, marginal voice until the last decades of the century, generally not even recognized as a voice of feminism. The dominant voice of feminism, which affiliated itself, albeit generally discreetly, with the westernizing, secularizing tendencies of society, predominantly the tendencies of the upper, upper-middle, and middle-middle classes, promoted a feminism that assumed the desirability of progress toward Western-type societies. (1992: 174)

Ahmed describes 'the alternative voice' as wary of and eventually even opposed to western ways, seeking a means to articulate female subjectivity and affirmation within a native, vernacular, Islamic discourse. However, this strict separation between the 'modern, secular and westernizing voice' on the one hand and the 'conservative, anti-western and Islamic voice' on the other obscures the overlappings, contradictions and complexities of discourses and activism that took place against a back-

---

[6] The exception is a group of feminist scholars, the Women's Memory Forum, who are involved in the reinterpretation of history. Their reading of history involves the special consideration of the contributions of women to Egypt's intellectual and cultural development.

ground of anti-colonial and anti-imperialist struggle. Even the early, upper-class, French-educated feminists such as Sha'rawi did not abandon Islam and were acting within and reacting against a complex web of solidarities and alliances.

The women activists today express many different views and interpretations concerning the 'indigeneity' or 'westernness' of the historical movement. Some activists distance themselves from the earlier activists, whom they perceive to be driven by 'upper-class interests and western agendas'. Others argue that the movement was deeply rooted in indigenous culture and that the charge of being too western was unfounded. This tendency can also be found in more recent publications on the history of the women's movement (Badran, 1995; Nelson, 1996). Margot Badran, for example, stresses the nationalist aspirations and indigenous framework for both Huda Sha'rawi and Ceza Nabarawi. The attempt to free the Egyptian women's movement from the powerful accusation of being western-induced and therefore inauthentic may work at the expense of glossing over the complexity of cultural encounters during and after colonization.

The debate over 'foremothers versus forefathers' (male reformers versus women journalists and writers) and the cultural background of 'the parents' (western versus indigenous) could be resolved by replacing 'a single parent' with 'a bi-cultural couple' – thereby allowing for the possibility that the women's movement was born to a combination of ideas, values and traditions. A different way of thinking about the intellectual origin of the women's movement, and consequently any kind of political struggle or contestation, would allow for the potentiality of a cultural encounter that is not merely confrontational and exclusive, but creative and incorporating. A step in that direction has been made by Baron, who looked at the critical encounter and resulting syntheses of western and indigenous values and thought.[7] While holding on to analytical categories of western versus indigenous, Cynthia Nelson's biography of Doria Shafik (1996) does also break through these dichotomies as it portrays the life of a woman who struggled throughout to synthesize her French and Egyptian cultural backgrounds. Her political activism as well as her poetry bear witness to the creative and innovative potentials of what only too often has been described as a clash of opposites. What becomes

---

[7] An ethnic and religious diversity, which reflected the varied composition of Egyptian and Arab society, also characterizes the founders of the women's press. Their journals presented a wide range of views. According to Baron, they 'were no doubt aware of the western colonial discourse, or more properly discourses, on gender, but were not completely swayed by them' and 'tackled issues related to culture, identity and change' (Baron, 1994: 7–8).

obvious in the case of Doria Shafik, and many other examples up to today, is that the perceived dichotomy of indigenous versus western is as much about class tensions and conflicts within Egypt as about differences in cultures.[8]

The complexities of the colonial encounter constitute generally a 'missing link' in contemporary scholarship, but present points of focus for Lila Abu-Lughod's recent edited volume: *Remaking Women: Feminism and Modernity in the Middle East* (1998). In her introduction, Abu-Lughod states her particular interest in 'the actual dynamics of colonial cultural hybridization', which calls for a close examination of the very conjunctures 'between the projects of Europeans and Middle Easterners and the actual role of European discourses in Middle Eastern ones' (p. 29). Rather than merely rejecting the western versus eastern opposition, she argues that the 'process of entanglement' might be a much more powerful and successful way to overcome binary opposition than to insist on the authenticity of social actors.

As my research concentrates on 'secular-oriented' women activists, it is not surprising that 'indigenous' and 'authentic' are not necessarily linked to Islam, even if many activists consider religion (both Islam and Coptic Christianity) as elements of Egyptian authenticity. Very few of the women I interviewed questioned whether the dichotomy of western versus indigenous was valid in the first place. Rather, this division has generally become naturalized in the sense of constituting conventional wisdom or common sense. Indeed, the construction of the world in terms of indigenous versus western has become such an incontestable fact that only very few Egyptian intellectuals and academics would actually question and challenge it. However, some women activists, who are trying to break out of prevailing frameworks and discourses, reject this classification altogether along these lines. One younger activist in her forties put it the following way:

Our struggle dates back much longer than Huda Sha'rawi. I would not frame it in a specific time, not western or non-western. People all over the world have been fighting against injustice. Framing it into this kind of dichotomy is harmful. It mirrors how both the Islamists and the West look at these issues and create their identities. Secular liberal thinking is portrayed as ownership of the West. We need to break through this.

Those who challenge the common dichotomy stress that women activists have faced very similar accusations from the beginning of the twentieth

[8] A refreshing and challenging new angle is provided by Kumari Jayawardena's latest work, *The White Woman's Other Burden: Western Women and South Asia during British Rule* (1995). She looks at feminist and anti-imperialist struggles of western women living in South Asia during colonial occupation in a way that profoundly dislocates the polemics of East versus West by either the previous colonizers or the colonized.

century – the accusations have only become worse and the context more threatening:

The accusation of being too western is much more potent today than it was before. In the beginning of the century modernization became the nation's project. Now we find a reversal of that process which is making those claims and accusations much more harmful. The only project that exists today is the Islamist's project of claiming authenticity. So it is much more difficult for us now, but at the same time there is a much stronger challenge to develop our own language and the essence of our own project. This forces us to look much deeper and find the essence of what we are trying to do.

Considering the specific circumstances of the emergence of the women's movement, that is, the struggle against the British colonial powers, the likelihood of transcending dichotomies of indigenous versus western was weak. The continued experience of imperialism in present-day Egypt, albeit in a less direct form, does not render it more likely today. Unfortunately these prevailing dichotomies have provided such a powerful idiom that it has been internalized by most of the different, and often opposing, constituencies within Egypt as well as by scholars writing about Egypt. As I have tried to show in the previous chapter, these dichotomies serve a purpose: they constitute elements of the symbolic capital that Islamist and nationalist constituencies use to mobilize allegiance and support. For women activists this has often resulted in the subordination of their agendas to wider concerns such as national liberation and class struggle.

The tendency to frame the women's struggle within the wider struggle of national liberation – and the inherent tension in this bond – appears to constitute a continuous thread in the history of the women's movement in Egypt. The late writer and activist Latifa Zayyad expressed this relationship in the following way:

The liberation of women goes side by side with equality in more general terms. This takes all social issues into consideration and does not single out women's issues. Women can never be liberated if the whole country is not liberated. Every important feminist movement, or individual feminist, reached certain rights only in collaboration with the nationalist movement. The woman who binds herself to a national movement requires rights and requires influences, the one who does not is easily excluded.

While some earlier historians came to the conclusion that 'feminism formed part of the content of nationalist thought' (Hourani, 1962: 215, quoted in Philipp, 1978: 277) and that 'women showed that they did not hesitate to participate in political struggles' (Badr, 1968: 51), it had gradually become 'clear to many feminists that during the nationalist struggle, and certainly afterwards, [that] men's nationalism had a patriarchal character' (Badran, 1988: 31). Philipp (1978) shows that the relationship between the nationalist movement and feminism was by no means as harmonious and positive as it may appear at first glance. Initially, male nationalists accepted women's nationalist activism (demonstrations, economic boycotts, etc.). However, 'after 1919, when nationalist pressures emerged in the wake of promulgation of a constitution for Egypt, women's political rights were not mentioned. Their equality with men was not discussed' (p. 278).

The picture that presents itself during the post-independence period (after 1923) is certainly a confusing one. Every shade of opinion regarding the emancipation of women was represented, and nationalists themselves were far from agreeing on the matter. Indeed, Kandiyoti argues that the nationalist project itself was ambiguous since it spoke both with the universalist voice of modernism and the anti-modernist, romantic impulse to restore the authentic community (Kandiyoti, 1991).

As mentioned earlier, feminist discourse and activism during the period of post-colonial state formation, and even up to the first half of the twentieth century, has repeatedly been identified with Huda Sha'rawi and 'the Egyptian Feminist Union'.[9] However, the most in-depth work on the history of the movement during this period encompasses a wider variety of voices and perspectives. Margot Badran offers a thorough analysis of the emergence and evolution of Egyptian feminism as an integral part of the history of modern Egypt in her book *Feminists, Islam, and Nation: Gender and the Making of Modern Egypt* (1995).

Based on the view that the first phase of feminist activism was merely elitist and philanthropic in character, Khater and Nelson (1988) had argued earlier that it was actually during the period from 1945 until 1959, which was to be neglected in many studies (Al-Sabaki, 1987; Berque, 1972; Jayawardena, 1986; Khalifa, 1973), that the women's movement came of age. Badran challenges some of Khater and Nelson's arguments by emphasizing that diversification in ideology and political consciousness were already characteristic of the earlier movement. However, with regard to her claim that the movement associated with Huda Sha'rawi and Nabawiyah Musa already transcended elitism, Badran's work fails to persuade. According to Badran herself, the eleven founding members of the EFU were mainly from wealthy land-owning families, raised within *harem* culture (Badran, 1995: 96). Moreover, a look at the magazine *L'Egyptienne* which was published by the EFU reveals that all its writers were either from the Egyptian elite or western women.

[9] Huda Sha'rawi founded Al-Ittihad Al-Nissa'i Al-Misri (the Egyptian Feminist Union) in 1923. The EFU's feminist agenda called for political rights for women, changes in the personal status law (especially for controls on divorce and polygamy), equal secondary school and university education, and expanded professional opportunities for women. Its activism was characterized by dynamic interaction and tensions between women's feminism and nationalism.

Considering class structures, distribution of wealth and the spread of literacy at that time, the question of the elitist character of the initial movement seems to be rather pointless to debate. Badran's concern to disassociate the beginnings of the women's movement from elitism is part of a general trend among both academics writing about the women's movement and Egyptian women activists themselves. One can detect an enormous pressure to give populist credentials to feminism and gloss over the elitist character of much of feminist activism. One might pose the question why it seems so difficult to describe the beginnings of the Egyptian women's movement as related to the aspirations of a rising nationalist bourgeoisie.

What needs to be explored more carefully, however, is the fact that the initially welfare-oriented movement linked to anti-colonial struggle initiated by Huda Sha'rawi, became more independent from male official party politics and more outspoken with regard to women's political rights. Some activists today perceive no essential break between Huda Sha'rawi's feminism and the feminism of women in the 1940s and 1950s. They contrast the beginnings of the movement with present-day activism, which, in their view, neglects some of the pressing issues. Leila I., founding member of the leftist group Ma'an, says, for example:

Historically, the women always used al-haraka al-nissa'iyya al-misriyya [the Egyptian women's movement]. *It was a politicized women's movement from the twenties to the fifties. It represented the nationalist women's point of view. From Huda Sha'rawi to Inji Aflatoun, women were interested in developing the law, and in creating new social, economic and political relations. In all this, they were trying to see how changes for women were going to improve the whole situation and all of society.*

The view of continuity up to the middle of the twentieth century is not shared by all women interviewed. Other activists' perceptions concur with those of various scholars, who have argued that the discourses and activities of feminists took on a different direction in the 1940s and 1950s (Ahmed, 1992; Botman, 1987; Khater & Nelson, 1988).

A new generation

The ongoing debate as to whether the feminist movement was interrupted with the collapse of Huda Sha'rawi's journals, *L'Egyptienne* and *Al-Misriyyah*, in 1940, and World War II (Badran, 1988) or whether Doria Shafik's activism and her publications radicalized the movement (Nelson, 1988) has gained new momentum since the publication of Cynthia Nelson's *Doria Shafik: Egyptian Feminist – A Woman Apart* (1996). Khater and Nelson had argued earlier that 'by addressing itself to middle class women and their problems, the Bint El-Nil Union reflected a pragmatic departure from the earlier elitist EFU' (1988: 469).

The Bint El-Nil (Daughter of the Nile) group was created in 1948 as an initiative for a new and invigorated Egyptian feminist movement whose primary purpose was to proclaim and claim full political rights for women. It also promoted literacy programmes, campaigned to improve cultural, health and social services among the poor and enhance mother and childcare (Shafik, 1955: 191). The campaign for women's political rights was linked to the campaign for social reforms (Khater & Nelson, 1988: 470).[10]

In comparing Bint El-Nil with the Egyptian Feminist Union of Huda Sha'rawi, one could categorize both associations as independent in the sense of not directly being associated with or directed by either a political party or other constituency. However, the friction between the EFU and the Wafd described earlier appears harmless in comparison to the confrontation between Doria Shafik and the regime. Bint El-Nil seemed to be much less inclined to accept 'official authority' as outlined in Molyneux's typology (see the introduction to this volume) and was much more independent than the EFU ever was, in that Bint El-Nil was not only autonomous from any political party but also openly challenged the state.

One year before the 1952 revolution, Doria Shafik and 1,500 other women stormed the parliament demanding full political rights, a reform of the Personal Status Law and equal pay for equal work (Nelson, 1996: 168–77). Shortly after the revolution, she declared to the Ministry of Interior that Bint El-Nil was reorganizing as a political party, which was initially recognized (ibid.: 186). In 1954, when the new military regime announced the formation of a constitutional committee on which no woman was given a place, Shafik went to the Press Syndicate and engaged in a hunger strike for ten days, joined by a number of other women (ibid.: 197). Her final and most direct confrontation with the Nasser regime took place in 1957, when she started a hunger strike in the Indian embassy to protest both against the occupation of Egyptian and Palestinian territories by Israeli forces and the (in her view) 'dictatorial rule of the Egyptian authorities driving the country towards bankruptcy and chaos' (ibid.: 238). The intervention of Prime Minister Nehru saved Shafik from prison, but she was kept under house arrest in her apartment in Zamalek.

---

[10] The extensive plan of social reform began with a campaign against illiteracy among adult women. Bint El-Nil founded centres in Cairo, Alexandria and several towns in the Delta where women were taught how to read and write, some elementary hygiene, and income-generating possibilities (Khater & Nelson, 1988).

Throughout her activism – as well as after her death – Doria Shafik has been subject to even more impassioned accusations than Huda Shaʿrawi ever had to endure. According to Nelson, the content and level of criticisms and denunciations are paradoxically linked to Shafik's precarious and problematic positionality:

From the moment she established her journals in 1945 until her final defiant act in 1957 protesting against the authoritarian regime headed by Gamal Abdel Nasser, Doria Shafik was engaged in a cultural critique that was simultaneously directed toward the Other (the west) and inward toward the Self (Egypt and Islam) in a project that was aimed to dismantle the distorted and stereotyped images of the oriental woman as well as the patriarchal frameworks in which these were embedded. (Nelson, 1998: 100)

Generally, Doria Shafik does not present a subject of debate among women activists today. However, when asked, some contemporary activists severely criticized Shafik for her close links to French culture as well as bourgeois upper classes. In an interview shortly before she died, the writer and activist Latifa Zayyad told me:

Doria Shafik is being glorified now. I know that Nelson writes a book about her. She was an aristocratic woman. She was very showy. She was divorced from me and my class. Doria Shafik had great sums of money from the American intelligence to publish her very chic magazine.

Zayyad herself opposed Shafik's orientation and approach as she was part of the communist movement in Egypt during the time of Shafik's activism. Women such as Inji Aflatoun, Soraya Adham and Latifa Zayyad, who had adopted socialist or communist ideologies, called for the more general struggle for social equality and justice (Botman, 1987; Khater, 1987).

Zayyad's view is widespread among many of the more radical leftist women activists in Egypt today. However, the majority of younger activists reacted to my question about Doria Shafik by shrugging. Many acknowledged their ignorance about either Shafik's struggles or the debates surrounding them. Several women stressed that they are waiting for Doria's biography to come out, as this would help them to gain insight into her activism as well as reappropriate her into their history.[11] Among the older generation, a few were sympathetic. I could detect a sense of nostalgia:

I believe that the gains of the early feminists are going down the drain with the new generation. If you see AUC[12] students now, they don't have any idea what these women were fighting for. I don't feel that among young women there's any kind of movement that is

---

[11] Doria Shafik's biography was published towards the end of my research in Cairo.
[12] Acronym for 'the American University in Cairo'.

going to replace the one that was before. I don't know why there isn't the spirit of fighting any more. When I was very young, I used to see the picture of Doria Shafik. I once saw her on the street in a car guarded by soldiers. It was inspiring. I really respected her and her courage. You don't see this any more. (Amal K.)

The sense of nostalgia was often expressed in terms of wider cultural, social and political vistas which allowed for a heterogeneous women's movement. The state's vulnerability and regular changes of government set the stage for a diversity of political voices; the most prominent of these were leftist forces which emerged alongside Islamist tendencies. Established by Hassan Al-Banna in 1928, the Muslim Brotherhood (Akhwan Muslimin) grew rapidly. It took advantage of the Egyptian view that the Palestinian struggle represented another western imperialist and Zionist crusade against Islamic peoples. Positioning itself as pan-Islamic, anti-western and anti-Zionist, the Brotherhood attracted increasing support from men and actively sought to increase its female membership.

It is during this period of the 1940s that the women's movement took different directions: the aristocratic, charity-oriented 'ladies of the salon' affiliated with Princess Chevikar; Doria Shafik's Bint El-Nil, a mixture between charity, feminist consciousness-raising and political protest; the Lagnat Al-Shabaat (Committee of Young Women) founded by Ceza Nabarawi and Inji Aflatoun to revive the fading Egyptian Feminist Union as it attracted 'pro-communist women who were prevented by the government to establish an organization of their own' (Nelson, 1996: 165); as well as the welfare and Islamist-oriented 'Muslim Women's Society' created by Zeinab Al-Ghazali.

The phase of militant and heterogeneous feminist activism of the 1940s and first half of the 1950s was followed by a period of quiescence. Egyptian feminist activism receded under the rule of Gamal Abd Al-Nasser as a result of the state's strict monitoring of political activism and the banning of any kind of autonomous organization. The state monopolized women's issues and formulated them as social welfare issues, especially through the activities of the Ministry of Social Affairs. Nonetheless, the position of women underwent great changes during the Nasser period due to the broader commitment to social egalitarianism as women were given increased opportunities and rights within the limits set by the government.

The Nasser period

As far as Nasser is concerned, the country was in a state of progress and development. Naturally, women were in a good state. The right to vote and to run for elections was very important. Nasser also gave women the right to work and to acquire economic independence. Whenever anybody graduated he had to be appointed by the state. All this accu-

mulated into progress. I would call anything that happened afterwards 'aftermath'. Of course, there were problems. But putting the pros and cons together, the pros overruled in the daily lives: women were allowed in the socialist party, in all the organization, but there were no independent organizations admitted, whether for women or for men. (Leila S.)

The tendency in both scholarship and political discourse to define Nasser's regime merely in terms of its authoritarianism and repression of organized opposition has recently been replaced by a more positive re-evaluation of the Nasser period. Various scholars have stressed that Egypt's 1952 revolution inaugurated a new age for women by altering the class structure and by the ideological, legal and practical inclusion of women in the new state (Ahmed, 1992; Hatem, 1992, 1994). Nasser's commitment to women's welfare as part of his wider struggle for social justice has been juxtaposed to his suppression of women's activism. Nasser's authoritarian regime prohibited all forms of independent political activism – including feminist organizations. The socialist-oriented activist Leila I. described a harsh rupture in the women's movement during the Nasser period:

During the Nasser time, the movement was hit. There were women in the institution of the regime: careerists. These women only represented the pragmatic needs of the Nasser regime. These were only women who spoke about women's rights: haqq al-mar'a bil ta'lim [women's rights to education], for example, or tahrir al-mar'a [the emancipation of women]. They would say that reactionaries were against tahrir al-mar'a. They were mainly listening to the authorities. There was the regime supporting change and women were making propaganda for the regime, but women were not allowed to be organized.

This description of the women's movement under Nasser fits in with Molyneux's notion of directed mobilization in which women's issues have been co-opted by the state. Even charitable organizations were placed under state control which resulted in a series of laws restricting any kind of independent activity. Although voluntary work has a long history in Egypt, it was only during the Nasser regime that the role of NGOs (non-governmental organizations), PVOs (private voluntary organizations) and LCDAs (local community development associations) came into sharp focus. Many laws and regulations, culminating in Law 32 of 1964 (still in effect today),[13] were formulated to organize and monitor the

---

[13] Law 32 restricts the formation and activities of voluntary organizations (e.g. women's or human rights associations) with regard to their fields of activity, number of members allowed, number of organizations within a particular region, record keeping, accounting and funding. Law 32 also gives the government authority to intervene by striking down decisions by the board of directors or even dissolving the entire board. The law itself has been the object of a human rights campaign in recent years. In May 1999 the Egyptian government passed an even more restrictive and undemocratic law than the 1998 NGO draft law, which had been rejected by Egyptian NGOs and civil companies. See http://www.geocities.com/~lrrc/NGO for details about the newly passed law and the campaign against it.

various activities carried out by all voluntary organizations. Mona Z., who was involved in charity work during the Nasser era, recalls:

Charitable and religious institutions grew. The political system was closed, so the only thing people could do was charity. All this was subject to the Ministry of Social Affairs. It was okay as long as they were not involved in any political activity, but only worked for the interests of their constituencies. Nasser's regime was based on 'corporatism': let people group, which makes them feel that they have power, but actually it is an easier way to control.

The lack of independent feminist organizations was paralleled by the state's appropriation of women's issues. Not only did the 1956 constitution and its revised 1963 version declare that all Egyptians are equal regardless of gender, but labour laws were changed to guarantee state sector jobs for 'all holders of high school diplomas and college degrees irrespective of gender' (Hatem, 1992: 232). Moreover, in 1956 the state granted women the right to vote and to run for political office. The education system was reformed to increase enrolment, both for primary and secondary education, which particularly affected female participation in higher education (Ahmed, 1992: 210). Hatem has labelled the state's formal legal or ideological commitment to women's rights 'state feminism'. The term also refers to informal state policies and programmes which introduce important changes in the productive and reproductive roles of women (Hatem, 1992: 231).

However, the impressive accomplishments of the Egyptian state in education, employment and social mobility, which accounted for the progressive nature of Nasser's regime, were accompanied by the preservation of the conservative Personal Status Laws of the 1920s and 1930s. Hatem argues that

state feminism under the Nasser regime produced women who were economically independent of their families, but dependent on the state for employment, important social services like education, health and day care, and political representation. While state feminism created and organized a system of public patriarchy, it did not challenge the personal and familial views of women's dependency on men that were institutionalized by the personal status laws and the political system. (ibid.: 233).

Views about Nasser and women's rights are very divided among contemporary activists. Many women I interviewed stressed Nasser's achievements in improving women's status in the context of achieving greater social equality and justice for all Egyptians. However, several of the women who were adolescent girls or young women during the Nasser period strongly challenged the idea of women's equality under Nasser:

The Nasserist discourse of equality and fraternity masked a lot of inequality. This was the atmosphere I grew up in. The work laws had changed, copying communist countries. When it came down to reality I felt that there was so much hypocrisy. I was brought up to be independent, but when I think carefully I had to resist everything I was brought up with. (Shereen M.)

The sense of hypocrisy and masked inequality characterizing the Nasser regime is particularly strong among women activists who do not perceive women's rights as limited to the rights to education, work and participation in decision-making processes, but also look to women's issues in relation to the Personal Status Law.[14] Today, some activists challenge the 'blind spots' of those continuing to equate women's participation with an improvement of women's overall status in society. Raga N., a researcher and activist, who lived through the Nasser period as a student and still very much admires Nasser, told me:

People who talk development are mainly Nasserists, who argue that if you give women rights in the public sphere, they'll be able to change their situation in the household. It isn't simply a matter of being integrated into the economy though. As long as there are discriminatory Personal Status Laws, women will be in a weaker position. Even my public rights are curtailed by my husband's right to put me into bayt al-ta'a.[15] *All Arab women are schizophrenic. By law I'm equal at work – we have a set of laws that stress equality in the public sphere – at home there's a very different situation though. My problem is with women who don't perceive this contradiction. It's sensitive because of religion, but it's a matter of interpretation. In Tunisia, for example, they banned polygamy. What we have isn't a matter of religion but power relations.*

While this particular criticism is not unique, throughout my interviews I noticed a widespread perception that Nasser's policies helped women to gain some economic, social and cultural strength through their increased participation in education and employment. A significant increase in women's cultural and political activities is often attributed to the new opportunities and options the Nasser regime offered to women. Siham A., of the same generation as Raga N., expressed the following position:

At Nasser's time, women were given the right to vote and to be elected. Women benefited as well from the wide range and free education. Because of the secular atmosphere women were respected and allowed in many fields. Another important element is that the state of women is closely related to the state of the country: when the country flourishes women's rights increase and we have not seen the case of women as bad as it is now.

The evaluation of Nasser is often phrased through the filter of juxtaposition with his followers: Sadat and Mubarak. In recent years Egypt has witnessed a wave of nostalgia for the Nasserite past. Intellectuals have

---

[14] Law governing marriage, divorce, child custody etc.
[15] *Bayt al-ta'a* literally means 'house of obedience' and refers to the right of the husband to force his wife to return to his house, with the help of the police if necessary.

increasingly replaced the earlier rhetoric associated with Sadat's 'de-Nasserization' policies with statements conveying their longing for 'the better days'. Even political activists, mainly communists, who were imprisoned and tortured under Nasser, express their admiration and retrospective support of Nasser.

Many articles expressing pro-Nasserist opinions and sentiments were published on the occasion of the twenty-fifth anniversary of Nasser's death in September 1995. The anniversary coincided with the signing of the Oslo treaty in Washington. Disappointment with the 'peace process', generally perceived by Egyptian intellectuals to have been at the expense of Palestinians and Arabs, has revived anti-Israel sentiments. These are linked to both a rejection of the Oslo 'peace' treaty – in many ways reminiscent of Sadat's earlier treaty with Israel – and the praise given to Nasser, who, even if having lost the 1967 war, did not engage with 'the enemy' as Sadat did. The pan-Arabic component of Nasserism, it has been argued, could be used 'to redress the present disequilibrium in the balance of forces between Israel and the Arabs' (Sid-Ahmed, 1998: 8).

The film *Nasser 56*, directed by a Nasserite (shown in 1996), features the famous actor Ahmed Zaki as Nasser. Produced in black and white, and interspersed with documentary clips, the film transported thousands of Egyptians into the glorious days of the nationalization of the Suez Canal. The success of the film cannot be attributed to either its cinematographic greatness or to Ahmed Zaki's performance – which was praised by those who had seen 'the real Nasser' – but has to be seen in the light of the extensive sense of nostalgia for the days when Egypt challenged not only the British, French and Americans but also its own perceptions of dependence and weakness.

The re-evaluation of Nasser suggests that issues of post-colonial developmentalism and modernity are being fought over the Nasserite legacy. Nasser has become a symbol for anti-colonial struggle and an 'independent modernity', which sharply contrasts the perception of dependence of contemporary Egypt. Many of the women activists who were too young during Nasser's time actually to remember much carry a very vivid image of Nasser whom they associate with progress, development without foreign help and secularism. Summaya M., a young member of the group Al-Mar'a Al-Gedida, praised Nasser for his policies towards the Muslim Brotherhood:

I believe that nobody fought the Muslim Brothers as he [Nasser] did and nobody knew how to defeat them. He met their logic with the secular logic independently, as opposed to Sadat and Mubarak. Now the government is sharing the same grounds and fighting with the same arms. This gives immediate superiority to Islamist groups.

While independent feminist activism only reappeared at the beginning of the 1970s – coinciding with the beginning of Sadat's era, the rise of *infitah* (open door) policies and the increased emergence of Islamist movements – this new generation of feminists actually gained their intellectual, social and professional experience under Nasser.

Sadat and *infitah*

Nasser co-opted those people who had authored the progressive project, whether they were feminists or leftists. Lots of the things they had demanded were written in the Nasserite frame. It was understood that all forms of political expression had to take place within the frame of the state. This stifled all opposition. People felt that it was justified because of the nationalist project and the war. With Sadat the incredible gaps began to appear. When people had no more hope in the national, social and economic project, the apparent unity was cracked open. Then people saw the political void. With the emergence of a political wave, people had to look back at least twenty years and ask themselves: how do you start your own organization. This is the main problem for Egyptians until today. (Randa S.)

Under Sadat, the role of the state as social and economic agent of change was reduced by withdrawing from the policies of social equality and equal opportunity, decentralizing the making of economic decisions and increasing the participation of the private sector. Not only were many of Nasser's official commitments to gender equality abandoned, but *infitah* (open door) policies[16] also led to an increased gap between rich and poor. Yet, paradoxically, it was under Sadat that the Personal Status Law was reformed in favour of women's rights. The initial promise of Sadat's rule entailed swinging an 'open door' to western and Arab investment. The liberalized economy would be paralleled by the softening of 'the most oppressive features of Nasserist authoritarianism', as Egypt would restructure 'the socialist economic mechanisms developed under Nasser' (Baker, 1978: 132). Sadat allowed private businesses to invest in the economy in the hope that the new technologies and increased finance would boost the economy. However, this form of development ignored such intractable problems as poverty, unemployment and the massive disparities between rich and poor. When tens of thousands of the urban poor flooded the streets in 1977 to protest at the reduction of basic food subsidies they were joined by students and workers who demonstrated against Sadat's economic policies, conspicuous consumption and western influence (Baker, 1990: 118).

Women were affected in different ways by Sadat's *infitah* policies. Their

---

[16] Not only did *infitah* constitute the declared economic policy of privatization and the open market, but its *laissez faire* undertone also extended into the realm of the government, administration, migration, foreign policy etc. (Ayubi, 1991: 17).

integration into the economy, which had been part of Nasser's 'state feminism', was replaced by high rates of unemployment and inequality of opportunity in the workplace.[17] On the other hand, labour migration, especially to the Gulf countries, not only provided economic betterment and improved standards of living for many families, it also forced many women to take over tasks that were previously carried out by their husbands (Hatem, 1992: 238). While a number of women might have gained autonomy as a result of the migration of male household-heads, some studies point to the demoralizing social and emotional effects of migration on working-class women (Graham-Brown, 1981; Hatem, 1992).

The different effects of Sadat's *infitah* on women are related to their specific class positions. Upper-middle-class and upper-class women certainly benefited more from Sadat's *infitah* than lower-middle-class and working-class women.[18] Sadat's *infitah* policies cut sharply in two ways simultaneously: it opened the door, for the well-placed few, to extravagant wealth, glib corruption and rampant consumerism. On the other hand, the rest of the population suffered from *infitah*'s broader implications – high inflation, chronic shortages of basic goods and housing, reduced employment opportunities and poor working conditions – intensified all the more by the state's reduction of investment in public service and job creation.

The social and economic changes brought about by *infitah* were paralleled by a distancing from the Soviet Union and rapprochement with the United States. The close alliance with the USA in particular and with the 'West' in general involved co-ordination with international organizations that reflected 'capitalist ideals' such as the International Monetary Fund and the World Bank (Ayubi, 1991: 299). Some of the older generation, upper-class activists think back to the 'better days' with sorrow:

During Sadat's time, Egypt was much more modern than it is now; women were wearing mini skirts, striped dresses. I myself was wearing those; at that time, there were just three girls at Cairo University who were muhaggabat *[veiled]; everyone was talking about them; they always stuck together; they called them* mutazamita *[rigid/conservative] and* mutakhalifa *[backward]. (Manal A.)*

The majority of the activists I interviewed, however, especially those who were involved in the student movement in the seventies, strongly criticized Sadat's economic as well as foreign policies. Camp David and the subsequent peace accord with Israel is viewed by many as '*Sadat's ultimate*

---

[17] Women were often not hired on the grounds that the provision of maternity and child care, stipulated by the progressive laws of the 1950s and 1960s, made their labour expensive.

[18] See Hatem (1992, 1994) for an in-depth account of the transformation of the Egyptian state from Nasser to Sadat and the different effects on women.

betrayal' and *'the end of Egypt's legitimacy as a leader in the Arab world'*. Another sharp reproach is related to Sadat's manoeuvring with regard to Islamist constituencies. There is a widespread conviction, especially among those women who are affiliated with the socialist Tagammu party, that an alliance between Sadat and the United States is responsible for the emergence of an Islamist movement:

I believe that many of the Islamic groups were armed and trained by Anwar El-Sadat and financed by the CIA in order to fight the communists and Nasserites. It's similar to Israel helping to finance and create Hamas in order to boycott Palestinian independence. The significant role of Americans in supporting Islamic movements isn't a rumour, it's a fact. Whenever you speak with Americans about it, they say that they want to be in contact with all the forces existent. (Hoda K.)

According to the literature, a growing sense of alienation – resulting from the rising imports of new ideas and consumer goods and a consequent rise in materialism – led many to equate *infitah* (open door) with *inhilal* (social disintegration). These effects as well as the further polarization of social inequality that resulted from *infitah* have often been mentioned as significant factors in the subsequent rise of Islamism in the 1970s (El-Guindy, 1981; Hatem, 1992).[19] Initially the Sadat regime co-operated with the Islamists, using the idiom of religion to gain support and legitimacy, as well as to take positions against leftists and Nasserites.[20] However, in 1977 the Islamists started openly to challenge the authority and power of the state with the assassination of the Minister of *Waqfs* (Religious Endowments), Dr Hassan Al-Dhahabi. Sadat's policy of manipulating Islamic groups as a means to weaken popular leftist forces led to an increasing Islamist revival which also galvanized women.

At a later stage, under the influence of the president's wife, Jehan Sadat, reforms to the Personal Status Law (governing marriage, divorce, custody, etc.) were proposed. These reforms spearheaded a two-pronged strategy of undermining the strength and legitimacy of Islamists and demarcating the state's social agenda from that of the Islamists as a form of internal and international mobilization against them. Internally, the state anticipated that the reforms would encourage the growth of a secular coalition of men and women; internationally, it hoped to use the law as a form of public relations to improve its image as a step towards gaining increased political and economic support, especially from the United States (Hatem, 1992: 242).

---

[19] The rise of religiosity among the Egyptian population has been commonly ascribed to Egypt's rout by Israel in 1967 (Ahmed, 1992: 216).

[20] The Sadat regime's attempts to undo Nasser's power elite and structures and discredit his regime in order to gain legitimacy have been labelled 'de-Nasserization'.

The Personal Status Law of 1979, labelled 'Jehan's Law', granted women legal rights in marriage, polygamy, divorce and child custody; it was implemented by presidential decree along with another law that introduced changes to women's representation in parliament. Jehan Sadat, the wife of Anwar Sadat, was instrumental in passing the 1979 Family Status Law that reaffirmed a woman's right to divorce, gave her the right to travel without needing her husband's permission and raised the legal age for marriage from sixteen to eighteen, among other things. The presidential decree created conflicts among women of different political persuasions and put them into a difficult position vis-à-vis this progressive law. Obviously, the common nickname 'Jehan's Law' delegitimized the reformed Personal Status Law by indicating the authoritarian and personalized manner by which it was passed. However, as the activist Siham B. remembers: '*All of us did not want this law to be abolished. We all preferred changes to take place in a democratic way, but within the context of state dynamics at that time it was a great achievement.*' Another woman objected to the linking of Sadat with a progressive law:

Jehan's Law was only a very small element of the Sadat regime. When we speak about Sadat, we speak about a general policy. For me, Sadat is responsible for the growth of the Islamist tendency. He armed and trained them and ended up being killed by them. The general policy under Sadat was against the possible liberation of women. Madame Jehan, on the other hand, managed to pass the new Personal Status Law. It was a good law, but it didn't last. It was changed. The point is: were organizations allowed during Sadat? We must admit the importance of the student movement which was against Sadat. He has no credit whatsoever for organizations.

Women basically lacked independent representative organizations of their own and were dependent on the regime's particular needs. The beginning of the UN Decade for Women in 1975 caused the regime, which was searching for stronger ties with its new allies, particularly the United States, to promote gender issues. Despite the progressive laws of 1979, the state lacked an overall programme to ensure women's rights and did not encourage independent feminist activism.

Post-*infitah* women's activism and the current state under President Mubarak

All in all, I think, Mubarak has learned the difficult way that women are the real force which can prevent the further growth of Islamist activities. Although this hasn't really been translated into some active policy. He hasn't been able to create a new atmosphere. It's being created again and again by the Islamists. What is most dangerous is that all places of authority are being infiltrated by Islamist authorities. Mubarak is terrified by the reactionary forces. He's ambiguous towards women. To his credit is the fact that groups of women are allowed to organize themselves. (Latifa Zayyad)

The increased confrontation with the Islamists over the implementation of the *shariʿa* (Islamic law) pressured the Mubarak regime to legislate and implement more conservative laws and policies towards women and to diminish its support for women's political representation. While Islamist forces continue to constitute a powerful constituency within the contemporary Egyptian state,[21] there has been increasing demand on the Egyptian government to adhere to UN conventions concerning women's rights. Economic dependence on aid from the United States and international donor organizations (IMF and the World Bank) compels the current regime to present itself as abiding by the values and ethos of democracy, human rights and women's rights – as promoted by Egypt's financial and political 'benefactors'.

Several political analysts stress that President Mubarak inherited a complex legacy from the Nasser and Sadat eras (Ayubi, 1991; Baker, 1990; McDermott, 1988). Ambiguity and contradictory signals have been features of a regime that has to struggle with competing forces within contemporary Egypt as well as the legacies of the past.

The early years of the Mubarak regime were characterized by a search for stabilization and consolidation. In 1985 the Personal Status Law, which had been at the centre of the debate concerning the state's legitimacy, was amended due to strong opposition from the Islamists who perceived it to be anti-Islamic. The revised law abandons many of the rights that women had attained in the earlier version (Bibars, 1987). A strong women's lobby used the 1985 Nairobi Conference – marking the end of the decade for Women – to protest and pressure the government to reformulate the law. Two months after its cancellation (just prior to the Nairobi Conference) a new law was passed which restored some of the benefits that the 1979 version had provided.

The re-emergence of women's activism has mainly been linked to the continuing battle over the Personal Status Law and the taking up of formerly taboo issues such as contraception and clitoridectomy (Ahmed, 1992: 214). However, in 1985, during the national discussion of the Personal Status Law, differences within the movement became more emphasized. While Nawal El-Saʿdawi defended the law and campaigned to maintain it, the Ittihad Al-Nissaʾi Al-Taqadummi (Progressive Women's Union, affiliated with the leftist Tagammu party) argued that it was passed unconstitutionally by Sadat and should therefore be annulled. In this debate nationalist leftist women, who opposed Sadat's policies

[21] Among its many manifestations in public life are the establishments of Islamic schools, hospitals, banks and social welfare organizations. In the realm of the 'private' a growing observance of religious rites and a stress on 'Islamic values' has particularly affected women (Zaki, 1995).

of *infitah* and rapprochement with Israel, could be found arguing on the same lines as the Islamists and the Azhar who were enraged by the reformed Personal Status Law. This debate very clearly showed the 'instrumentality' of women's issues and their submergence into broader political questions. What was at stake was not the actual substance of the issue, but a joint opposition against Sadat's general policies.

This episode is also reflective of the heterogeneity and frictions among women representing different political convictions and ideologies and having conflicting interpretations of the actual content of *qadiyyat al-mar'a* (women's issues) and how to go about promoting women's rights. However, it does not only show that women activists were just as ideologically and politically divided as men were, but also demonstrates the existing gaps between the various strands of the women's movement.

The very act of forming an emergency coalition, when the constitutionality of the Personal Status Law was challenged in 1985, represents a break from prevalent nationalist– and liberal–modernist discourses within Egypt. These discourses had only focused on women's rights in the public sphere as part of 'the process creating new modern societies' (Hatem, 1993: 42). However, prevailing perceptions of women's rights were very closely tied to the modernist discourses of earlier male reformers, such as Qasim Amin, and the more recent development discourses. According to Mervat Hatem, these discourses accept 'women's public space, where they were expected to pursue public activities like education, work and some form of political participation, especially suffrage' (ibid.: 40). Women's rights within the 'private', family sphere are not only ignored, but also considered as standing outside the legitimate struggle for *qadiyyat al-mar'a* (women's issues). During the post-*infitah* period these previously unchallenged premises on women's rights started to be challenged from various directions, even if they still constituted the most widespread interpretation of women's rights.

One of the earliest and most powerful challenger of modernist–nationalist discourses on women was Nawal El-Sa'dawi. Like other women of her generation she had significant 'formative experiences', first as a medical student and then as a medical doctor during the Nasser regime. Her activism and her writings suggest a combination of both: an ambivalence about imperialism and the local patriarchy. After she brought out her book *Al-Mar'a wa Al-Jins* (Woman and Sex, 1971), she emerged as a prominent and courageous activist for women's rights. A number of the women I interviewed recalled the turmoil and uproar that El-Sa'dawi's book and lectures stirred up. Many felt that she was the victim of society's double standard. As Azza L. expressed it:

I used to attend her lectures at the Naqabat al-Attibaa' [the doctors' syndicate] *every two weeks until they threw her out. Imagine, they threw her out, because she was writing a scientific book about virginity and circumcision. The book was called* Woman and Sex. *She was trying to save women who were naive and ignorant. It was a medical and scientific book. Today you see all these books about sex. The other day I was really shocked. I walked downtown. You know the Café Américain on Imad ad-Din street? In front of the café there was a guy selling sex books with pictures. Nobody is doing anything about this. The Islamists aren't doing anything, but they did threaten Nawal, because she's trying to empower women.*

In this controversial book, and also in her fiction, El-Saʿdawi attacks the patriarchal control of female sexuality. She made taboo issues such as clitoridectomy, sexual abuse and exploitation public issues, and initiated a kind of feminism different from previous trends. While the majority of activists today distance themselves from El-Saʿdawi's activism, either because they view it as 'too western', 'too radical', 'too elitist' or 'too authoritarian', there were only very few who did not acknowledge Nawal El-Saʿdawi's courage, her influence on several generations and her pioneering role. '*We all read Nawal El-Saʿdawi*' or '*she was always on top of our list for readings and lectures*' were common statements among women of several generations.

Aside from enlarging the perspective from a national to a more regional level, El-Saʿdawi also supported another group of women activists in their struggle.[22] Gamaʿat Bint Al-Ard (Daughter of the Land Group) had emerged in 1982 in Mansoura in the Egyptian Delta. It was made up of a number of young women who had been involved in public protests against the Israeli invasion of Lebanon (1982). While the broader solidarity movement dispersed after a period of campaigning against Israeli aggression and fund-raising for its victims, the members of the women's committee continued their meetings and shifted their focus to women's issues, such as consciousness-raising of adolescent girls, literacy, legal awareness, women's rights in Islam, etc.

It became clear throughout my interviews that, despite the gratitude expressed by various women who had been supported by El-Saʿdawi, there was also a sense of difficulty about working with her on a teamwork basis. The clash between authoritarian and hierarchical styles of decision making and more democratic aspirations is not unique to El-Saʿdawi and younger activists, but characterizes the relationship between many

[22] Aside from Jamiʿyat Tadamun Al-Marʾa Al-ʿArabiyya (Arab Women's Solidarity Association), several other formal and informal groups started to emerge by the mid-eighties: e.g. Gamʿat Bint Al-Ard (the Daughter of the Land Association) Al-Marʾa Al-Gedida (the New Woman), the Communication Group for the Enhancement of the Status of Women in Egypt and Rabtat Al-Marʾa Al-ʿArabiyya (the Alliance of Arab Women).

of the older charismatic figures in the movement and the new generation.

Overall, I found that the younger generation (those in their twenties or
early thirties) tended to show much less appreciation of Nawal El-
Saʿdawi's role and contributions than did older activists. However, the
widespread negative reactions expressed about El-Saʿdawi often lost
ground when I inquired about their actual contact either with her written
works or the person herself. Very strong opinions could often not be sub-
stantiated by anything other than 'what one had heard about her'. This is
only one of several examples:

I have read Nawal, but very little. I only read her sociological analysis of the Jahaliyya
[pre-Islamic] *time. I don't like her. I disagree with everything she's doing. She's so outspoken that it works against her. It is this aggression that I hate. She only speaks about
the sexual aspect. I feel this is very superficial. I haven't read any of her fiction. (Niveen
H.)*

The lack of knowledge among younger activists about El-Saʿdawi's
writing and activism was very noticeable in the course of my research.
During the last months of my fieldwork, El-Saʿdawi returned to Egypt
after living and teaching in the United States for two years. She gave me
the following explanation for the level of ignorance and frequent misconceptions concerning her writings: '*My work has been prohibited during the
sixties and seventies, although my books are still there. Later under Sadat and
Mubarak I've also been censored. I've been in exile. I haven't been in the media
in Egypt. There are many young women who have never read my work.*'

El-Saʿdawi expressed anger and disappointment to me on several occasions. While part of her anger is related to the government and the
Islamists, who were the reason for her self-imposed exile, she spoke a
great deal about the current women's movement:

*We don't want the older ones and we start from zero. There is no continuity. And this is
why there's no history. In the national movement they've a history. The history must be
known, there must be building. Everyone speaks about Hoda Shaʿrawi, but they're afraid
to mention anybody else. She was conservative and pro-regime. She was very bourgeois.
These are the women who are considered by the regime. There is only an official history;
you don't find a non-governmental history of women. Most of my work is in Arabic, but
only when I travel abroad they mention my name, when they talk about 'foremothers' of
the feminist movement, they mention me.*

El-Saʿdawi's experience reflects a more generational shift in which older
women activists, who initially struggled for women's rights in the frame of
nationalism and anti-imperialism, feel sidelined by a group of younger
professional women. Their feeling of being upstaged actually parallels the
experience of many more radical western feminists, who do not identify
with some of the newer feminist trends. In Egypt, a generational shift

coincided with a radical transformation of the institutional infrastructure in which women's activism takes place. When Nawal El-Saʿdawi started out with AWSA in the 1980s her organization was one of the first re-emerging women's rights advocacy groups. Meanwhile, a flurry of independent, associational and directed organizations arose with a variety of agendas: some are advocacy groups while many constitute apolitical service delivery organizations. The increased level of the professionalization of women's activism is directly linked to donor-led agendas which often direct mobilization from outside Egypt. However, it would certainly be unfair merely to define the younger generation in terms of the influence of foreign donors and their agendas. Older women activists, including El-Saʿdawi, are also taking part in the struggle for funding and resources.

The reasons for the banning of AWSA by the Ministry of Social Affairs in 1991 have been the subject of much debate. Mona Helmi, the daughter of El-Saʿdawi, recalls the accusations against AWSA as a continuous element throughout the existence of the organization: '*We were accused of separating men and women; of not focusing on the national issue and class aspect, but being only interested in the patriarchal aspect; and being influenced by the West. We were called Islamists. We were accused of obscenity, immorality and westernization. Both Islamists and leftists were against us. We were accused of exactly the opposite of what we advocated in our seminars and writings.*'

It has been argued that AWSA's feminism was 'highly visible and confrontational, and outspokenly critical of Islamist positions on gender' (Badran, 1993: 142). Many women I interviewed, even those opposed to the banning of the association, argue that rather than the content of Nawal El-Saʿdawi's seminars, writings and speeches, it was the actual form of the organization that made it an easy target. Some activists point to a lack of administrative and organizational skills on the part of El-Saʿdawi which, later on, were taken against her when the government felt threatened by her discourse.

However, even many of those who were critical of Nawal El-Saʿdawi and her organization disagreed about the way the association was dissolved, which fuelled the ongoing debate about Law 32 and led to the establishment of a coalition called 'the Committee to Change the Law of Associations' (D. Sullivan, 1994: 35).[23]

Despite Mubarak's official pro-democracy policy, repressive measures have not only been directed towards Islamic militant groups and communists, but also towards women activists. A number of laws, most notably the Law of Associations (32), first established under Nasser, continue to

---

[23] For a detailed discussion of Law 32 see S. E. Ibrahim (1996) and D. Sullivan (1994).

regulate the establishment of voluntary groups, associations and organizations under the supervision of the Ministry of Social Affairs. These laws oblige women activists to operate either as informal groups or as officially registered organizations which are subjected to the control of the Ministry of Social Affairs.

The level of control varies depending on the political climate. The influence of state power on civil society organizations through the Ministry of Social Affairs and the apparent randomness with which organizations are allowed to operate is being restrained by the international arena. The influence of the international community became more pressing during the preparations for the United Nations' International Conference on Population and Development in Cairo (September 1994) and the International Women's Forum in Beijing (September 1995). One year prior to the ICPD Egyptian NGOs experienced a breakthrough in their tension-ridden relations with the government as the latter recognized and supported an elected National NGO Committee for Population and Development (NCPD). The ongoing ambiguity of the Mubarak regime concerning women's rights was reflected in the flaring up of the continuing debate over Law 32 during the preparations for Beijing.[24]

It is within the context of increased pressure from NGO circles within Egypt as well as international donor organizations abroad that the Egyptian government decided to propose changes to the contested law in 1998. However, as an Egyptian NGO position paper on the draft Law of Associations (32) points out, the proposed amendments only aim 'to tighten government control over non-governmental organizations by filling the loopholes in Law 32 of 1964 and extending the law to include, and stifle, all forms of civil work'.[25]

The increased influence of the international agencies and bodies has triggered a fierce debate about the external links of previously independent organizations. In the typology mentioned in the introduction to this book, 'directed collective action' 'applies to those cases where the authority and initiative clearly comes from outside and stands above the collectivity itself' (Molyneux, 1998: 229). While there is certainly room for negotiation over goals and means, it is obvious that the international women's movement as well as agendas of funding agencies does influence

---

[24] Several women's groups preferred to circumvent Law 32 and the danger of being dissolved by the Ministry of Social Affairs and registered with the Office of Property and Accreditation as research centres or civic non-profit companies as opposed to PVOs or NGOs, thereby avoiding the control and restrictions set by the Ministry of Social Affairs.
[25] 'Defending the Autonomy of Civil Associations'. NGOs' position paper on the draft Law of Associations (27 May 1998).

and partly direct the contemporary movement in Egypt. This relationship takes different forms and might be more reciprocal in some instances than in others. One of its main effects has been the professionalization of the previously voluntary welfare sector. Being a woman activist can be a 'career' in contemporary Egypt, where a new field for jobs has been created within the wider NGO movement. Unfortunately, professionalism and careerism often involve competition for job opportunities, funding possibilities and travel grants, which, in turn, may breed envy and rivalry.

The international arena and power relations within the state have also had an impact on Islamist conceptualizations of women's rights. There is an increasing number of Islamist women activists who have managed to gain a voice within the mainstream Islamist discourse and to criticize and challenge their male counterparts for misinterpreting Islam.[26] A number of scholars have already explored the issue of Islamism and women's rights which I do not want to recapitulate here (Badran, 1991, 1994; El-Guindy, 1983; Karam, 1993, 1994, 1998; Zuhur, 1992). However, I would like briefly to outline some of the tendencies of Islamist women activists.

The literature reveals that the most celebrated women have remained ambiguous about what constitutes an adequate role for women within an envisioned Islamic state and society: for example, Zeinab Al-Ghazali, the most prominent Islamist woman and founder of the Jama'at al-Sayyidat al-Muslimat (Muslim Women's Association, 1936), and Safinaz Qazim, a journalist and former leftist who committed herself to Islam in the 1970s. While Al-Ghazali and Qazim find no contradiction between women's public involvement (education and work) and private lives within the family (wives and mothers), they have remained antagonistic to feminism (Badran, 1994: 209).

A new generation of Islamist women have been more outspoken and confrontational about the way they view women's role in an Islamic state. They stress Islam's compatibility with UN-stipulated standards of women's rights and point to persisting traditions of pre-Islamic times as being responsible for the discrimination against women (Ahmed, 1992). Zeinab Radwan, for example, a professor of Islamic philosophy at Cairo University and author of the book *Islam and Women's Issues*, told me that she would spread her convictions through newspaper articles, in public lectures, TV programmes and in lectures at Cairo University. In her view,

---

[26] The term 'gender activism' has been coined by Margot Badran to conceptualize an activism that 'transcends ideological boundaries of politically articulated feminism and Islamism' and constitutes a 'response by women deciding for themselves how to conduct their lives in society' (Badran, 1994: 202).

the movement of *tahrir al-mar'a* initiated by Huda Sha'rawi only addressed issues such as education and veiling, but failed to address women's rights and position in the family, which she sees as clearly defined by Islam.[27]

Heba Rauf Ezzat, one of the youngest and most prominent Islamist women's activists, is certainly the most outspoken in the call for the launching of an Islamic women's movement. Feeling closest to the more moderate Akhwan Muslimin, rather than some of the more radical tendencies, she clearly expresses her objective to change society from within in order to realize her vision of an Islamic state. *Ijtihad*, the reinterpretation of the sources of religion and traditional values and the examination of Islamic history are the methods chosen by Rauf to evolve an Islamic theory of women's liberation.

Rauf rejects being labelled a feminist since she perceives feminism to be 'anti-men' and negating religion (Badran, 1994: 213). Yet she does not categorically dismiss feminism, but acknowledges that women have not been able really to obtain their rights in Islamic societies, which explains the successes of 'western' feminist movements within Egypt (ibid.: 214). Rauf says:

> The Islamists always considered women's liberation a western idea. This prevented them from making their own interpretations about women's problems. It is time to launch a new women's liberation movement – an Islamic one, not only for the benefit of Muslim women and Muslim societies but for all women everywhere. If Islam is a universal religion and a way of life, then this movement too should aim at universal goals. It should parallel a struggle for economic and political liberation from the colonialism of the new capitalist world order. (*MERIP*, Nov./Dec. 1994, p. 27)

Central to Rauf's thinking is her search for 'authenticity' and a rejection of 'western eccentricities and immoral behaviour', such as the acceptance of homosexuality (Karam, 1998: 222). According to Azza Karam, all three of these Islamist women, Heba Rauf, Zeinab Al-Ghazali and Safinaz Qazim, perpetuate dichotomous Islamist thinking, 'with all its resulting exclusion of the ideas of "the Other", that is the "West"' (ibid.: 231).

Conclusion

The 'revival' of women's activism during the recent past cannot be reduced to a defensive action against Islamists' calls for women to return to the home, even if the 'climate of fear' might enhance efforts to organize

---

[27] For a detailed and interesting analysis of and comparison between Zeinab Al-Ghazali, Safinaz Qazim and Heba Rauf see Karam (1998).

secular middle-class women. It is important to stress that the flurry of pro-feminist activism during the recent past – and articulations of new perspectives and demands on such issues as women's political participation, women's equality in the workplace, and the more sensitive issues of women's reproductive rights and violence against women – took place in a profoundly transnationalized global context where the government felt pressured by international constituencies to prove its commitment to women's equality. Moreover, resources and people were mobilized around both the International Conference on Population and Development (September 1994) and the International Women's Forum (September 1995).

In some instances individuals seem to have grouped only temporarily in response to funding possibilities generated by international agendas, and dissipated after both conferences ended. However, some issue-oriented networks, such as the FGM (Female Genital Mutilation) Task Force and a network of organizations working on a project called Women and Violence did not only persist, but also seem to have maintained their momentum. These various issue-oriented networks actually typify a new organizational form in the history of the women's movement in that they consist of associational linkages in which the various groups maintain their autonomy and, to some extent, acknowledge the differences among them. The Women and Violence project, for example, includes an independent women's rights advocacy group, a legal aid group, a human rights group, a centre for victims of torture and a health NGO.

Throughout history Egyptian women activists have been discredited by different constituencies by being labelled western agents of colonialism or imperialism. Inherent in some of these attacks is the lack of agency attributed to Egyptian women. However, the struggle to improve women's status and redefine their roles is not monopolized by western women, nor are struggles against social justice the domain of western men only. Egyptian women activists, as varied as they might have been in their ideological inclinations, were active agents in their specific cultural, social and political contexts. It never fails to astonish me how women activists continue to be discredited on the basis of their class affiliation and links to European culture and education, while male political activists, especially communists, do not seem to be exposed to the same degree of scrutiny concerning their class or educational background.

But we also have to go further than notions, as suggested by Badran, for instance, that 'Egyptian feminism was not a subtext of colonialism or "Western discourse", but an independent discourse that simultaneously engaged indigenous patriarchy and patriarchal colonial domination' (Badran, 1995: 24). Perhaps it is about time to abandon the defensive and free ourselves from the need to legitimize a movement by proving its independence from western thought. A new, and certainly more constructive, approach opens up possibilities of cultural and ideological contestations which do not necessarily result in a bounded unchanging and imposing whole, but could be moments of selection, absorption and reformulation, as well as creation. Rather than holding on to essentialist conceptualizations of 'culture' and 'identity', a post-colonial analysis with an emphasis on hybridity, dynamics and exchange offers a more constructive approach than claims to authenticity.

The continued redefinition and reassessment of the roles and status of women has been one of the most distinctive features of Egypt's modern history. An insight into this history reveals that the most dramatic changes in the redefinitions of these roles and status have occurred during those moments when the country itself was passing through political, social or economic crisis (Nelson, 1984: 223–4). The 1919 revolution, independence in 1923, the 1952 revolution, the 1967 defeat, the October war of 1973, the *infitah* economic policies of 1974 and the impact of Islamist discourses and growth of Islamist activism in the 1980s, the ongoing economic crises and the increased influence of international agencies in the 1990s, have been important periods of transition in the history of the country as well as important landmarks in the history of the Egyptian women's movement.

The state is not only far from being homogeneous and static, but its relation to women's organizations differs from context to context. In Egypt the changing role and policies of the state vis-à-vis women's issues were paralleled by the continuous pressure women exerted on the Egyptian state to respond to their demands and needs (Hatem, 1992: 248). The Egyptian state poses a threat as well as offering resources to the women's organizations. Connell's conceptualization of each state embodying as well as creating 'gender regimes' provides a useful analytical tool to understand the changing and ambiguous relationship between the Egyptian women's movement and the state (Connell, 1990). Throughout its history the Egyptian state was actively engaged in constructing gender through its policies and legal provisions. The debate about the Personal Status Laws is a case in point, as it shows the shifting and ambiguous role of the state concerning gender relations. The state can be both a means to challenge existing gender relations (by reforming the conservative Personal Status Laws and granting women more rights with regard to marriage, divorce and child custody) or it can reinforce oppressive gender relations (by abolishing the reformed laws).

As Badran has already pointed out, 'historically, there has been room in Egypt for the competing discourses of the state, Islamists and feminists on the "woman question"' (Badran, 1994: 205). In the 1990s the state and pro-feminists have increasingly had to take into account Islamist social and political activism, discourses and demands. Meanwhile, agents of globalization, i.e. the international constituency of policy-makers, development agencies and UN-related organizations, also shape contemporary women's activism.

3 Self and generation: formative experiences of Egyptian women activists

Yes, it's painful to talk about it. Every time I do talk about it, it leaves me devastated. Every time, I had to pull myself together. Every time, I had to wonder: did this really happen to me? Is it the present me to whom all that happened? And finally: what is the real link between the 'I now' and my 'I' in the past? My 'I now' will tell the story, that is herstory. Not only am I telling it for your research, but also for the sake of the 'I now'. The 'I' has to get rid of it, once and for all. I have to say it now, imbued with all my biases and personal drives. I don't promise you it's going to be objective; it's going to be very subjective. You'll have to struggle with it to come out with some logical conclusions and scientific results. Indeed, this is what your research requires: logicality, historicity and, most important, objectivity. They are the three rivets of the male phallocentric culture. Yes, you'll have to struggle, because it will be irrational, ahistorical and illogical. (Samia E.)*

Sitting cross-legged on the bed of Samia E., sipping the Nescafé she made every time I came to visit her, smoking her cigarettes, looking at all the old newspapers stacked up and all the books lying around, I often forgot about the actual 'purpose' of these meetings. Samia's narrations of her experiences regularly transported me into other worlds: the apartment where she spent the first years of her childhood with her mother and father as well as her father's first wife and children; the gloom of the flat to which she moved with her mother after her father's death, the scrutinizing looks and comments of her relatives, her boredom and despair living in Saudi Arabia where her mother was trying to make ends meet by working as a teacher. Samia's talent for story-telling, the way she moved all of her body and used her voice as well as the content and details of her stories totally gripped me and often left me with the same sense of astonishment she herself expressed: 'Is this really the same person in front of me who experienced all this?'

Samia, as well as nine other women activists, had agreed to have their life-stories recorded by me after I had interviewed them several times for my project. As mentioned in my introduction, my criteria for choosing these particular women out of the approximately eighty women I met and interviewed were linked to some 'objective' factors, such as generational differences, political orientation and organizational belonging, as well as religious affiliation. However, equally important were 'subjective' factors: there had to be a certain 'chemistry', a personal curiosity and interest, and it had to exist on both sides. I was chosen by the women activists whose life-stories I recorded as much as I chose them.[1]

Samia and I became very close in the course of my research. Soon she knew as much about my life as I knew about hers. I sometimes felt uncomfortable, because I feared that she would interpret my concern and interest in her life as the sheer curiosity of the researcher. This fear induced me to downplay this role in our relationship, even though Samia never actually seemed to have a problem with it. As our friendship grew, it became harder and harder to actually get 'some business done' and continue taping her life-story. Was it not much more interesting to discuss our visions about feminism, talk about the latest news, sometimes gossip, or commiserate about our respective 'heartaches'? Whenever we did record parts of her life-story, however, Samia really let me and the tape-recorder share in her experiences. Unlike the women with whom I did not develop such close friendships, Samia did not just tell me about her parents' professions and roles in her upbringing, her education, how she became involved in politics in general and women's rights in particular, her career, her family and her involvement in the women's movement; she also told me about her dreams and fears, her problems and insecurities, her happy moments and painful ones. After some months of meeting up and talking about her life, she told me:

Do you know now why and how I became a feminist? Feminism was there all the time. It was there when I hated being shouted at, being beaten, being accused of things I have not done. It was there when I said 'no' to illogical orders and 'no' to tailored marriages; when I insisted on going out and when I yelled back. It was there with its twin: the sense of guilt. Both are here now. They have adapted peacefully. They are even decorated with many theories, seminars, conferences, papers, workshops and discussions. The sense of guilt, however, will come to the foreground, disguised as Mr Anger and Mr Depression. Now, I

---

[1] While often used interchangeably, I use the term life-story as opposed to life-history or biography as it more adequately describes the method of selecting excerpts of a woman's life, rather than presenting a chronological account of a woman's past. The life-story, according to Marcia Wright, is 'ambiguously authored, and may be more or less actively composed by a mediator who arranges the testimony and quietly supplies explanatory interventions' (Wright, 1986, quoted in Reinharz, 1992). Life-stories, then, are narratives that grow out of interaction with a researcher and are distinct from an interview in that they deal more broadly with a person's past rather than a particular phenomenon or experience (Reinharz, 1992: 130). Like life-histories and biographies, life-stories can be subsumed under the more general term 'oral history'.

am a pessoptimist[2] secular feminist with whom some feminists do not feel comfortable, because I am not conforming to the norms. And I won't.

But how did other women become activists? What does it take to become involved in women's rights struggles and continue to do so over a long period of time? What are the individual trajectories and what is the historical context? And how do they relate to one another? These and related questions were at the back of my mind when I listened to Samia and the nine other women who patiently gave me glimpses into their lives. Their complex and often moving tales require much more space and consideration than is feasible in this work, but I hope that my brief excerpts will provide some insight into the variety of experiences, motivations and incentives that spark contemporary women's activism in Egypt.

The web of meaning

Almost unnoticed, it appears that yet another dichotomy has entered through the backdoor of our discipline. In his review of six works of 'new Middle Eastern ethnography' (Abu-Lughod, 1993a; Bowen & Early (eds.), 1993; Burke (ed.), 1993; Hammoudi, 1993; Messick, 1993; Munson, 1993) Charles Lindholm passionately argues that the focus on personal narratives and life-histories often works at the expense of 'any possibility of theory building or comparative work' (Lindholm, 1995: 805). Underlying his criticism is certainly a very disconcerting tendency within what is called Middle East scholarship: its unwillingness to look beyond itself in terms of region and in terms of a theoretical and methodological field of study. However, Lindholm's disapproval also seems to be based on the anxiety that Lila Abu-Lughod's insistence on studying the particular, as articulated in her well-known article 'Writing against Culture' (1991), excludes any grounds for generalization and comparison and aims to deny any kind of boundary: 'between self and other, autonomy and participation, unity and plurality, male and female, equality and subordination' (Lindholm, 1995: 818). This hardly seems to be what Abu-Lughod (and 'many younger Middle Eastern specialists', as Lindholm puts it) had in mind when she suggested a focus on individuals and the particularities of their lives (1993a: 27). Rather than 'an argument against generalization *per se*', Abu-Lughod's approach entails 'a refusal to accord generalizations objective or omniscient status' (Jackson (ed.), 1996: 19). Personal narratives and biographies, just as much as sta-

---

[2] Samia is referring to a novel entitled *The Pessoptimist* by the Palestinian writer Emile Habibi, whose main character is struggling both against the Israeli occupiers and norms and traditions in his own society.

tistical information, can be tools to learn about historical events, political processes and social phenomena, as long as this is what the researcher intends to do with them. The line between individual and collective experiences is blurry and difficult to draw. Historical contexts, particular political events and discourses provide a backdrop and set the scene for individual consciousness and activity, but they cannot be reduced to or be determined by them. There is no fixed and finite set of rules, only a repertoire of possibilities.

Personal life-stories may shed light on particular political epochs and historical periods, their prevailing world-views and forms of actions. These might culminate in experiences that gain particular significance in forming a person's consciousness, actions and political involvement. Even if shared, these 'formative experiences' have been lived and narrated individually and with great variation. Borrowing Marx's vivid image, Michael Jackson put it well, when he wrote: 'The frozen circumstances are forced to dance by us singing to them their own melody' (ibid.: 1996: 20).

The dialectic between individual experiences and historical context, or 'objective' events, has constituted an ongoing unresolved concern for many thinkers and, in fact, continues to be a headline problematic in the social sciences. Variations on this theme range from articulations of the tensions between human agency and structure (Berger & Luckmann, 1967), processes of 'structuration' (Giddens, 1979), the relationship between sociology and history (Abrams, 1982) to issues of individual and collective consciousness (Marx, 1959; Merleau-Ponty, 1962). It is beyond the scope of this chapter to examine this extensive debate;[3] I would, however, like to quote Maurice Merleau-Ponty, whose phenomenological philosophy underlies his outlook on personhood, which entails two coexisting aspects of experience:

To be born is to be born of the world and to be born into the world. The world is already constituted, but also never completely constituted; in the first place we are acted upon, in the second we are open to an infinite number of possibilities. But this analysis is still abstract, for we exist in both ways at once. There is, therefore, never determinism and never absolute choice, I am never a thing and never bare consciousness. In fact, even our own pieces of initiative, even the situations which we have chosen, bear on us, once they have been entered upon by virtue of a state rather than an act. The generality of the 'role' and of the situation comes to the aid of decision, and in this exchange between the situation and the person who takes

---

[3] For a brief summary of the debate, see Philip Abrams, 'Preface and Introduction', in his *Historical Sociology* (1982). Among the various writers who have dealt with the issue of human agency and structure, Abrams mentions Marx (1959, 1962), Durkheim (1960), Weber (1930, 1949), Merton (1957), Berger & Luckmann (1967), Elias (1978) and Giddens (1979).

it up, it is impossible to determine precisely the 'share contributed by the situation' and the 'share contributed by freedom'. (Merleau-Ponty, 1962: 453)

In line with this view, notions of 'subjectivity' versus 'objectivity' become nonsensical as individual experiences always vacillate between a sense of oneself as subject and as object. Moreover, as we deal with 'reality', engage in our everyday lifeworld, try to master and react to it, our very actions change what appears to be naturally and socially given (Schutz & Luckmann, 1989: 1). Life-stories, then, are narrated by people whose individual knowledge and experiences of self always take place in relation to others as well as being shaped by general circumstances. Women's autobiographical accounts and self-narratives are never just private and subjective: 'The categories and concepts we use for reflecting upon and evaluating ourselves come from a cultural context' (Patai, 1991: 18). This interrelatedness creates the context, or 'web of meaning', within which we live and act.

In the following sections I shall explore both the individual experiences of women activists and the actual contexts that shaped their consciousness. On the basis of the ten life-stories I recorded and my interviews with more than eighty Egyptian women activists it was possible to detect several distinct periods that represent different arenas of engagement and different formative experiences. These have influenced both the types of their involvement and their outlooks on the women's movement. The eldest generation of contemporary Egyptian activists on women's issues (in their seventies and eighties) emphasize their early involvement in community and welfare projects in pre-revolutionary Egypt. The Nasserist era of revolutionary transformations and experiences connected with the Nasser regime constitutes a later period of mobilization, followed by the disillusioning experience of the 1967 defeat at the hands of the Israeli army (age group: fifties and sixties). Many of the women I interviewed mentioned experiences related to the student movement during the Sadat period as crucial in their personal and political development (age group: forties). The increased influence of international organizations and donor agencies and the involvement of women activists in internationally sponsored projects, as well as personal experiences of oppression, characterize the entry point of the 1980s and 1990s (age group: twenties and thirties).

The activities characterizing these periods of mobilization are certainly not mutually exclusive, nor do these represent clearly defined periods. I shall give examples of the formative experiences typical of each period by looking at the various life-stories. I do not intend to suggest that such experiences fully determine a particular woman's attitude towards and involvement in the women's movement. Rather, I intend to sketch certain tendencies and forms of commitment, which, while rooted in specific historical developments, also represent current strands and sources of variation within contemporary women's activism in Egypt.

I shall also explore recurring themes in the various narratives, which shape and influence women's daily lives and political consciousness. Here I will address the roles of parents, relationships with husbands, responsibilities towards children and friendships. I will show that while women have to struggle simultaneously on many fronts, their closest relationships and bonds could be as much a source of hindrance as they could be a source of strength and courage.

Social welfare and public-spirited elites

For those activists who grew up during the 1920s and 1930s, involvement in the women's movement is very closely linked to their early commitment to welfare and charity work. Many were encouraged by parents as well as teachers to 'help the poor', 'do community work' and 'make themselves useful'. Hoda A., an activist with a long history of voluntary work within Egypt as well as a long career within the UN system, recalls the summer she first became involved in community work:

My father was liberal in giving my mother full freedom to get involved in community services. She was also involved in political life as she was active in the first women's movement connected with Hoda Sha'rawi. The whole family supported that, because two of her best friends, who happened to be her cousins, were also very active in the Hoda Sha'rawi movement. When I was a bit older and started school in Cairo, maybe I was around fifteen, and my mother asked just before summer was around: 'What are you going to do with your summer?' I said: 'I am going to have fun. I am going on a holiday.' She said: 'It would be good if you became a bit busy and made yourself useful.' I talked to my friends and we started thinking: 'Why don't we give our summer to teaching some poor children in our surroundings?' By that time my parents had moved to Cairo and we lived in Zaitoun, in my old grandfather's house, which had a huge garden. So we brought these poor children. We were about five young volunteers. Some of the children were older than us. We knew how to convey in a simple way what is cleanliness: 'Why do we have to comb our hair? To wash our faces? And why do we have to know how to read and write?' We also took them out on picnics and we had a lot of fun with them. At that time, Zaitoun was semi-rural and the children used to walk through the fields to come to us.

Among the group of friends who used to do voluntary work together was Nadia M., another woman activist today. Like Hoda, Nadia grew up being exposed to social and welfare work. However, her first remarkable experience in the field of voluntary work took place somewhat later, after she had finished high school and accepted a teaching job for a year at the American Junior College (now Ramsis College) in Cairo:

I accepted an offer as a social case worker, since I was not working full-time as a teacher. It was an NGO[4] that was working with the families of TB patients. They recruited me to go and collect information about the families so that they could give them assistance. They were mainly patients from the Kasr El-Aini hospital, who were very sick, so I used to collect names and investigate these families. I took my work very seriously and I had some very interesting incidents. One afternoon, for example, it must have been around 2 o'clock, I went to Imam Al-Shafei.[5] I was very ignorant, because I was following an address given to me and it took me hours to find the place. Then I knocked at a door, one person answered me and asked what I was looking for. I told him I was looking for a place and showed him the address. He then told me that I had to look for a tomb. At that time, it was in the year 1945, people were living there in tombs. At last I got the person I was looking for, but not in that tomb. It was just scary, because it was getting late and I was wearing two golden bracelets. I was alone and people told me later that I could have been killed. Then I told myself that I will never again wear any gold.

Both Nadia and Hoda, like many of their best friends then, were raised in upper-middle-class families. They remember that their initial involvement in social welfare work involved an encounter with people, lifestyles, customs and values that seemed far removed from their own. Both express their initial shock at becoming aware of the big gap between their own and the life circumstances of 'the poor'. In some instances their experience of difference was related not only to their upper-middle-class status, but also to their religious affiliation. For Hoda and Nadia belonging to the Coptic church also contributed to their early commitment to welfare work, in that volunteer work was greatly encouraged by the church as part of community life. Both women recall being active in Sunday school while growing up. However, Hoda and Nadia stress that many of their best friends, who were Muslims, were equally involved in and concerned with social welfare work.

Muslim–Christian relations figure in their life-stories differently. Nadia narrates an incident which she describes as significant for her later development:

The incident happened in Boulak,[6] in a building called 'El Rabaa'. It was a building with strange corridors, which are used like streets and every room housed a different family. In one of those rooms, there was a TB case and I was investigating the family. Two men came inside, and they were talking of an accident which was caused by one of them while riding a motorcycle. He mentioned that he hit a young girl. The other asked him the name of the girl and when he mentioned the name, it turned out to be a Christian name. His friend said: 'She is Christian, let her die and go to hell.' When I heard this I was scared. They did not know my name and I felt that I had to run away for my life. It was not a safe place, but this really helped me to see and to carry myself in such a way as to cope with this.

[4] The introduction of the clearly anachronistic term 'NGO' is Nadia's own usage.
[5] Imam Al-Shafa'i is a low-income district in south Cairo.
[6] Low-income area close to central Cairo.

Nadia does not use this incident to articulate an overall sense of feeling discriminated against or feeling threatened. Rather, she uses this and other incidents to illustrate the development of her strength and the multi-layered nature of her anger and subsequent struggle. Another element of her early sense of marginalization and impulse to resist different forms of discrimination is related to her school education. Nadia, who went to a government school for her first school years, remembers the way people of her background would look down on government schools. Her experiences in the government school, as well as her family's attitude towards schooling, shed light on some of the prevailing values of the time:

I was in the house until the age of seven. Then I got the uniform to go to the school run by French nuns, like my other three sisters. But my mother got very upset with the school, because my sisters became so religious and the nuns made them follow all the Catholic rites. My older sister, who was sixteen or seventeen years old at that time, wanted to become a nun. My mother, being from an orthodox Coptic family, was so upset and she took all her daughters out of that school. She got them tutors for a couple of years at home. She decided that I was not going to any place other than a government school. At that time our own family members looked down on government schools. When I used to mention that I was going to Ghamra Primary School, people used to comment how terrible that was. This made me really strive to imitate my sisters and work on my French, because I felt that I was the black sheep of the family. In the school it also helped me to really distinguish myself, because not only was I in a government school, but we were only two Christian girls in the class. Although those times were not like the present days of fanaticism, the Muslim teachers and the mistresses used to say that the worst thing about me was being a Christian.

Hoda, on the other hand, stresses the harmonious relationship between Muslims and Christians: '*The pre-war period was a time when all of us mixed together without thinking who is who. We attended each others' classes. There was no such division as there is today. So the unity among religions was also very much supported by the schooling. Of course, I was lucky. I went to a private school.*' Later on, Nadia also switched to a private school and joined Hoda in the American Junior College (now Ramsis College). The influence of this high school went beyond the actual school curricula, as both women repeatedly emphasize that their values of social justice, serving the community and tolerance were very much shaped by the spirit of the American Junior College.

The school, as well as Hoda and Nadia's respective families, and friends, encouraged their international outlook early on. Debates on international relations, political developments and different cultures in school, summer camps in Alexandria, conferences in various Middle Eastern and European countries for students and an open family house with people visiting from all over the world were all part of Hoda and

Nadia's upbringing. Both women spent a considerable amount of time studying and working abroad in international forums.

At the end of World War II Hoda finished university in Cairo. She wanted to study abroad and, as the United States had just set up several scholarships, she applied and received a full scholarship to study abroad.[7] In America, Hoda enjoyed her studies tremendously at Bryn Mawr College. She was the first Egyptian to be accepted to the famous women's college in 1946. Aside from being exposed to a variety of courses in various subjects, she had her first introduction to the UN charter which triggered her curiosity to learn more. Hoda's teacher helped her to become a junior trainee at the newly established UN Department of Social Affairs in 1947. A year later she had started post-graduate studies, but had to go back to Egypt because her mother passed away. Before she returned, some of the people she worked for as a trainee in the UN asked her to stay on: '*They asked me if I could stay, because they had no other Egyptian. I said: "No, I have to go back." I am very "green". I just came from University. I know nothing of my country's problems. They said: But you are here to think internationally. I said: "No, I must go back and finish my graduate courses."*'

Three years later, in 1952, by which time Hoda was working for the Egyptian Ministry of Social Affairs, she went to the United States for a conference and was once again approached by the UN to stay and join. When Hoda refused this time, she met persistence: '*They told me to speak to the head of my delegation. He was a great man, and I said to him: "They offered me a job in the UN." He said: "You take it." I said: "No, I am committed to the Ministry of Social Affairs." He said: "You leave the Ministry. We need you there."*' This moment constitutes the beginning of Hoda's UN career, which lasted for thirty-one years (1953–84).

As she was appointed to different postings, doing various kinds of work (mainly in Africa and Europe, in addition to the UN headquarters in New York), Hoda's successful international career is certainly unique in its length and its breadth of experience. However, many of her childhood friends also worked at an international level for some time. Some, like Hoda, also represented 'the first Egyptian woman' to be recruited for a particular job internationally. Nadia, for example, was the first woman who worked as a general secretary for the ecumenical movement of the World Council of Churches in Geneva. What is significant here is the conjuncture between the first period of state-building in post-colonial and post-revolutionary Egypt and Hoda and Nadia's education. Hoda's

---

[7] After World War II the United States actively sought to increase its influence and began a massive propaganda campaign, which involved the development of closer commercial ties, military assistance and the establishment of scholarships for Egyptian students.

entry into the UN system and Nadia's work in Geneva precede the recruitment of educated middle-class women in response to the state's need to expand new cadres. Hoda and Nadia were both part of an educated upper-middle-class elite which became increasingly aware of the country's realities and problems. The post-revolutionary regime provided an encouraging background for many educated women to challenge traditional gender roles. The beginnings of Nadia and Hoda's careers coincided with a more general reorientation of a previously more sheltered elite, or one that was mainly involved in welfare work, to a more exposed and professional elite.

One might pose the question whether Hoda and Nadia's religious affiliation to the Coptic church contributed to their international outlook, but it is apparent that many of their contemporary Muslim friends also became professionals working on an international level.[8] While Nadia mentions experiences of discrimination as a Copt, both she and Hoda stress that incidents of confessional tensions and discrimination were not as intense and widespread during their youth than in later times. In the 1930s and 1940s, Copts and Muslims generally united in their efforts to rid the country of continuing British control and military presence. This period has often been described as a time when Egyptian politics was subsumed under a more general banner of 'national patriotism and unity' (Zaki, 1995: 196).

Both an early involvement in voluntary work and experience in the international arena are important aspects of Nadia and Hoda's involvement in women's activism today. Now, like many of their friends in their age-group, officially retired, they are even more busy and are working harder than ever. Nadia is a board member in an NGO called the Association for the Protection of the Environment, working among the *zabaleen* (garbage collectors) in the Moqattam Hills. She initially joined the fieldworkers to get to know the community. Later on Nadia tried to link up with other organizations internationally and created a health and development committee. She was one of the first women activists in Egypt concerned with the issue of female genital mutilation (FGM), and has been at the forefront of the campaign against this practice. In 1976

---

[8] The unilateral declaration of Egyptian independence by the British in 1922 restricted Egypt's sovereignty on a number of points and allowed for ongoing military presence and political intervention. Among these points was the continuation of the protection of 'minorities and foreigners'. This policy triggered contrasting reactions among the Coptic community: some welcomed the protection by the British, while others, committed to national unity, vehemently opposed it (Carter, 1986: 58–88). Despite widespread Coptic involvement in nationalist politics and anti-imperialist struggles, and despite the common rhetoric on harmony and national unity, Copts have been continuously identified with foreign and alien powers and threats.

Nadia wrote one of the first substantial papers exploring this issue after receiving a one-year scholarship to do research in England.

During the preparations for the International Conference on Population and Development held in Cairo in 1994, Nadia's organization became part of the planning committee:

We were appointed by ministerial decree and therefore did not work as an NGO. We worked on FGM and we were hosted at the Ford Foundation. The person who was pioneering the issue is a Sudanese doctor.[9] *She knew about my previous work on FGM. One time she approached me and said that we need to organize a task force here in Cairo, and she said that it would work only if I became the co-ordinator. I said, 'I'm ready for that, but we need a legal umbrella.' So we were accepted under the NCPD.*[10] *Now the group is very active, and we are proceeding very well, even if there are some problems, because the NCPD is appointed by the government. The FGM task force doesn't behave in line with the government, but always behaves against the interest of the government. The same people, who have been members of the NCPD, have now formed another independent association.*

Nadia acknowledges the tensions inherent in her commitment to both governmental and non-governmental organizations. She does not believe in direct confrontation with the government, but makes it very clear that her struggle remains independent and is often on a collision course with government agendas. Hoda perceives her own involvement in different constituencies as less problematic than Nadia's: '*I've been very involved both at the NGO level as well as having had the privilege of being a national delegate for the official Egyptian delegation for both the ICPD and the Beijing conference. I sit on the national commission here on co-operation with NGOs, which is now fully supported by the Ministry of Health and Population. So one could say that I'm as busy now as I was at the UN.*'

After having lived abroad for over thirty years, Hoda decided to return to Egypt:

Why? Everybody wondered, with all this long international career. You could place yourself in Geneva or New York in a more international atmosphere. Well, my feeling was that I wanted to go back to my roots, and after serving the world for so many years it was time to go to my home country, back to my base. I knew that it would be hard to adjust at the beginning, but I made plans for myself in terms of purchasing a flat and staying and preparing for my retirement. Ever since I came back, I've given a lot of time to various projects and organizations.

Women activists of younger generations, especially those who were involved in the student movements in the 1970s, often describe the older

[9] Nahid Toubia is a Sudanese woman activist and medical doctor who has been at the forefront of campaigns against FGM. She is currently an associate for women's reproductive health at the Population Council in New York. She also founded an NGO concerned with reproductive health issues (RAINBO).

[10] NCPD is the abbreviation for National NGO Committee for Population and Development.

generation as 'moderate', 'non-political' and 'non-confrontational', which carries both negative and positive connotations. For some it means being 'too compromising' and 'working too closely with the regime' or 'buying into neo-imperialist policies', while for others it involves 'the ability and willingness to build consensus' and 'to work with a long-term vision'. Some activists mentioned the existence of a minority of women belonging to Hoda's and Nadia's generation, who in the 1940s and 1950s, did not get involved in social work, but chose instead to become politically engaged.

For Hoda the past, especially when compared to present times, was characterized by tolerance, respect, openness and an eagerness to learn. She misses some of these qualities in the younger generation:

We did not feel any barriers. Today there are barriers, why? Maybe we were not exposed enough. I don't know. I can't figure it out. We keep saying to each other, look at our generation, we studied so thoroughly. We mixed with boys, without worries. But today, life is much tougher in many ways. Maybe there are shifts, there are fundamentalists in both religions, in Christianity as well as Islam. Now people tend to question each other, rather than accept and respect each other. Maybe our groups were more exclusive. I don't know. The history books are going to analyse that. My nieces used to teach at Cairo University, and they're a generation younger than I am. They speak of how difficult it is to convey ideas to students, concepts they're not interested in, like different ways of life, backgrounds to Shakespeare books or to any author. They're impatient. Life today is a race after income, because the cost of living is high, and they're impatient to think and read and conceptualize and to rationalize, to compare each other's ideas. They're insecure today. I don't know if we're proud to say that we're at the height of science and technology. There's a race with that, and they're leaving behind certain basics in life that gave us the wisdom and the confidence to grow. I'm impatient when I stand or sit with any young person, who's not interested to reflect and think why is it this and not that.

Hoda's reflection on the difference between her generation is a comment on the considerable opportunities and openness that characterized the period of her upbringing and early career. She also gives evidence of the class homogeneity of those women who made up the early elite cadres in post-colonial Egypt. Today, by comparison, economic hardships combined with the increased influence of conservative forces contribute to a general sense of crisis and lack of opportunities. Nadia reflects on the change of ethics, which she relates to a deterioration of the education system and a fierce competition in the job market today:

When we first started there was a level of competition too, but we respected each other's domain. In terms of work or recommending people we had a sort of ethical system. What we may say about our time is that we were friends, who deeply understood each other, but we never recommended a friend [for] a job, however strong relationships were, because we considered this nepotism. Regarding generational differences, we know that most of us, who started at the American College, have been more inspired by public service and by giving services. Only some are career-oriented. That's why in our generation you find them more willing to volunteer and to serve the people. This was the time people were exposed to education. We developed the love of creativity, because there were more choices. Because of that there was less competition. There's less sense of engagement now. Nowadays in the eighties and nineties, many young people turned to religious fundamentalism, and few to human and women's rights activism. There is a lot of professional jealousy and show. I don't see in the new generation a sense of what they want to do, followed up with precision and seriousness. I think, it should be attributed to a failure in the education system.

Hoda and Nadia's thoughts reveal that the cultural gap between different women activists widened with the participation of women from a broader class base than had been the case during their early social welfare work. Their initial involvement, in contrast to today's activism, grew out of the spirit of voluntarism and was based on a homogeneous class background, where lifestyles, social standing and life opportunities were more similar. Rather than judging the younger generation of women activists, who, through access to foreign funding, now have the opportunity to get involved in activism professionally, both women stress how the different social circumstances and economic conditions today render voluntary work extremely difficult. They acknowledge the struggles and hardships facing most Egyptian men and women in supporting and maintaining their families. For Hoda, the biggest challenge right now is '*to motivate young people to give their wisdom, their time, their experience and knowledge to the bigger communities surrounding them*'.

Encounters with the revolution and the Nasser regime

By the time Hoda had finished her university years she had started to work for the Ministry for Social Affairs and was about to join the UN. At that time (1952) Siham B. had just finished primary school. She remembers vividly the 1952 revolution, an event that for many Egyptians symbolizes the final break with Egypt's colonial past:

When I was very young, during the period of the national uprising against the British occupation and the palace between 1946 and 1951, I remember hearing that the students were demonstrating and that the faculty of medicine was leading the students. My brother was in that faculty. The day the police governor was killed my father said: 'I am going to the police station to get Gamal.' He was arrested in one of the demonstrations and a part of an exploded bomb had hit his shoes. When he came home, everybody was looking at his shoes, while he was telling us what had happened. I remember a general feeling of excitement and admiration. Later, when the 1952 revolution took place, the whole family was happy. My second brother Ma'moon, who was a law student, got to know the members of the revolutionary council. I remember a picture of him and the revolutionary council. My brother was with them representing students. How? I don't remember. He was very enthu-

siastic about the revolution. My father was happy with the revolution too. The revolution entered our house and became part of our daily discussions. When I was at secondary school many political events occurred, and often the whole school went out for demonstrations. We had a physics teacher, who was a really good speaker, and during these events, he would give fiery speeches about the revolution. My level of awareness might have been simple, but I was involved. When the 1956 war broke out, I was in the school National Guard. We had military and first aid training. I felt I was part of what was happening around me.

Siham, like many of her fellow students, became involved in politics even before entering university. The high level of organized activities within the schools was part of a larger campaign which aimed at consolidating the regime's power base by creating loyal cadres among the youth. Nasser introduced many changes in order to create a more comprehensive and populist education system than the elitist and fragmented system inherited from the *ancien régime* (Abdallah, 1985: 101). Among others, these changes included the nationalization of most foreign schools, the abolition of school fees and the restructuring of secondary education and its curricula. The expansion of state education also involved giving greater attention to girls' education (ibid.: 104).

Throughout my interviews I noticed a widespread perception that Nasser's policies helped women to gain some economic, social and cultural strength through their increased participation in education and employment. The significant increase in women's cultural and political activities is often attributed to the new opportunities and options the Nasser regime offered to women. Siham recalls:

During the time of the war [1956], I joined the National Guard outside of school. We learned how to shoot rifles, and we were collecting donations from people. I joined the committee of civil defence. My older sisters also joined the committee: Neam, who was studying journalism and working as a trainee in Akhbar El-Youm *newspaper at the same time, and Nagah, who was a housewife and active in voluntary social work. I remember going on a lorry with my two sisters. Neam, the journalist, had a megaphone, and was telling everyone what is happening in Port Said. She spoke so beautifully that we got a few lorries of donations. People were crying on the balconies. Every day we collected things and we went to hospitals for training. I attended the birth of a child by a Sudanese woman in Ahmed Maher hospital. I also attended the appendix operation of my brother once. All these things happened when I was in secondary school. So when I went to the university, I was prepared to be socially active. I was known in the family to be older than my age to the extent that our neighbours gave me a nickname, which meant 'old woman'.*

Siham's family and friends all appeared very politicized and supported her political activism. While her family did not object to her political involvement, Siham remembers her struggles for greater freedom of movement. She could not just come and go to and from the house as she liked, but had to ask for permission every time she wanted to leave and had to return at certain hours. However restricted her movements were, Siham recalls a constant engagement in political events. Aside from activities related to 'the national cause', she remembers how the feeling of Arab solidarity and unity was part of her upbringing:

When I was in secondary school, there was a magazine called The New Generation. *It had a corner on the last page entitled 'Remember this Name!' They used to go to schools and ask people to nominate active students. They would put these students' pictures and some information about them in this corner. I was nominated, and when the journalist came to interview me, one of her questions was: 'What is your wish for the future?' I answered: 'I want to become the first female guerrilla fighter in the liberation of Palestine.' I do not know why I used the word 'guerrilla fighter', but I remember that it was a very spontaneous answer. The Palestinian question was on my mind all the time as part of the national and anti-colonial struggle. I actually got a letter from a Palestinian man saying that he was touched by what I said, and another letter came from Saudi Arabia. During the same period I was in the girl guides, a youth group which organized camps. I participated in a camp of the Arab girl guides in Alexandria. There I met girls from different Arab countries. We felt like sisters. I still have a picture leading the Egyptian girl guides and carrying the flag of Egypt.*

Siham's early involvement in both regime-related youth organizations at school and clandestine political organizations at the university has influenced her political outlook to the present day. Unlike Hoda and Nadia, who grew up to think 'internationally', Siham has mainly been thinking 'regionally' ever since her school years. Her high school and university education coincided with the blossoming of Arab nationalism. Pan-Arab sentiments grew into a key ideal of the Nasser regime and were officially endorsed from the mid-1950s onwards. Among the various policies, reforms and forms of indoctrination that helped to spread pan-Arab sentiments, the official academic curriculum included a compulsory annual course entitled 'Arab Society' (Abdallah, 1985; Beattie, 1994; Erlich, 1989).

With the rapid spread of Arab nationalism in the whole region, various pan-Arab organizations, such as the Ba'ath party, acquired a following among Egyptian students. But despite its Arab nationalist principles the regime opposed these 'foreign' parties, which had emerged outside Egypt. State repression forced these pan-Arab groups and their followers into clandestine activism (Beattie, 1994: 140):

Getting involved practically in politics changed my outlook and my way of thinking in many ways. First, I started believing in my public role, and that we have to work for our countries. This was our duty, and those who did not do it were not living a full life. I believe that my patriotism extended from Egypt to other countries. I felt very Arab at that time and I learned to be true to myself. This is very important, because it has to do with my later development. Then it taught me to take risks, because my political work was largely underground. We were going on demonstrations and I knew that I was blacklisted and I was under surveillance. This also taught me the fact that one can face the risk and it should not hold you back from doing what you want to do. Whenever the leadership of the party came, we used to sit and talk to them and discuss. So in a way this was a training in dealing with leadership without being intimidated. Politics became an important thing in my life and I did not hide anything from my family.

During her upbringing she was taught to see the region mainly in terms of 'the Arab nation' but, later on, while studying in Europe, Siham also became interested in Africa and 'the Third World'. She recognized her lack of knowledge about Africa when mingling with African students and professors at the Institute of Social Studies in The Hague. Increasingly, Siham became involved in post-colonial African politics. However, most of her professional research and political activism has been framed either by a national or an Arab regional context.

Siham's experience of new opportunities and prospects parallels Raga N.'s recollections, in that she also praises Nasser for providing better conditions and access to resources for the majority of the Egyptian population. She even remembers being nicknamed 'Mrs Nasser' during her time studying in The Netherlands. Looking back to her childhood and college years, Raga stresses the regime's aim of 'national unity' between Copts and Muslims and the abidance of the secular slogan '*Al-Watan lil Gamiyyah wa Al-Din lil Allah*' (The Nation for Everyone and Religion for God).[11] Growing up as a Copt in Nasserite Egypt, Raga did not feel discrimination, because of her religious affiliation: '*At the time, we were not busy with religious differentiation. The majority of Copts gained rights under Nasser just like other Egyptians did. No differentiation was made with regard to rights and employment. But the Copts were not a homogeneous group and the wealthy landowners were hit in their economic interests just as the wealthy Muslims were.*' Like Siham, Raga's political convictions are deeply rooted in pan-Arabism and socialist ideals.

In Raga's view, the 1967 defeat by Israel presented a break in the way Copts were treated during Nasser's era. Her experiences at the university in Cairo are intertwined with her first conscious experiences of discrimination:

I scored very high in the thanawiya amma.[12] *I wanted to enter the faculty of literature and study French, but my father refused categorically. He persuaded me to study at the faculty of political science and economics. I had an excellent economics professor, who made a great impact on me during the first year. So I decided to specialize in economics, and I graduated top of my class. I was appointed as* muwid, *which is a job with tenure. You are a research assistant, teach and study for your Master's and Ph.D. When I wanted to travel abroad in order to continue my studies, they wouldn't let me go. For the*

---

[11] This slogan was originally coined by the Wafd party. See chapter 2.
[12] Final exams at high school.

first time I felt that it was discrimination, that they wouldn't let me travel because I was a Copt. But I got myself a personal scholarship outside of the 'bahathat system'[13] of the state. I went to The Netherlands to get a diploma at the European Institute. The diploma equals a Master's in Egypt, but they didn't accept it when I came back. I had to do another Master's in Cairo. Again, my diploma was not acknowledged, because I was a Copt. While I was doing my second Master's, I looked for a way to get a Ph.D. scholarship. Again I was bypassed and they took the second best. I somehow managed to get a scholarship to get a Ph.D. in economics at Clark University in Massachusetts. From that time on I've felt that there's a difference in the way Muslims and Copts were treated. I felt discriminated against.[14]

Despite this account, Raga stresses that there was no systematic state policy during the Nasser period that led to discrimination against Copts. Rather, she speaks about a *de facto* practice of discrimination by certain people after the 1967 defeat. Her perception concurs with Moheb Zaki's reflection on Coptic–Muslim relations and state discrimination since Egypt's independence. Zaki argues that despite the Nasser regime's discriminatory practices against the Copts, particularly with regard to jobs in the higher offices of the government, there was little sectarian strife or tension at the time (Zaki, 1995: 196). He attributes it to the regime's authoritarianism and appropriation of politics (ibid.) rather than the commitment to 'national unity' as argued by Raga. However, he also views a radical change between the Nasser regime and the Sadat regime concerning policies towards Copts.[15]

Raga's experience of discrimination based on her religious affiliation within Egypt during her student years found painful resonance in her experiences abroad where she felt condescending attitudes towards her: '*People consider you sub-human, just because you're an Arab. I actually felt more Egyptian in the States than in Egypt. I was the only Arab student among many Jews.*' These experiences triggered in Raga an interest in revolutionary theories, such as Marxism, theories of dependency, neo-colonialism and issues related to ethnicity and minorities. When she returned to Egypt she was struck by the level of poverty, which had become much more apparent and horrifying to her than before her studies abroad. She became increasingly involved in issues related to development before she also turned to gender issues:

A personal tragedy opened my eyes to discrimination against women. I got married very young, just when I graduated from the university. I travelled after forty days of being

---

[13] State scholarship for studies abroad, established under Nasser for outstanding students.
[14] Raga's account parallels the descriptions of discrimination against Copts by Shawky Karas, an upper Egyptian Copt who immigrated to the United States. In his view, the government actively privileges Muslim over Christian candidates in granting teaching positions and study grants (Karas, 1985: 120).
[15] For an insightful account of sectarian strife during Sadat, see Farah (1986).

married. It had been a traditional marriage, not a love match. But it had not been imposed on me. I was so obsessed with my career and I thought that my husband would support me in that, but actually he wanted to stop me. When I came back from The Netherlands, I started the divorce procedures. The only way for a Copt to get a divorce is for one spouse to change the church from Coptic orthodox to Greek orthodox. There is a law saying that if there are two different churches the Islamic shariʿa will rule. Then I experienced a terrible insult. My ex-husband tried to force me to stay with him by using bayt al-taʿa.[16] I never thought that something like this would happen to me. He tried to stop me to go to the States. I needed his permission to travel. But how could I get permission during a divorce battle? It was really just because of a bureaucratic mistake that I got an exit visa. They thought that he had given me permission. All this triggered my concern with women's issues, but still my dominant research interest was related to development.

Raga's more consistent involvement in the women's movement started in the mid-eighties, when there was a renewed interest in women's issues. Just like Raga, Siham only became interested in gender issues through her political activism and professional career. She presents her entry into women's activism as an outcome of her professional work and research, rather than political conviction. She links her emerging interest in *qadiyyat al-marʾa* (women's issues) to an invitation by the women's committee of the Arab Lawyers' Union to speak at a conference held in Tunis about Islam and Women's Labour (1984). Slowly Siham became a spokesperson on women's issues in Egypt and the Arab world in international fora. However, she stresses her conviction that women's liberation is only possible in context of a wider social transformation:

But I also believe that we can work in parallel on society and on women within the society. I still don't believe that I can work for women only. I'll never be a feminist in that sense. Women's issues are important, but I can't emphasize them at the expense of dependency relationships or the international economic order or globalization. I believe that we still need much more work looking at the relationship between public policies and the daily lives of women. So we should really make the connection between how women could be liberated in society, or how the situation of women could change, if the society changed, and the dialectic between these processes.

Siham's outlook on feminism and the significance of 'wider issues' of national liberation, social justice and imperialism is common to most of the Nasserite and leftist generation I interviewed. This perspective can be described as a radicalized version of the 'national liberation discourse' associated with the anti-colonial struggle of the 1920s and 1930s, in which women are dealt with as part of the struggle for political and economic decolonization (Hatem, 1993: 42).

Despite nostalgia for 'Egypt's glorious days' associated with the Nasser period, there are ambivalent and critical voices among Egyptian women

---

[16] Bayt al-taʿa or 'House of Obedience' allows a husband to obtain a judge's order to forcibly return his wife to the marital home and to refuse divorce proceedings.

activists, particularly among the younger generation who did not experience the early years of the regime. Azza H.'s first years at university coincided with the 1967 defeat and the later stages of Nasser's regime, when it is often described as having transformed itself into a police state. The desolation brought about by Egypt's defeat during the Six-Day War created a deep sense of shock and immobilization among the whole population. Many students felt contempt for the regime, which had continued to broadcast fictitious reports of victorious Egyptian troops at the outskirts of Tel Aviv while the Egyptian military was being defeated. Nevertheless, on 9 June, when a visibly shaken Nasser took responsibility for the defeat and announced his resignation, students led the demonstrations that called for him to stay on (Beattie, 1994; Erlich, 1989).

Azza's experience of the Nasser regime is therefore decisively different from Siham's:

We had youth organizations, which were mainly organized by Nasser to develop the cadres for a new socialist system. We used to meet in every college and school. The first thing was the cleaning of the school buildings during summer. But I remember that we were hit by the 1967 war. It was really this sort of feeling that you've been cheated and deceived and your morale came down. At the beginning, we were walking from Sayyeda Zeynab to Abbasiyya,[17] which is a long walk, getting our military dresses and trying to do something. We were discovering that the whole army was being killed and that we had been deceived as a nation as well as individuals. We got out of this state of shock and paralysis when we asked Nasser to stay. This happened at 3 o'clock in the morning. We had no phone at home, so my family got really upset with me. I think this was one of the important stages in my life. I was so upset that I walked on the streets and cried. The children were scared and they were playing in the streets. I thought that they were cheated too. This was a terrible time.

Despite this spontaneous expression of support for Nasser, in the aftermath of the defeat students became increasingly militant in their protest against the ruling establishment and its repression of independent political forces. Massive demonstrations, strikes and sit-ins were organized as an angry reaction to the humiliating defeat. Students, in general, did not question the ideals of the Nasserite regime but rather the way the state attempted to suppress any kind of autonomous political activism and the level of surveillance by the regime. Azza recalls:

We were being approached by the secret police. Those were cadres that Nasser was building to face conservative reactionary forces whom he didn't trust. He now wanted the support from all the people who really loved socialism. But actually he used the various organizations to spy on people. We were very critical and we wanted to do something for this nation. They wanted us to write reports. They called it a public opinion report: what people were talking about, what jokes our colleagues were cracking etc. We soon felt that

---

[17] Sayyeda Zeynab and Abbasiyya are areas within Cairo.

we were not just cheated on a political level, but that they were trying to mock us. It's somebody who thinks that you are only an informer. It was terrible and we announced public refusal. Everybody refused to work, not really strike, this was when we began to be approached by leftist groups. This was a shift. This was the end of the sixties, beginning of the seventies. I had a woman friend, whom I trusted very much, and we were always together. That helped me to take a position. We began then to be more involved with the leftist groups and started to study Marxism.

In addition to the call for the withdrawal of intelligence personnel from the universities and the request for an investigation into police intrusion in universities, students also demanded freedom of expression for the press and the promulgation and enforcement of laws establishing political freedoms (Abdallah, 1985: 152). These demands actually led to the lifting of a number of restrictions which had hindered independent student activism. Especially significant was the increase in uncensored university wall-magazines which student activists utilized to criticize the regime, spread their ideas and mobilize their fellow students.

The student movement and women's increasing dissidence

After Nasser's death in 1970 the limbo 'no war, no peace' with Israel continued, and triggered strong reactions from a frustrated population. Student activists, in particular, organized broad protest movements criticizing the Sadat regime for its lack of action around the Palestine question (Baker, 1990: 127). However, the sense of loss and frustration was soon to be overshadowed by a new enthusiasm and political activism related to the student movement. Despite the fears and hardships associated with the political activities of students during the 1970s, many women describe their involvement as a positive experience of shared struggle, hope and optimism.

The involvement in leftist politics in general and the particular experiences related to the student movement during the Sadat era seem to be crucial for a whole generation of women including a large number of contemporary women activists. Hania K., who went to school in Canada, returned to Egypt just at the time the student movement started to flare up. For her, the movement and all the activities related to it helped her to find her feet again after a period of feeling lost:

I decided that I had to come back to myself and get involved in the nationalist struggle. I was arrested for the first time when I was seventeen years old. The first three years of my return to Egypt were a great turning-point for me. My father really broke down, because all his fears were related to the Nasserite period, where people were arrested and never came back. My mother was very strong, although she always appeared weak. My brothers were first arrested during sit-ins at their universities. My father was just scared of what would happen to them. This was repeated again the following year in mid-1972. That time the police came and arrested my brothers at home, and then they arrested other students at the university. This constant confrontation became part of our existence, and my father had to adjust to it, because he believed in what they were doing.

Students' mothers became increasingly involved by pressuring the regime to release their children in detention, and also by hiding student activists, who were on the run from the police. Hania became the spokesperson of 'the mother's movement' when she was very young:

All the women involved in this movement were incredible. They were ready to do many things, like going to demonstrations, prisons and so on. Among the things they would do was taking messages from prisons to people outside and vice versa. My mother did not like that duty, but she and other mothers tried to accompany us whenever they could. I was also arguing with some of the officers, and we would all organize sit-ins in the court house. Our mothers would try to avoid these confrontations, but we would not allow it. Once we were cornered, arrested for some time, taken to interrogation and released in the evening. These events continued for years during that time of instability.

Azza also has recollections related to her mother's involvement in the student movement. While her father was working abroad political activities brought Azza closer to her mother:

My relationship to my mother improved during the student movement, because, during that time, without my father being there, friends and colleagues used to come to sleep at home overnight. My mother used to cover for somebody for two days, and then she was really beginning to feel herself. Until now, if you talk to her, she tells you: 'These were very great days.' I remember the first time my father returned. I do not know exactly what he said at the time. But my mother answered back strongly and he was just shocked at how she could dare. I remember this very well, because he was carrying food and he just threw it into her face. This ended up on the wall, and it stayed there for a long time. My mother was feeling that she gained some sort of strength and self-esteem. That is the meaning of empowerment to me. She was part of the mothers' movement. The mothers of students went together into courts and to the state security offices, collected money and smuggled letters into the prisons. My mother began to feel that she was part of my life and I was part of hers.

In the early 1970s, a fully fledged student movement grew, demanding the liberation of the Palestinian occupied territories and the democratization of the Egyptian political system (Abdallah, 1985: 176). Another issue tackled by the movement was Sadat's withdrawal from socialist ideals and the resulting changes in the socio-economic structure of the country. In Hania's view, the initial enthusiasm and energy related to the national question was slowly overshadowed by burning social and economic issues:

I went to university in 1973 and studied English Literature. There I met people who are still my close friends. We were all holding a very clear political position, but at the same time the energy we had was gradually eroding. The 1973 war was a turning-point for many people with regards to the whole issue of the land [Sinai]. *It was a time of reflections and discussions, but among us there was that kind of belief existing that the revolution was still around the corner. We actually tried to push hard until, at last, we broke. This actually happened very gradually, and we were working till the end of 1970s. In 1977, although we tried to broaden our horizons, we realized that the focal point was no longer the national question, but social and economic problems. There was the rise of fundamentalism, and there were individuals who were retreating into their private worlds.*

In retrospect, Hania perceives her years in the student movement as being enclosed in an *'almost ghetto-like safe space'*, from which she and other activists began to think of the outside world as unreal. She recalls a sense of alienation with the world outside the student movement. Once the movement disintegrated, Hania and many of her friends felt very lost, especially since their activism had prevented them from actually getting involved in their university studies:

So many of us started putting their lives together in the 1980s. I then decided to search for a different path in my political struggle and broadened my understanding of what politics is all about. At that time there were no independent organizations, but parties, which formed offices in different places. We became involved in the elections and other activities tying us to the government. Then this whole issue of parties and structures became part of our discussions and reflections for each one of us.

Parallel to the creation of organizations and groups outside the frame of political parties,[18] some of Hania's friends started to meet regularly and discussed various issues, such as the history of the women's movements in Egypt and other Arab countries or the development of women's position in society. During these gatherings, Hania's friends did not merely discuss new issues but also explored new methods of decision making and power distribution, which constituted a break from the more hierarchical and undemocratic ways in which the student movement as well as political parties had previously operated. When they were challenged by members of the Tagammu party and other leftist activists about the actual content and purpose of their gatherings, they started to publish a newsletter.[19]

Hania, as well as other women activists who were involved in the 1970s student movement, stresses that before the 1980s women's issues were sidelined or discussed within the framework of socialism: '*We were looking*

18 Hania mentions two new models which emerged in the late 1980s in two different districts in Cairo: the Helwan Community Centre which provided services for working-class men and women (women especially use the centre's services, e.g. reproductive health care, literacy programmes) and a community-based and -owned health centre in Waeli, which was established by a group of medical doctors who shared a common vision regarding health policies.
19 Here I refer to the gradual establishment of the group Al-Mar'a Al-Gedida (the New Woman) which has been active for over ten years and whose histories I will present in chapter 6.

for change and social justice. The whole thing of women's issues seemed to be part of a broad mosaic. It was not politically correct to just speak about women's issues.' However, some women activists rebelled against the norms and moral codes imposed on them by their male colleagues. Fatima R., for example, started to become involved with women's issues because she saw that men were contradictory in their attitudes, *'pretending to be your friend and talking about you behind your back. There was moral judgement: the girl who did not have male friends was the better person. Women's opinions were not taken as seriously as men's.'* Azza's memories of cross-gender relations within university during those years of common political struggle give evidence of the strict norms and values concerning a 'proper' woman's behaviour:

We had men and women sitting together in the cafeteria. It was called 'ghorza', it means a place people go and smoke hashish. It used to be a traditional cafeteria, and no girls would go there. So we first began to occupy the corridor leading to this place, and then we began to occupy the wider hall, and finally we had girls and boys sitting there. This was new to the faculty. But it was known that we were very straightforward girls. We were very conscious about our behaviour. Especially me, because my father was originally from the village. So I knew how people who are not from Cairo look at girls. It was very important for us, because many of our schoolmates came from villages. Remember, at that time, the faculty was open to all social classes and all people were there, and they came from villages and the countryside, with all their feelings and preconceived ideas about women, and particularly women of Cairo. City girls, and especially those who are socially emancipated, were usually too liberal. But we felt that we really want to be models to be followed, and encourage other men and women to join the group.

When some female student activists concerned with the moral codes and contradictions with respect to gender relations proposed to hold a seminar on women the prevailing reaction was negative. Fatima was one of the women who wanted to challenge the general conviction that women's issues need to be addressed as part of wider social problems:

Many girls and boys told us that this was feminist, and that as socialists they believed that women's problems would be solved along with the other social issues. They wanted to work more in the direction of liberating the working class. We gave in and were a bit worried, and so our project was put off for a while. However, it was never ruled out. Later on, we decided to have a women's magazine.[20] I realized that this was important when I worked in factories during the summer and found out that women workers had different problems than men. I was still more interested in politics though, as my husband was directly involved in political work. He was constantly detained. But when I got married I realized that my personal freedom was also linked to the freedoms of so many other women.

Several women confessed that their personal life painfully showed them that *'there is something called women's issues'*, which has to be tackled inde-

---

[20] The magazine referred to is called *Al-Mar'a Al-Gedida*.

pendently of the general struggle for social justice. The realization that even 'progressive' men oppress women – either within the context of party politics or within the institution of the family – is a turning-point in the lives of many activists. Some activists also mentioned the marginalization of women in political struggles internationally, e.g. in Algeria, Palestine and the former Soviet Union, as the main reason for reconsidering their original approach.

In Azza's view, the shift to a more serious consideration of 'women's issues' as worthwhile and significant is related to the 1985 UN conference on women, held in Nairobi:

I think Nairobi was really useful whether women realize it or not. For me personally this was a turning-point: getting involved in the preparations, exerting lots of positive efforts, and becoming familiar with readings about women. All this wasn't really a concrete attitude at the time, but then I began to be convinced, and I felt much stronger about women's issues by the time of the Nairobi conference. And it wasn't really Nairobi itself, because I didn't actually go. What was more significant were all those activities, which took place in the mid-eighties. From 1983 to 1985 there were lots of organizations. I wasn't a member of any of them, but I was entangled in many of their activities. I got involved in the campaign to maintain the 1979 Personal Status Law, called Jehan's Law. I was part of this group that was created, the 'Family and Women's Committee'. There was a big movement. We were meeting in different homes and places and drafted some sort of amendments to the law and put it to parliament. Lots of things happened at that same time: the preparation for Nairobi, working for the report and working on my research for that regional meeting on Arab-African women. All that was just something that polishes you very quickly. Also, Nawal El-Sa'dawi had her first meeting about Arab women. UNICEF asked me to come and present something about young women's health. It was a lot of digging, a lot of reading about the issue. Health was my entry point into women's rights activism.

Azza gives evidence to emerging convergence between professional work and women's activism as well as the growing interconnection with regional and international fora. She makes also reference to the influence of Nawal El-Sa'dawi, whose lectures and books addressed women's emancipation as an important issue, without perceiving it as contradicting either class struggle or national liberation, as already indicated in the previous chapter.

It becomes apparent that the gradual shift towards women's rights as a legitimate issue in the 1980s is rooted in multiple causes, such as the general crisis of socialist ideology and particularly a disappointment in the actual implementation of socialist values by male activists. More and more women activists started to reject conventional male political structures and increasingly discredited the moral codes and double standards imposed on them either by male fellow activists or their 'progressive' fathers, brothers or husbands. The revolt against restrictions on their personal freedom coincided with the expansion of international agendas and fora, which continues to have an impact on the lives of women activists in the 1990s.

Personal traumas and international agendas

It is difficult to understand, but I think there's something wrong with the younger generation. They don't have the same drive and initiative that we have. Whereas we felt that we really had a goal, and we were rushing towards it, this new generation doesn't have that. They're not going towards anything, instead they're waiting. Yet we feel that we're tired and we want some people to come and take over the struggle, but there seems to be no one to do it. When we started out, we attacked the older generations. We took the initiative, in a productive not in a destructive way. Hopefully there will come a moment where people will be able to see something to go forward to. (Hania K.)

Hania's thoughts on the 'new generation', that is women in their twenties and thirties, find resonance among women activists from her own and previous generations, who often describe younger women as lacking enthusiasm, motivation and the will to engage in political struggle. While the crisis in socialist ideology, after the break-up of the Soviet Union, provoked many of the older leftist activists to be more concerned with women's issues, there appears to be a general sense of disillusionment and lack of collective incentive on the part of younger women. In view of the lack of broad-based opposition movements outside Islamic frameworks, secular-oriented women do not become active as part of a larger political movement, but are driven by either career opportunities or personal rebellion against their oppression as women.

Another flaw perceived to be typical of the younger activists is the high level of careerism. Older women contrast this either to the spirit of voluntary work or to political militancy, which characterized the motivations of activists of their generations. As alluded to earlier, the increased influence of international development, women's and human rights organizations as well as funding agencies has certainly contributed to a high level of professionalization among contemporary women activists. However, it would be misleading to imagine that only the youngest generation combines political activism with paid careers. Most women activists of older generations have also become part of the complex system of development work, women's activism and strategizing to attract foreign funding.

Nevertheless, many of the young women activists themselves regret that they were not born into the previous generation of women who '*knew what they were struggling for*'. Niveen B., an activist in her early thirties, told me: '*The worst generation is ours. We have virtually no common struggle or leadership at all. Although, in the beginning, our generation had all the poten-*

tial. But when foreign aid started to come to Egypt, and lots of centres and asso-
ciations were established, many individuals in our generation changed their per-
sonalities and ideas.'

Perhaps Niveen's pronounced nostalgia for times she never lived in is
related to the way she started to get involved into the movement. Unlike
other women of her generation whom I interviewed, Niveen did not
grow up in Cairo, but in Mansoura, a city in the Delta. There she came
into contact with a group of women activists belonging to the 1970s
generation:

A friend of my brother introduced me to two women with whom I later worked in Bint Al-
Ard [Daughter of the Earth], the activist group I belong to. I was sixteen at the time.
The other women were a bit older. It was a great experience at the age of sixteen, having a
fascinating project like this. It changed my life. I started to be familiar with the cultural
scene in Mansoura through the group. Before that, in high school, I was only involved
with the student union. Being with the other women activists, I started to have a view of
things and a political attitude. I got to know what feminism is. The group taught me the
meaning of team work. Ours was a very unique experience in this respect. Maybe I had
the potential for it, mentally and educationally, but it was also very important to practise
this and at such an early age. This was a stage of formation of my character. I owe 70 per
cent of my mentality to the group.

Niveen emphasizes the uniqueness and privilege of her political experience with women of an older generation. In her view, these special
circumstances distinguish her from other younger activists and generated
in her a sense of belonging to the generation that became politically active
during the era of Sadat. Niveen also expresses a sense of alienation with
respect to the extent that public events, such as conferences and seminars, take place in Cairo. At the same time, she acknowledges that her
move from Mansoura to Cairo was largely motivated by a higher level of
activity and increased career opportunities found in the metropolis. As
Niveen is trying to establish herself in Cairo, working with different
groups and increasingly becoming involved with international organizations, she maintains close links with the women who initiated her into
politics. However, Niveen realizes that she is departing more and more
from the type of activism and principles that distinguished the group she
first belonged to.

However difficult it is to judge the actual impetus for individual
involvement in political activism, it seems inevitable nowadays to consider ways of making a living while being politically engaged. Certainly,
there are women who are more driven by the prospect of both financial
reward and fame than any genuine desire to advance women's rights. But
even if few in number, there are young women activists who struggle for
their rights as passionately as the older generations. When asked about

their incentives for their involvement in women's activism, most younger activists were not sure when and how their interest started, but each of them had a sad story to tell. Mona A., for example, grew up very sheltered from the outside world. Both of her parents imposed very rigid rules of *'how to behave properly as a girl'*. Initially, Mona did not question any of her parents' norms and morals, and even remembers arguing, during a debate in school, in favour of women staying at home:

I really don't know what triggered my rebellion and when it really started. I was always rebellious, but in a sense, up to a certain age, I very much believed my father, who always told me that a woman's place is at home. I stopped believing him when I considered his unhappiness. My mother stayed at home and my father was still unhappy. It had nothing to do with whether she was home or not. My friends at school, whose mothers used to work, were far happier than me as a child . . . My mother was very violent and I think this is partly the reason for my rebellion. I could have been a demure nice little girl, but I was not. She used to beat us until quite late in age. I remember the last beating I ever got was when I was fourteen. I remember I told my sister one night that I am very ashamed of being beaten being fourteen years old, while my friends at school were never beaten. One time I told myself: if she beats me I will beat her back. And this is what happened. She slapped me and I slapped her back. So she slapped me again. It went about five times back and forth. She slaps me and I slapped her too, and she was so shocked that she just couldn't believe the reaction. She never beat me again after this incident.

Mona was not exposed to social welfare work or political organizations while growing up. She perceives her own feminist engagement as an outcome of her personality, her sense of justice, her compassion as well as a series of painful experiences, mainly related to her mother and later her husband. For many years Mona worked in a job that was totally unrelated to women's activism. After her marriage she quit her job and stayed at home for a number of years. It was during that time that she started voluntary work with Nawal El-Sa'dawi's association, AWSA. Her next job was related to a women's income-generation project, before she settled in her current job in a human rights centre: '*I like the work here, although people think it's a volunteer job. But I prefer it even [to] professional work, because it's my hobby. This is what I love to do. I've gained a lot from working here. From the narrow perspective of feminism, which is just one aspect of human rights, it made me develop into a broader experience. I feel happy with my position here in that I'm a human rights activist and a feminist.*'

A human rights perspective has become a widely accepted framework for women's activism in Egypt today. For many political activists of the 1970s, like the founder of the institution Mona works in, the notion of human rights presented an alternative to earlier forms of socialist struggle. In the very recent past, however, the mushrooming of centres working on human rights is probably one of the most obvious outcomes of the influence of international agendas and donor organizations.

Just as Mona views her current involvement in women's activism as an extension of her earlier rebellion against the beatings by her mother, Samia E. also describes her own involvement in the women's movement as a development linked to her previous sense of being oppressed and the resulting defiance against her mother's, relatives' and fiancés' expectations:

I was brought up believing that women should get married and have children, even though my family members were highly educated. I got engaged twice. It didn't work out. Every time something went wrong with a big problem, because my two fiancés were trying to frame me, they tried to impose their image on me. But there was always that sort of hidden rebellion. I kept insisting that I was looking for a 'normal' life. My mother and the rest of the family used to say that it was only because I was doing my Master's, my Ph.D., because I was too mature, or because I had too much freedom.

Both Mona and Samia were not particularly interested in politics prior to their involvement in women's activism and had no clear ideological frame. As different as their respective experiences and current involvement might be, they share the sense of having been marginalized and oppressed in the past. Mona describes how her mother and her sister used to treat her as 'the ugly duckling', because of her darker complexion. Mona recalls an incident only six years ago when she went to Germany to give a series of lectures: '*I had my mother with me to baby-sit my son. When we would walk in the streets, people used to turn round and look at me not at my mother. My mother told me that they were looking at me because I am dark.*' However, the sense of feeling different from everyone else is much more profound than just having different looks. Mona describes herself as an introvert who always found it difficult to make friends. Her current work brings her into contact with many people, but Mona is still very selective with her friends and prefers to work quietly, despite having become well known.

Samia, on the other hand, chose another path. She now is enjoying the public attention related to her involvement in women's activism. For her, becoming a feminist also meant becoming extremely sociable and extrovert. Like Mona, Samia recalls a sense of 'not fitting in' when growing up: '*I was very quiet. I didn't know how to speak. I was horrible and miserable. I was very fat, more than eighty kilos. I was studying and eating all the time. I had no social life.*' Later on, at university, Samia still felt like an outsider, even though she received very high grades and lots of attention from the male students: '*When they said I was beautiful, I thought they just want to flatter me. I was still very shy and I was only interested in studying. They thought I was arrogant.*'

After a number of failed relationships Samia felt increasingly frustrated and depressed. Her sense of being a misfit reached a climax before she changed her attitude dramatically:

Suddenly I had a moment of what they call 'epiphany' in literature, or illumination. I felt that I was the one who was right, the others had the problem. I met all these women, who were living a life they hated. Women who hated their husbands. I used to have this horrible sense of guilt. At some point I felt ashamed of myself. The strength of that feeling gave me the impetus to break out of it all.

Shortly after this change of heart, Samia got into contact with the group Markaz Dirasat Al-Mar'a Al-Gedida (the New Woman's Research Centre) which then provided a theoretical and political framework to explain her painful personal experience:

It was more a matter of luck. I met Al-Mar'a Al-Gedida by coincidence. I was attending a seminar on the image of women hosted in the British Council. I didn't have a theoretical framework. I admired them. I started to attend their meetings and slowly I became part of that group. They taught me a lot. It helped that I'm originally in academia, so research was familiar to me. I believe that the two lines meet at some point. They shouldn't be separated. I believe in solidarity: alone you cannot do anything. The strength of Islamic women is their solidarity. Gradually feminism became my vision and style of life. Ever since then things started to work for the better.

Samia derived a sense of empowerment from the realization that many other women besides herself were suffering from feelings of guilt and alienation. Since her encounter with Al-Mar'a al-Gedida she has discovered a safe space in which she can express herself freely and where she found women who could provide her with the necessary conceptual tools to analyse the context of her own oppression. Her description of women's activism as being similar to academic research is indicative of one of the features of contemporary activism in which scholarship, development work and political activism tend to conflate. The accusation of being too theoretical at the expense of concrete political action is common among various opponents of this strand of women's activism, such as leftist constituencies, Islamists, and also NGO members who are working closely with what is called 'the grassroots'.

Samia stresses that the group only provided a platform, an opportunity to concretize the potential that had been in her all along. Only a few years after her initial encounter with the group Samia was transformed into a public figure. It would certainly be unfair to describe Samia's or other women activists' initial impetus as being related to career opportunities. Without doubt though, the economic and social context of women's activism in the 1990s, with its international links and increased media attention, does produce an atmosphere in which careers and fame can develop rapidly. Women activists react to this situation in different ways: some may be more seduced by the new opportunities than others.

Personal circumstances: opportunities and dilemmas

The selected excerpts of women activists' life-stories contain much more than evidence about different entry points into activism related to particular historical moments. The narratives also offer insight into personal circumstances and obstacles, which shape the everyday life of any social actor. Although the life-stories told are by individual women and contain idiosyncratic experiences beyond a general historical and political context, they do raise general issues. The narratives I have collected are too complex to allow me a comprehensive exploration of all the recurring aspects and themes. However, I would like to single out a number of issues that were addressed by almost all activists as particularly significant aspects of their lives. These issues are mainly related to women's immediate surroundings: mothers, fathers, relatives, lovers, spouses and friends. In some cases, they can be sources for support and strength; in others, they could pose serious obstacles and create additional burdens. Often, they present an odd mixture of both in the course of a woman's life, sometimes encouraging her growth and development, at other times restricting and hindering her.

This phenomenon is especially notable in the way the activists depict their fathers and the impact they had on their lives. A number of women drew attention to the positive influence their fathers had on their development and their supportive attitude towards their daughters' education. Azza remembers one of her favourite books given to her by her father:

When I was a child, my father was telling me about books and allowed me to go to the public library. One of the most important books he gave me, and I still remember it and I bought it for my daughter, is Amelia Earhart. *She was the first woman pilot. The book was about her life. When she was a child she refused just to be a girl and played boys' games. She was very persistent and strong. My father was hoping that I would be a strong woman like her.*

Azza, like Siham and Niveen, stresses an enthusiasm and interest in education. Studying and books are not the only aspect of high school and university education described as being critical to their development as women activists. An involvement in extracurricular activities was mentioned over and over again. Hoda recalls various discussion groups, projects involving community work and summer camps as part of her education. Siham was not only very active in sports and in the 'National Guard', but was also involved in many cultural activities apart from her political involvement. Azza joined the drawing and acting classes inside university, she was part of a journalism group, and wrote poetry and joined reading competitions before she became involved in the student movement. All of them, in various ways, were outstanding, active, enthusiastic and compassionate students who wanted to be part of and influential within the circumstances and changes going on around them.

It becomes obvious that for many women education, in its widest sense, provided the means to transcend narrowly prescribed gender roles. The link between education and 'being like a boy' was very crucial in Siham's upbringing and experience of herself:

I was allowed to walk to school. Maybe I was trusted, because of my appearance. I looked very young, and I think I didn't develop as a woman when I was in secondary school. Boys were outside of my thinking. My family considered me as a boy when I was small. This was because I was the youngest and talked like a grown-up. My brother used to call me when he had his friends around and talked with me in order to show off. They asked me questions and I answered in a very articulate way. My father liked that. He always answered my questions. This made me think that my brains are very important in order to be loved. It was a very important discovery for me when I grew up. So, because I was praised all the time, because of what I was saying, I thought all the time: the way I think and talk are part of my assets. I am intelligent, and I was encouraged, that is why education for me was normal. When I was thirteen, I had to get a permission when I wanted to go out. And if they said 'No, you cannot', I realized that my brother used to go out when he wanted. So I started asking: 'why?' I was taken seriously in my education, and maybe this registered in my mind that I would be taken seriously like my brothers. But I was not allowed the freedom they had. Maybe I felt that I was, in a way, a boy, without the rights of a boy. Maybe education for me was kind of wanting to be like them. Since an early age I was aware of the different rights given to men and women. Another thing which was important in my upbringing was that my father, being a good reader, believed in participation in public life, if not in an organized way, but a kind of commitment that we have to be concerned with what is happening outside the house. He used to discuss politics with his friends while I was sitting with them. I remember when I was very young that my father would bring the newspaper and tell me: 'If you read this bit I will give you a penny.' So I sat and read and I hear my father talk about politics and I grew up to feel interest in public life. All of us were not cut off. We were not a traditional family in this sense.

As supportive as fathers like Azza's and Siham's could be with regard to their daughters' education, they nonetheless set up the barriers that prevented them actually behaving and moving around freely 'as boys do'. A sense of feeling discriminated against by the mere fact of having been born a girl pervades many life-stories, regardless of the level of support given by the immediate kin. Often the fluctuation between support and hindrance is perceived as a contradiction which actually contributed to personal forms of rebellion and to involvement in more organized forms of struggle. Some, like Nadia, for example, view the times of difficulty as a blessing in disguise as it helped them to gain intensity and force in their later struggles:

I came as the fourth girl when they very much wanted a boy. I was very unlucky, because I was born as the unwanted girl, darker in colour than the rest of my sisters and at a time when everybody was grieving over the death of my grandfather. So I grew up accepting my lower status, and my brother who came a year and nine months later was the joy of the family. But later I took this as a privilege. The interesting part is that I had the stronger personality and my poor brother had to follow me.

Nadia, like others, stresses that her personal experiences of gender discrimination sensitized her to all forms of oppression and induced a deep aversion against any form of exploitation. But Nadia also acknowledges that these incidents might lead to insurmountable complexes and interior barriers in the course of a woman's life. In Hania's case, contradictory signals were given from different parts of her family. While she generally felt supported by her father, who would treat her as an equal to her brothers, Hania's mother kept reminding her '*to behave like a girl not a boy*'. She also remembers that her brothers, with whom she grew up, playing with them and their friends, objected to her first boyfriend.

These contradictory signals might lead to a sense of confusion, but in the cases of these women activists in fact resulted in increased self-knowledge, moral strength and political insight. What needs to be stressed, however, is that a supportive father is by no means a necessity for a woman to become an activist. Mona, for example, describes her father as a '*male chauvinist who believed that a woman's place is at home and that her primary duty is to her husband and then her children*'. Despite this portrayal, Mona does not hold any grudges against her father: '*My dad is such a sweet person, but he's so disturbed in his thinking concerning women. I think it has to do a lot with his upbringing. His mother died, and he was an orphan who had to fight for his life.*' The person she really despises and holds responsible for causing her lots of pain and difficulties is her mother:

My mother is the main problem relationship in my life. She hates women and that shows how much she hates herself. I can tell you that now, because I can see and understand things with analysis. She always wanted a boy, which is very typical. My mother never worked and she wasn't very educated, but she was a very beautiful woman. She's the typical pretty woman, who made her husband and children very unhappy precisely because she stayed at home. It was very frustrating for her, but even if she got chances to work she wouldn't do it, because she didn't believe in it.

From the restrictions, insults and beatings of her childhood and teenage years to the more recent interferences in her marital life, Mona's mother has caused her continuous pain and hurt. Some of her stories are too gruesome and disturbing to repeat here, but the continuous humiliation and attack by her mother led Mona to the decision to stop talking to her: '*I decided to put her out of my life because I couldn't take it any more.*'

Even though their cases were not as drastic as Mona's, both Samia and Niveen have experienced serious relational difficulties with their mothers. Both lost their fathers when they were rather young and were brought up by their mothers and close kin. Samia's father died when she was only four: '*I was brought up in a house where I had a father, my mother, my father's first wife and a half-sister.*[21] *I remember that I loved the first wife of my father very much. I think my mother was very jealous of that. I thought it was normal and I have very beautiful memories of the times spent in this apartment.*' When Samia's father died she and her mother moved to another flat. Life became very difficult on many levels as Samia's mother was trying to make ends meet. When Samia was nine, she had to go to Saudi Arabia where her mother got a job as a schoolteacher: '*It was very awful there. Just food and consumption, and one had to mingle with the worst Egyptians. My mother adapted to them and became very conservative.*'

Samia's teenage years and twenties were full of struggles with her mother, who tried to impose strict rules on her and made her feel '*that there was something wrong with me, because I was different*'. This became particularly pronounced in the episodes of Samia's two failed engagements. The mother did not only urge Samia to get married and lead a 'normal' life, but also enlisted other relatives into putting pressure on her. At some point the mother's concern with Samia's unconventional behaviour went so far as to become a conviction that her daughter must be possessed by a *jinn* (spirit). This, in Samia's view, contributed to her extreme self-consciousness and concern with the image she projects in front of other people.

The troubles of Niveen are rather different from either Mona's ordeal with her mother or Samia's difficulties. But Niveen also experienced great pressures from her mother, especially concerning marriage: '*My mother had some sort of depression and she used to treat me and my sister as the cause of it. She behaved as if we didn't want to give her happiness.*' When Niveen's mother and the rest of the family started to introduce her regularly to various men, as potential husbands, she decided to avoid an arranged marriage by looking for a husband herself.

However different Niveen's, Samia's and Mona's experiences with their mothers might be, the three women share the determination never to become like their mothers, whom they ultimately see as part, or even victims of, prevailing patriarchal structures. Of course, mothers do also present positive models and provide support for their daughters. Sometimes, as in Azza and Hania's situations during the student movement, mothers struggled alongside their daughters. In other cases, as in Siham's, the mother's care and love strengthened the daughter in her struggle and helped her to feel comfortable and in harmony with herself.

While some mothers pressured their daughters into marriage, hus-

---

[21] Samia's father had been married to two wives who were cohabiting in the same flat.

bands themselves could be a great source of anguish and stress. Niveen is one of the women who believes that the pressure exerted on her '*to become a wife*' is one of the reasons for her unhappy marriage. She met her husband at university and started to go out with him. He was neither a leftist nor interested in Niveen's women's activism, but '*he was moderate*', '*more understanding than the other guys*' she met, and he worked in Cairo, the place she wanted to move to. Niveen observes: '*This was not good logic, but it was one of the reasons, especially since none of the guys I met impressed me. I wanted to know a man who would be interested in the women's group I belong to. There were no such men. None of them could move my feelings either. Ahmed was not a leftist, but he was moderate and we could manage one another.*'

Niveen acknowledges that, unlike many more politically progressive male activists, her husband does share responsibilities in the upbringing of her daughter: '*He always tells me that many men would refuse the things he's doing for me. I don't know how I would have handled a husband who wouldn't take care of the child at all.*' Overall, Niveen expresses a sense of having to compromise all the time to the extent of feeling overstretched and pressured. This partly derives from her husband's wish that Niveen should stay at home instead of being engaged in women's activism:

I had a three-day conference in Paris and I wanted to go, but he refused and was very obstinate about it. When he refused I didn't want to have a big hassle, but there was already a problem between us. I didn't think it was good to go against his will, as this could reflect on our daughter and our relationship later on. So I decided to give in. That was in March. I went to Morocco in April. He didn't want to bother me all the time, so he didn't object on that occasion and let me go. I then told him that he was holding a chain: letting me go and holding me back at different points.

At the beginning of their marriage Niveen tried to discuss her concerns and interests with her husband, but stopped after she found out that their world-views were totally different: '*Now, I share my interests with my friends, and occasionally with my sister, if she has the time, but not with him. I don't argue any more. I know already that we're different. We hardly have discussions about general human issues.*' Sometimes the feeling of leading two totally separate lives, one as a woman's activist and one as a wife and mother, becomes almost unbearable for Niveen. But divorce does not appear to be a solution, as she is worried about her daughter's future and the trouble and social condemnation a divorce might create: '*I am scared of doing my daughter wrong. I was fatherless and know how important a father is psychologically. He is as important as a mother is, and not less as they usually say. So long as I can cope with the situation, why not? But sometimes, I think that I would have been better on my own.*' Niveen's concern about her daughter's future and well-being parallels Mona's experience in her marriage:

My problem with my husband is summarized into two major problems. He is a horrible miser and we think totally differently. If he would be nice and kind, or some sort of generous and warm type of person, it might be easier to deal with our different ways of thinking. But nothing of that is there. The only good side and the only thing that is keeping me with him is my son. He is a good father to Hany. He loves him and plays with him.

Responsibilities to children often pose a dilemma for women activists. In the cases of Niveen and Mona, the main anxiety stems from the struggle between leaving a non-supportive husband and remaining with him for the sake of the children. But problems also arise on a more practical level: juggling the time spent with children and time for work and politics. A perpetual sense of guilt seems to be some women's most dogged companion. Many women expressed their sorrow at having to leave their children in the care of others for long periods. As mentioned earlier, husbands play different roles, but most women describe their husbands as sharing in childcare. For those with more limited financial resources, nurseries and schools provide outlets in the sense of time for their political activism. Those with greater financial means also rely on paid help in childcare. For some women, the extended family, that is siblings, their own parents, uncles and aunts as well as friends provide a kind of childcare network which takes off the burden to some extent. Hania, whose parents were initially against her marriage, depicts the birth of her daughter as a turning-point in her parents' attitude:

After my daughter was born, my family began to change their thinking towards our marriage and they began to accept it. With my daughter, we had two years of real enjoyment in our life. I stopped working for a year and then I resumed it. But I maintain that my child is a priority in life not a secondary issue. Sometimes it was difficult to manage, especially after I resumed my political activism. There were times when everything was calm and I could cope, but other times there were conferences and we had to cram. At those times I had to find a way to do both. In the last seven years it has become increasingly difficult, and I've been giving less and less time to my family, but my husband has been very supportive. He fills the space whenever I'm not there, and my daughter enjoys his company, so I don't feel any great sense of guilt. She is also growing and starts to have friends of her own. Inevitably, something gets lost, either you can't meet deadlines for your work or you have to neglect your family and children. This constitutes a continuous pressure for women who work and are involved in politics. What helps is that we live in an extended family household. There's always someone to watch over the kids, and there are lots of other children to keep each other entertained. When both me and my husband are busy, my mother carries the whole load.

In the various accounts of problems and joys related to children, the extended family was mentioned over and over again as constituting a significant element in women's ability to '*juggle with childcare, work and political activism*'. Neighbours and friends, as well as parents of the children's friends, play an important role too. It would be inaccurate to perceive children as a burden, as all the women I interviewed stress the great joy they derive from their children. Mona, who is particularly fond of children and always wanted to have many, regrets that she could not have more children, because of her unhappy marriage:

I love children so much, and I think they're the best things in the world. I could have had twelve children and not be annoyed. I have been more or less adopting children in that every child that comes near me I attend to. Obviously I love my son beyond anything and I wouldn't do without him. I don't find it difficult in terms of managing work and the child, because I find a lot of pleasure in sitting and discussing things and watching him grow. The way he and children in general perceive things always fascinates me. He has given me a lot of strength. At some points in my life in the past, I could have committed suicide. But just looking at him makes me want to be on my two feet for as long as I can. I don't lead my life as recklessly as I would have done without him. I don't drink, for instance, precisely because I don't want to endanger my life for his sake, just because I don't want him to be without a mother. I want to bring him up, as he is actually the major thing in my life. I never put him on the same level as work.

Despite Mona's great love and desire for children, she did not want to have a child for the first five years of her marriage, because she did not get along with her husband. They separated for a year and then Mona decided to go back, because she wanted a child: '*At that time, I didn't believe in divorce and remarriage. If I wanted a child I had to get it with this one person or else not at all. In retrospect I believe that I could have got a divorce, married someone else, lived happily and had a child, but this is not the way I was brought up.*'

As much as Mona and Niveen experience overriding demands and hardships in their relationships with their husbands, the anger and pain caused by the marriage constitutes one driving force in their wider struggles. Other women are much luckier with their husbands and found partners with whom they could actually share their lives. Nadia never wanted to get married, as she considered herself too outspoken and unwilling to compromise: '*In my generation, men were afraid to speak to women like me, who were able to express their opinions. Also, I was already considered to be too old to get married.*' When Nadia was thirty-three years old, a forty-one-year-old widower with two children approached her; Nadia had known him all her life and referred to him as 'uncle'. Despite her initial refusal and resistance to family pressures, Nadia gave finally in to the marriage proposal after about three months of serious contemplation:

I actually prayed in the sense that if this was part of God's will for me then he would bless that marriage. Suddenly I felt that this is what was meant for me. I took it very seriously and had a really beautiful family life. He was a wonderful partner and was very empowering. My husband encouraged me to be active and to do things. We planned to have our children immediately, because we were already getting too old and so we had two boys, one after the other. My husband was considerate and helped me a lot with the children. He was really recognizing the role of women and wanted total partnership. When the second child was ready to go to kindergarten, I went to join the MA programme at the American University in Cairo, and he encouraged me very much. But then after I joined, there was so much work to do between term papers, taking care of two children with two years' difference between them, having people coming to the house and entertain them. It was too much, so I decided that I couldn't go ahead with my studies. But he disagreed, and said that once I started I had to go ahead with my decision. He helped me to pull through and at the end it was really the most important thing I did.

For Nadia, marriage turned out to be a rather different experience from everything she expected and had seen around her. She attributes it to the uniqueness of her late husband as she believes that his considerate ideas and behaviour were rather subversive and unusual characteristics at the time and are still not widespread. But Nadia is also critical of some interpretations of equality: *'I'm very careful about this concept of partnership, because I see certain cases in the States, where it has been totally reversed. Women expect that they sit in the house and the husband does everything, because she's talking about women's rights. I dislike that. I like sharing things on an equal basis.'*

Her friend Hoda, who went to the same high school and is only a few years older than Nadia, did not want to take a chance and opted out of marriage. She was attached to someone, and thinking about marriage and settling down in Egypt, prior to her job offer in the UN. In her view, not too much has changed in the past forty years concerning men's unwillingness to follow their wives around the world:

Until today, we're gender biased and take it for granted that men can decide to take along their wives wherever they go. But the day hasn't yet come when the wife can decide to take her husband when she's transferred at work. In some places, like Sweden, wife and husband decide who will look after the children and who will work, depending on who has the better job. I tell you, the day might come when they will do that here in Egypt, but it's very far away.

Hania, who has a partnership and friendship with her husband, tells one of the most positive marriage experiences. She got to know her husband at university, but *'didn't like him very much then'*. It was ten years later, in the 1980s, that they became friends and then fell in love. Hania's parents were opposed to the marriage, mainly because her husband is Muslim, while Hania is Copt by birth, but also because her husband did not have a proper job:

He was always interested in writing. He was one of the people who got involved in the literary movement in the 1960s. But this was not his career. When we were thinking of getting married he got into his father's business. From all points of view it was a very unsuitable marriage. Anyway, we went through it very quietly and we got married in front of the Shaykh. The first years, we lived quite remote from my parents. We became very close by sharing a lot of ideas and discussing a lot of issues, although we have very different characters. We always left a space for each other. We don't need to move in the same social circles. He was a very anti-social person. He likes to stay alone and can deal with people on the one to one basis or two at most. This can be a bit of a problem, especially at the beginning until you realize that you don't have to be identical, that you don't have to go together everywhere. He can have his friends, and I can have mine, but we can be together at certain points. We don't have to present ourselves to the world as a couple all the time.

What might at first sound like another version of 'leading two separate lives' is quite a different arrangement. Hania shares all her ideas and work with Marwan and vice versa. Discussions about their respective concerns, interests and problems are part of their everyday lives. Hania feels that both she and her husband have evolved with each other and are able to allow for difference in opinion within their relationship: '*We discussed a lot of things and this has solved many problems in our personal life. In the beginning of our marriage, we used to fight and got into emotional battles, when he couldn't understand my views and I became very angry and felt like smashing him, as I had the sense of right on my side.*' With time the relationship has grown more harmonious and settled, especially since Marwan shares Hania's interest in gender issues and power relations. On a practical basis, they share household chores and raising their daughter.

The dilemma evoked by an unhappy marriage can be one of the most serious obstacles and strains in a woman's life, whether she is politically active or not. For women activists, the conflicts created by a relationship with an unsympathetic or non-supportive husband might lead to a sense of internal conflict as women lead two completely separate lives inside and outside the home. One way to compensate for the lack of encouragement and sympathy at home is to seek support and solace in the networks of female friends and fellow activists. This need has created a new kind of women's world, different from the old segregated *harem* of passive and oppressed women, a world in which women have become creators of their own culture, or at least sub-culture. Friendships often cut across generations as Nadia, who herself is in her seventies, describes:

I feel particularly privileged, because I have a lot of friendships across different generations. I have friends among women, who are in their thirties and forties, and now I even have friends from among young women of my granddaughter's age. This is because I'm particularly interested in fostering human relations. So, I feel that it's part of my rights to break down the age barriers. My only condition for friendship is that we can be sincere and articulate as much as possible. Age isn't a barrier for me, but the barrier very often occurs when we're not doing the same work, when we have nothing to share with each other. One problem is that one can't see friends who are not moving in the same sphere or operate in the same activities.

The close links between working relations, women's activism and friendships do not only provide a safe cushion and backing, but also produce an arena of fierce struggles and tensions. Personal differences and conflicts are often disguised as political discussions, and vice versa. Rivalry and competition feature side by side with team spirit and encouragement. At a time where visions are less clear-cut and paths less well defined than in earlier periods, friendships often carry a heavy burden. Hania explains the problems of evolving friendships that were originally based on shared political convictions and aspirations:

> We are speaking of hundreds of people who came together, but throughout the years this has been getting smaller, because nobody remains with the same ideas or feelings. At one point a lot of people have chosen different roads. It affects you when every time you see someone he or she is going away from you. A lot of people fell out with each other. We had gone through a period in which we sensed defeat, hopelessness, confusion and loss and this has its implications on your own personal choices. You come together on the basis of certain efforts and moral qualities, and all of a sudden you find that these are no longer there. So either you continue with people that you've been friends with before or quit, if you feel that there is no common ground any more. The only thing that remains is that we have been together twenty-five years. I've taken the decision that having been friends with some people in the past is not enough to continue the friendship in the present. You don't have to be involved in exactly the same things, but at least share some concepts, emotions and ethics.

Several activists cautioned me on a number of occasions not to romanticize networks and relationships between women activists. In the course of my interviews some women even gave me the impression that they actually lack the kind of friendship that would allow for a completely open and intimate exchange. Considering the complexities and sensitivities involved in mixing political activism, professional careers and friendships, it is not surprising that some women find it difficult to discuss very intimate aspects of their lives with other women activists.

Contemporary activism: layers of differences

The diversity of motivation and experiences should have made it clear by now that I do not intend to sketch a profile of 'a contemporary Egyptian woman activist'. Rather, I see these short excerpts from the life-stories as leads into the background experiences and motivations prompting various forms of engagement in women's activism. They are also emblematic of how particular historical conjunctures, and the experiences embedded in them, might inflect and colour ongoing political involvement. These conjunctures are not merely contingent in the lives of women activists but have a meaningful relation to them. They do not determine political action, but they shape likelihoods, suggest possibilities, generate tendencies and frame choices. Political orientations, goals, agendas, and forms of engagement in the women's movement, as well as in national and international agendas, are all affected by general trends and historical events. Family relations, friendships and support networks are not happenstance either, but are subject to the same social and political changes that have affected each of the activists.

Ideas come and go. People are not static in their beliefs; and beliefs and practices are not always mutually congruent and consistent. All activists have continuously accumulated new experiences, which further shaped their involvement. However, what has become evident in the cases of these activists is that their formative experiences appear to have left a particularly enduring mark.

Other experiences need not necessarily be linked to historical events or general societal shifts. Certain events, which are personally traumatic, such as feeling mistreated as a child, betrayal by friends, a broken relationship, infidelity by a husband or partner, divorce or death, represent disjunctures, which also change the awareness and *Weltanschauung* of people. Many of the women I interviewed referred to a series of 'decisive moments' which worked in conjunction with the general mood of particular political eras to shape their consciousness.

This leaves me with the question of what general statements I can make on the basis of these examples. Are the fragments of life-stories I chose representative of their era? The quotes I presented contain themes that elicit commonality from many of the other activists I interviewed. My choice then was neither for the representative nor the unique, but for the exemplary. My strategy has been to seek out formative experiences related to particular periods. I mainly selected turning-points in order to look at the possible relationship between these experiences and 'public political activism'. Any attempt to generalize from the personal experiences of any woman activist necessarily obscures the level of idiosyncrasy and uniqueness. The question that arises for me, however, is how far I can do justice to people's lives by utilizing 'case studies'. And related to this is the quest for the personal, the unique, 'the person behind the example'. It is certainly beyond the scope of this work to attempt to make any statements about the personalities of the women whose lives I selected here. Yet what needs to be stressed is that while a woman's sense of self is embedded in the collective memories of a particular political epoch, it also emerges from an awareness of uniqueness. I suggest that this context calls for a particular research methodology, which merges personal and political biographies while taking into account broader historical and cultural developments.

In this chapter I have attempted to add a biographical and subjectively experienced level to the more general historical context presented in chapter 2. The shift from public-spirited welfare work to various forms of political engagement, ranging from anti-imperialist, Arab nationalist and socialist to feminist frameworks is related to socio-economic changes and political transformations on a national and international level. Transformations in post-colonial and post-revolutionary Egypt provided the backdrop for many educated women to challenge gender roles by leaving the sphere of traditional voluntary welfare work and enter the job market. Their involvement up to today is very much coloured by the spirit of social services, voluntarism and international networking – all elements of their first involvements. For the next generation, pan-Arab and socialist ideas, experiences of the revolution itself and the immediate changes connected to the Nasser regime became decisive in shaping consciousness. It should be stressed that various phases of the Nasser regime were experienced differently as the later phase coincides with the 1967 defeat in the war against Israel and the increased defiance by student activists against the surveillance of and corruption by the regime. The student movement under Sadat introduced a whole generation to political activism and has shaped the consciousness and involvement of many contemporary women activists. As much as the student movement of the 1970s presents an entry point and is often connected with a series of decisive formative experiences, it is also described as a period in which political structures and agendas were mainly set by men who prevented women from pursuing independent issues by subsuming and sidelining women's issues to anti-imperialist, anti-Zionist and anti-class struggle.

The lack of any influential secular opposition movement, an increased connection to international organizations and funding agencies and the professionalization of previously voluntary work characterize the period that brought forth the youngest generation of contemporary Egyptian women activists. Those of older generations tend to comment negatively upon the youngest generation, criticizing them for their lack of enthusiasm and political consciousness, their careerism and striving for fame. However, young women activists can be as enthusiastic and passionate about women's rights struggle as their older counterparts. Different personal experiences of oppression and discrimination pushed many women to seek solidarity with other women and to find a more organized form of rebellion. For others, professional work coincides with personal interests, a situation that is certainly not unique to younger activists. Moreover, even the youngest generation consists of women with different motivations and goals and cannot easily be subsumed under one category.

The various frames of activism often work in conjunction with each other and women activists demonstrate a great level of selectivity and eclecticism, rather than replacing one set of beliefs for another. Many of the women I interviewed expressed their distress at the common tendency among scholars, as well as political activists and intellectuals within Egypt, to attach labels, thereby distorting the multi-layered and heterogeneous character of their activism. This tendency becomes particularly pronounced with regard to the label 'secular feminist', which is frequently used to describe any woman activist who is not Islamist. The use of the word 'feminist' is problematic, as I explained in my introduction, and this has been discussed by several scholars (Abdel-Kader, 1987; Badran, 1994, 1995; Karam, 1998), but what has been systematically overlooked is the misleading use of the term 'secular'. From our perspective today, with Islamism on the rise, secularism has increasingly become homogenized and abstracted, glossing over distinct discourses and forms of activism. In the following chapter I shall examine more closely the different interpretations and practices of secularism among contemporary women activists.

4   Secularism: challenging neo-orientalism and 'his-stories'

When I was growing up, secularism – 'almaniyah in Arabic – did not mean what it means now. It was used in relation to all the nice things Egypt had been proud of: the 1919 revolution, the Wafd party and so on. All of a sudden, in the last five to ten years, it started to have these terrible connotations. Before that 'secular' did not mean being against religion, it referred to the laymen as opposed to religious authorities. Now it is used as an insult by Islamists, who changed its meaning. It's now widely understood as 'being against religion', being a mulhid *[atheist]. Farag Foda was the first victim of this distortion, through him the Islamists really forced the idea of a secular meaning a person who has to be murdered because he is against religion.*[1]   (Mona A.)

Almaniyah *is based on the idea* fasl al-din wa al-dawla *[to separate religion and the state]. It has always been like that in Egypt. Those arguing against it now, do they want an Islamist country like Iran? I do not want to live in another Saudi Arabia or Iran. If you really want to apply the* shari'a *like in Saudi Arabia, of course, you will first ban alcohol and you will confine women to their homes. So it won't be the* hal *[solution] for women. From our point of view, all the public space will be taken away. No Islamic rule would prevent a wife to be beaten. A husband would just beat his wife and then go to the Friday prayer.*   (Samia E.)

I am a believer; but if you would ask me if I could transcend religious beliefs to make my choices, I would say yes. Religion has been used badly, but religion is not my enemy. If I look at the core of any belief, I feel that it is liberating for humanity. However, I make a big difference between the core of religious teachings and the way it is practised. I am against religious dogma in any way, that is: following the teachings of religion by an official institution blindly. 'Secular' does not mean that you do not have faith, but that you transcend the narrow teachings of any religious institution or authority. It also means accepting humanism, human rights and pluralism.   (Nadia M.)

---

[1] The secular intellectual and outspoken opponent of political Islam Farag Foda was shot and killed in June 1992 by two Islamist militants.

Introduction

Mona, Samia and Nadia leave us in no doubt that they have mulled over the issue of *'almaniyah* (secularism) and that an adherence to this concept is part and parcel of their women's activism. But what does being secular actually signify in the Egyptian context and how has it been used? Does it originally refer to 'laity', as Mona suggests? Or is it based on the notion of separating religion and state, as Samia says? Has the concept changed its meaning and significance over time, and if so, why? For many, and Samia is one of them, opposition to the implementation of the *shari'a* is the most obvious evidence of secularism. What role, if any, does religion play in the lives of 'secular-oriented' women activists? According to Nadia, the concept 'secular' primarily denotes a non-dogmatic view of religion, but does not imply that one is without belief. However, as Mona points out, Islamists have repeatedly used *'almani* (secular) interchangeably with *mulhid* (atheist) or even *kafir* (infidel), and their definition has gained discursive power and acceptance in contemporary Egypt.

Hardly any other concept has evoked as much contestation, objection and confusion as the term *'almaniyah*. During the past decade intellectuals, political figures and religious authorities within Egypt engaged in often fierce debates about the origin, meaning and value of secularism. Scholars and journalists commenting from outside Egypt have, by and large, contributed to the level of confusion and ambiguity surrounding the concept. Surprisingly, many writers fail to define what they actually mean when they address the notion of secularism. This lack of definition is frequently paralleled by an undifferentiated and homogenized presentation of 'the secular constituency'. The increased interest in Islamist movements, their various manifestations and tendencies, does not generally take into account that, far from presenting a singular category, secular tendencies display a range of positions, political affiliations and attitudes towards religion.

Likewise, very little attention has been paid to one of the main implications of secularism for modern citizenship in Egypt, namely that it defines varied groups of citizens as equal before the state and the laws – ideally, that is. Secularism is intended to play a positive role in ruling over multiethnic and multi-religious polities, such as Egypt (with Muslims and Copts). Unfortunately, many post-colonial secularisms have failed to grant equal citizenship to religious minorities, and often only strengthened the legitimacy of the majority religion, albeit in disguise. In some cases, as Amrita Chhachhi argues for India, nationalism was far more communalist than secularist (1991: 155). In Egypt, however, most proponents of secularism emphasize the link between secularism and 'national unity' between Copts and Muslims. As I have argued elsewhere (Al-Ali, 1997), the crisis of secularism in Egypt coincides with crises related to the national identity being threatened from 'within and without'.[2]

My own interest in secular women activists had been partly triggered by the realization that the current emphasis on Islamist constituencies often worked at the expense of differentiated and in-depth depictions of secular political actors and discourses in Egypt. My involvement in women's activism had not only shown me that there are great differences among groups and activists with regard to their political outlooks, their approaches to women's subordination and their activities, but I also suspected that variations existed concerning the interpretation and manifestation of secularism in their politics and lifestyles. This realization did not prevent me from feeling surprised during my fieldwork when I encountered a wide range of understandings and displays of secularism.

In my introduction I described a 'secular-oriented' tendency as the acceptance of the separation between religion and politics, and stressed that it does not necessarily denote anti-religious or anti-Islamic positions. Furthermore, I suggested that secular-oriented women do not support *shari'a* (Islamic law) as the main or sole source of legislation; rather, they also refer to civil law and the resolution of human rights conventions, as adopted by the United Nations, as frames of reference for their struggle. This definition has certainly found resonance among many of the women I interviewed. However, my research findings indicate that this definition glosses over the heterogeneity of understandings and manifestations of secularism among Egyptian women activists, and it also fails to analyse the continuum between religious and secular beliefs and practices in women's everyday lives.

In what follows, I hope to be able to illustrate some of these different views on and understandings of secularism among Egyptian women activists. I will also explore how these conceptualizations translate into political practice and individual lifestyles. But before engaging with the specific conceptualizations and practices of the women I interviewed, I would like to situate my discussion in the context of more general debates about Islamism and secularism. Linked to these debates is the unequivocal equation of secularism with the 'West' and Christianity, which, in my

---

[2] The 1994 conference on minorities, organized by the Egyptian Ibn Khaldoun Centre for Development Studies, is a case in point. The conference, which was to discuss ethnic and religious minorities in the Middle East, included a panel on Egyptian Copts. The conference organizer was severely attacked for undermining Egyptian national unity and paying lip service to foreign interests. The famous political analyst Muhammad Hussain Haykal, for example, actually initiated the discussion by stating that major international powers may exploit the 'illusion' of a Coptic minority to strike at Egypt's sovereignty, possibly even militarily, under the cover of protecting minority rights (Zaki, 1995: 29).

view, constitutes an essentialist presupposition that has to be challenged. I shall also briefly examine accounts about secularism in the Egyptian context.

The 'Muslim spirit' or 'spirits of orientalism'?

Far from having overcome those ahistorical generalizations so character- istic of earlier orientalist scholarship, many recent works exploring the 'nature' of Muslim societies and their compatibility with western notions, such as the nation state, democracy or secularism, evoke images of unchanging and ever-present characteristics of Islam (Bill & Springborg, 1990; Crone, 1980; Crone & Hinds, 1986; Gellner, 1983a; Kedourie, 1992; Pipes, 1983, 1992; Vatikiotis, 1983, 1987). In the same fashion, one can find that more recent political developments, particularly the increased popularity of Islamist movements and their demands, are fre- quently being explained in terms of their religious framework – Islam. The motivations and approaches might be altogether dissimilar but, as Sami Zubaida shows, many authors evoke the notion of a 'continuous his- torical essence of Islam' (1993: xiii).

On the other hand, one finds that a widespread argument among Islamists, secular Christians and some scholars is the notion that there is a natural and inherent link between Christianity and secularism, under- stood as the separation of religion and the state. This argument – which serves to stress the essential difference of Islam and its special relationship with secularism – ignores both the historical development of secularism and its political contexts as well as the multifarious and changing mani- festations of secularism in predominantly Christian countries today. Nikki Keddie challenges the notion of an inherent and self-evident model of secularism within western Christian cultures and points to the conver- gence of intellectual, societal and government-sponsored secularization which, far from emerging naturally, has been a matter of contestation and struggle over centuries:

While secularism is frequently traced to intellectual roots, in Locke and Mill on toleration, or Voltaire and other Enlightenment figures who attacked the Church and organized religion, it could equally be traced to Henry III, who confiscated monasteries and increased state control of the church, to enlightened despots who sponsored power over the Church, and certainly to the activities of the French Revolution, Napoleon, the new American republic, and increasingly secular European Governments. These governmental actions included measures of toler- ation such as the emancipation of Jews – and of Catholics in Protestant countries and vice versa – and reduced privileges for the majority religion . . . By the seven- teenth or eighteenth century, religious conflicts, whether in the religious wars in Europe or in persecutions in US colonies, had come to be seen as bloody, indecisive and inimical to national unity, so that it was increasingly felt best by all Governments to find a place for all religious groups. (1997: 36)

In the same way that Sami Zubaida (1994) argues that there is nothing inherently western about the notion of human rights (see chapter 6), Keddie also contends that the concept of secularism evolved historically and continues to be a site of contestation. The gap between adopted human rights resolutions and their actual application parallels the gap between articulated conceptions of secularism and their concrete deliberations. Most people in western countries would probably define secularism as the separation of religion from the state. However, as several authors have shown, western countries display a great deal of diversity in their specific approaches to religion and its relation to the state (Forster, 1972; Keddie, 1997; Rossiter, 1992; Saghal, 1992; Saghal & Yuval-Davis, 1992; Yuval-Davis, 1992) and the strict separation between state and religion cannot be found in any western country.

In Germany, for example, the former ruling party, the Christian Democratic Union, can hardly be called secular in the common sense of the term, as its very name is based on a religious identity. Religion enters state politics in a variety of ways, such as the state's collection of religious taxes which are used to support the church, or the Catholic bishops' constant meddling into politics, especially in Bavaria, Germany's conservative south. The boundary between religion and the state becomes even more blurred in Britain where there exists not only an established religion with the queen as its head but also a blasphemy law, which is meant to protect the Church of England (and no other church or religious group) from attack.

Gita Saghal and Nira Yuval-Davis in their introduction to *Refusing Holy Orders: Women and Fundamentalism in Britain* (1992) – a conglomeration of articles analysing Christian, Jewish, Hindu and Muslim fundamentalism in Britain with respect to their specific orientation towards women – consider Britain far from being a secular state:

The Christianity of Britain, however, is not just a question of religious affiliation or even just a part of British nationalist ideology. It is anchored in law, and extended beyond the symbolism of the queen being the titular head of the Churches of England and of Scotland. First, the church hierarchy participates in the British legislative process. The two archbishops and twenty-four bishops are members of the upper house in the British Parliament, the House of Lords ('the Lords Spiritual'). It is the Prime Minister's duty to appoint the Archbishop of Canterbury, and as debates in the media before the appointment of the last archbishop pointed out, the Prime Minister's religious affiliation and attitudes have to be accommodated in [an] appropriate manner. Moreover, in the Jewish yearbook, in the section on British laws which specifically concern the Jews, it is claimed that lcgally it is unclear whether a Jew (or any other non-Christian, for that matter) can become British Prime Minister. The case has never been tested in British history (Disraeli converted to Christianity). (Saghal and Yuval-Davis, 1992: 11–12)

The authors are members of a London-based group called 'Women against Fundamentalism' (WAF),[3] which consists of women from across the world with a wide range of religious and political backgrounds. The group uses the term 'fundamentalism' to describe all forms of religious extremism which, in their view, share a series of commonalities, among them the perception of women 'embodying the morals and traditional values of the family and the whole community' and the struggle to control 'women's minds and bodies' (*WAF*, 1995, no. 6, back cover). Homi Bhaba describes WAF as subscribing to a 'subaltern secularism' as opposed to 'liberal secularism', which he defines as being based on the premise of 'a world of equals who determine their lives, and the lives of others, rationally and commonsensically' (1995: 6). Bhaba uses the notion of 'the subaltern' to refer to the oppressed minority groups against which majority groups define themselves, but which are in a position to subvert the authority of those who have hegemonic power. In his view women of religious minority groups 'are caught in the cross-fire of multi-faith, multicultural society, where, invariably, the shots are called by the male members of the community who become the recognisable representatives of the "community" in the public sphere' (ibid.). Therefore, they do not have the choice and freedom upon which liberal notions of secularism are based, but as Saghal (1992) argues, are in need of secular spaces to ensure choice and ethics of coexistence.

While examining religious movements worldwide, WAF is also concerned with those aspects of British society that contravene the notion of secularism, such as the establishment of the Church of England, the blasphemy laws, the imposition of Christianity in state schools, including Christian assemblies, and state funding of religious schools. Clearly, the notion of secularism remains a contested issue in Britain and cannot simply be reduced to 'the Christian model'. Not just Christian, but also Jewish, Muslim and Hindu members of WAF (as well as men and women throughout Britain) challenge their own religious communities' and the state's outlook on religion and secularism, and the debates are far from settled.

Even in the United States, which comes closest in constitutional stipulations, laws and state policies to the common definition of secularism, the separation of religion and the state is not always strictly enforced. Despite being illegal, prayers are still conducted in many schools in

---

[3] I myself have been an active member of WAF since 1995.

several areas of the USA (Keddie, 1997: 25), and churches and religious sects increasingly attempt to alter and influence school curricula. Church schools and religious institutions are exempted from taxes and supported by different forms of subsidies. One might also add the widely broadcast church visits of President Clinton and his wife Hillary, particularly during times of crisis, as an aspect of ambiguous state–religion relationships.

The rise of Christian fundamentalism, the growth of 'born again Christians' and the flourishing of various Christian and non-Christian sects, religious groups and churches illustrate that the notion of 'the separation of church and state' conceals a far more complex constellation of secular and religious elements and forces than usually portrayed. In polls and in church membership figures, according to Keddie:

the US has always been shown to be far higher in religious belief and church membership – including regular church attendance – than any western European country. This means that what is probably the most secular of major western countries in its legal practice is also the most religious whether this is measured by church membership and attendance or by religious opinion. (1997: 39)

Analysis of secularism in the United States and in other western countries has to take these complexities and variations into account, and also has to pay attention to practice as opposed to rhetoric. Moreover, an analysis of secularism in the United States also reveals the necessity to differentiate conceptually between personal religious observance and politics.

It has not been my intention to engage in a theological study of Islam and Christianity in relation to the notion of secularism; this would not only be overambitious, but it is also my argument that neither religion can be considered outside its specific interpretations and practices. In other words, the question of whether Christianity is more compatible with secularism than Islam presupposes reified religions while ignoring *de facto* realities. The establishment of nation states, struggles for survival, global media exposure, mass education and industrialization are all secularizing factors which shape the everyday realities of people living in any society, whether Christian or Muslim. Egypt is no exception: intellectual and political debates about secularism and Islam have been paralleled by concrete societal and government-directed secularization, such as disassociating the *'ulama'* from most education, increasing state control over Al-Azhar, establishing a new military elite, seizing control of *awqaf* (religiously stipulated donations of land and goods) and religious taxes, along with various other secularizing factors mentioned above.

Nonetheless, intellectual debates about secularism within Egypt are generally framed within those arguments resting on essentialized notions about Islam on the one hand, and Christianity and the 'West' on the other. Proponents of secular views have been increasingly put on the defensive by growing Islamist trends, which have severely limited the discursive horizons of any discussions.

Egyptian secularism: official his-stories

It is generally acknowledged that open discussions of secularism have become marginal after the assassination of the secular human rights activist and writer Farag Foda in June 1992 by Islamic militants. Today many secular intellectuals feel threatened enough to abstain from openly articulating their views. The accusation of apostasy brought against the university professor Nasr Hamid Abou Zeid, the subsequent trial, and Abou Zeid and his wife Ibtihal Younis' flight abroad did trigger widespread outrage and expressions of solidarity among intellectuals and artists. But this tragic episode also illustrated once again how precarious and beleaguered secular positions in contemporary Egypt have become.[4]

Some thinkers and writers, formerly secularist figures such as Hassan Hanafi, Safinaz Qazim, ʿAdel Hussain, Mohamed ʿAmara, Anwar Abdel-Malek, Magdi Hussain, Khaled Mohamed Khaled to name just a few, now subscribe to political Islam (Flores, 1988: 28). Whether the individual motivations for this shift are based on newly found religious conviction, accommodation, opportunism or fear remains an open question. Their backgrounds and views are too varied to speak about a 'school of thought', yet their shift towards Islamism and an interpretation of Islam as the core of an 'eastern heritage' which they must defend against western cultural imperialism is a common denominator.

ʿAdel Hussain, a formerly leftist thinker and political activist who is now propagating Islamist ideas as the editor-in-chief of *Al-Shaʾb* newspaper, argues that 'now it is very hard to find a single intelligent young intellectual who is not for an Islamic solution' (1996: 5). He predicts that all proponents of 'a western secular future' will eventually disappear in favour of a new elite unequivocally committed to Islam. Hussain perceives Islam not only as constituting the religion of the vast majority of the population, but also as 'the basis of the national culture for all Egyptians, on which all their behaviour and their social institutions were built' (ibid.: 2). After the 1919 revolution, Hussain argues, Egypt's elite adopted western liberal ideas, which in many ways meant a replacement of Islam

---

[4] While public debates about secularism have declined in recent years, several cultural periodicals and magazines, such as *Al-Kitaba Al-Ukhra* (The Other Writing), *Al-Garad* (The Locus), *Zarqaʾ Al-Yamama* (The Blue Dove), *Al-Nidaʾ* (The Call) and *Alif-Lam* (The) have emerged in the past years as a secularist reaction to an encroaching Islamization.

in areas previously dominated by Islam – a process not acceptable to the Egyptian masses.[5] Hussain does not equate the West with Christianity, however, and emphasizes that, after a period of hostile confrontations between Islam and Christianity, it is now time for intensive communication: 'True believers in Islam, Christianity and Judaism may discover that they have important agreements against the present dominant materialism and secularism, which threaten all religious values, and threaten the very existence of nations, starting from the very basic social infrastructure, i.e. families' (ibid.: 7). Without doubt, remnants of Hussain's past political convictions concerning the opposition to capitalism can still be detected in his current denunciation of materialism.

Secularism, in Hussain's opinion, is external to Egypt's national culture, a western imposition, simultaneously alien and alienating. This view is not shared by the philosophy professor Hassan Hanafi, once an outspoken advocate of secularism and rationalism, who in recent years has been trying to fuse leftist and Islamic political ideas (Flores, 1988: 27). In an interview I conducted with Hanafi in spring 1995 he asserted that secularism constitutes an integral part of Islam. However, in his view the very debate and the attempt to separate religion from the state is a purely western phenomenon:

Things did not go well with that Christian model of unifying religion and the state. They won human rights, social contracts, democracy and freedom and the concepts of the French revolution. In our context, if you understand the spirit of Islam – and I am speaking as an expert in the history of religions, who reads papers on the subject internationally – you see that it is the most secular of all religions. We do not have religious authorities, like the clergy or the pope. I think that Luther and Protestantism have adopted some of the concepts of Islam, such as a direct relation between man and God and a free interpretation of the scriptures. You only have to know the language to judge for yourself. If secularism was against the power of the church, this does not apply here. Secondly, Islam, by nature, is realizable and using Hegelian Christian concepts it is an ideal that can be implemented . . . I do not see Islam as a religion in the sense of being the domain of rituals, dogma, institutions, supernatural forces. Islam is a socio-political structure. That means it is a law and a society with social justice. Secularism is from within Islam. We are projecting a western problematic on a culture that is by nature secular. We are conservative and consider religion as a sacred domain from the profane, so it looks as if we had that problematic. That, however, is not true. Islam handles causality in human action and it is a very positivistic religion. We do not need to secularize our life to be modern but rather to

---

[5] While Hussain objects to the 'uncritical absorption of western culture (in particular British and French enlightenment)', he states that the western liberal notion of the nation state was not alien to Egypt's national culture and helped to gain independence: 'I may remind you here that the liberation of the Muslim nation from foreign domination is one of the basic principles of Islamic thinking based on the Qur'an and Sunnah' (1996: 2). His muddling between the concept of the Muslim *umma* (community of believers) and the nation state reflects a wider trend among Islamist thinkers which refutes the argument that Islamism is inherently anti-nationalist.

understand Islam in an enlightened way to really understand its objectives from within this formula.

Hanafi's outlook differs greatly from that of ʿAdel Hussain and other Islamist proponents who perceive secularism as antithetical to Islam. Indeed, his view seems to be closer to those of the secular intellectual Hussein Ahmad Amin, who argues that nothing in the Qurʾan is opposed to earthly or temporal affairs, and that there is no religious authority set up in order to subjugate temporal institutions in Islam (1987: 89–100). Unlike the Al-Islami Al-Yasari (leftist Islamist) Hanafi, the secular leftist Amin distinguishes between religious doctrine and practice, stating that in reality there emerged a powerful religious establishment, the *ʿulama ʾ* (religious scholars), who used their privileged social and economic status to control the community of believers. Similar to the Christian clergy in medieval Europe, the interpreters of the *shariʿa* have appropriated the 'true interpretation' of religious texts and, in the name of religious orthodoxy, have been opposed to change and have promoted rigid traditionalism (ibid.).

Hussein Ahmad Amin is one of several secularist intellectuals, like the late Farag Foda, Fuʾad Zakariya, Muhammad Nur Farhat and Muhammad Saʿid Al-Ashmawi, who argued publicly for a secular state with Islam being restricted to a creed and to the sphere of spiritual and moral values. Although now muted to a large extent by the assassination of Farag Foda and the verdict of apostasy against Nasr Hamid Abou Zeid, in the mid-1980s there was still a lively debate with numerous exchanges, revolving around the question whether secularism could be reconciled with Islam (Al-ʿAzm, 1981; Flores, 1988, 1993; Gallagher, 1989)[6]. Intellectuals such as Amin, Zakariya and Foda refuted the Islamists' claim that secularism is unique to the European experience and rejected the notion that medieval Christianity was fundamentally different from the conditions prevailing in Islam (Flores, 1993: 33–4). Many of the debates about secularism the 1980s revolved around the crisis of national unity and addressed the position of Copts within the national fabric (Al-Ali, 1997: 186–7). According to Farag Foda, one of the greatest dangers of an Islamic state would be an increase in sectarian strife, and discrimination against Copts who would be regarded as second-class citizens (Foda, 1987: 23, quoted in Flores, 1988: 29). The issue of national unity has become even more vexed during recent years in which Islamist attacks on Copts were paralleled by fierce intellectual debates as to whether Copts constitute a minority in Egypt.

---

[6] For a more detailed account of these debates see Flores (1988, 1993). A description of a specific event is given in Gallagher (1989).

In the context of disputes with Islamists, secular-oriented intellectuals appear to articulate a series of values, fears and concrete political demands. However, they might not necessarily share a common conception of the term 'secularism'. One of the ongoing debates is related to the question whether the Arabic term for secularism is derived from the word ʿalam (world, earth) or from the word ʿilm (science, knowledge). The controversy of ʿalmaniyah versus ʿilmaniyah goes far beyond matters of pronunciation, as it presents two very distinct approaches and world-views. ʿIlmaniyah can be compared to positivism in which science and scientific thinking have gained the absolute authority of 'the truth'. ʿAlmaniyah, on the other hand, represents a broader concept which takes its point of reference in worldly, earthly matters. Sometimes, as in Zakariya's definition, secularism is understood to mean temporality, in the sense of temporal matters being related to what happens in the world and on this earth as opposed to spiritual matters. The particular interpretations of what constitutes 'worldly matters' range from human activities in general to particular social, political and economic conditions. It stipulates an independence from a merely religious epistemology, but does not necessarily view a contradiction between science and religion. Moreover, it allows for the acknowledgement that science itself is not unaffected by traditions, subjective premises and biases.

Differences concerning the interpretation of secularism are related to the complex history of liberalism and modernism in Egypt, particularly in relation to colonial and post-colonial experiences. In the 1920s and 1930s, secularism – promoted by intellectuals such as Salama Musa or Taha Hussain, for example – was deeply rooted in the belief in progress and rationality. The prevailing discourse of modernism was perceived to be the language of reason and 'objective science'. Freedom from the fetters of tradition and history was seen as a precondition for development and progress (Meijer, 1995: 25). Religion (equated with 'backwardness') and science (equated with 'progress') were largely regarded as incompatible. Many radical secularists looked to fascist regimes for inspiration, viewing dictatorship as the only form of government that could ensure industrialization and radical change (ibid.: 29).

This discourse stood in stark opposition to the discourse of authenticity articulated as an 'easternism' which rejected the interferences and influence of the 'materialist and immoral West'. Both conservative liberals and the Muslim Brotherhood considered Islam as a mere prerequisite for progress in Egypt. In the late 1930s, some of the radical secular modernists such as Hussain Haykal, for example, shifted from their initial positions and adopted a discourse of authenticity which replaced the focus on science with a cultural orientation. Science, however, was not rejected, but accommodated within an Islamic framework (ibid.: 28–9).

Through socialism and communism notions of equality, democratic rights and social justice entered the discourse on secularism in the 1940s. This new generation of secular thinkers such as Muhammad Zaki Abd Al-Qadir, Ibrahim Bayumi Madkur, Mirrit Butrus Ghali and Rashid Al-Barrawi not only promoted parliamentary democracy and liberal institutions, but also believed in an interventionist state that would implement reforms to attenuate the striking differences in wealth and ensure equal opportunities for all members of society (ibid.: 40–1).[7] Spreading secular education was seen as one of the major foundations for a standardized and homogeneous culture which would allow for social mobility and legal egalitarianism. Rationalism, secularism and nationalism constituted the pillars of this modernizing project.

A split between authoritarian and democratic strains can be detected in the various secular modernist discourses in Egypt's history. Whether Arab nationalist, socialist or liberal, many secular thinkers and politicians up to the present have to be characterized as authoritarian, oppressive and intolerant. In other words, there is nothing inherently democratic or pluralistic about secular thinking. Furthermore, the elevation of science as 'the authority' and the belief in the objectivity of the scientist is still a widespread assumption among many secular thinkers. However, the faith in science and modernization should not be equated with an uncritical espousal of the West and its values as many secular intellectuals, whether from the liberal Wafdist party, Nasserites or the communist movement, all have been extremely critical of western policies, particularly imperialism.

Many of today's secular intellectuals and activists do not abide by the blind faith in progress and science characteristic of early modernist stipulations. The more general break with modernist conceptions of society and development finds particular resonance among Egyptian women activists. Some women view the modernist project of rationality and progress and its linked conceptualizations of secularism as another male strategy to discriminate against women. They oppose the nationalist and liberal-modernist discourses which only addressed women's rights in the public sphere as part of the process of creating new societies. Likewise, they reject authoritarian and undemocratic tendencies among both Islamist and secular constituencies.

What appears obvious is that academic debates are flawed by the tendency to limit discussions about secularism to its male proponents or adversaries. Many of the women I interviewed hold secular attitudes

---

[7] A detailed account about these thinkers and early secular thought in general is given in Meijer (1995).

which are reflected in their political struggles and daily lives even though they take no public position in this debate. As in the case of civil society, which is by and large assumed to be populated by male actors, secularism constitutes yet another domain in which women's voices and actions are rarely being heard. In the following section of this chapter, I shall attempt to unsettle this perception of secularism by adding women activists' interpretations and practices to the discussion.

Problems of categorization

Mona, Samia and Nadia, who were cited at the beginning of the chapter, suggested three different understandings of secularism. Mona associated ʿalmani (secular) with people who are not part of the religious establishment. Samia evoked the slogan fasl al-din wa al-dawla (to separate religion from the state), and Nadia made a case for transcending the narrow teachings of religion and challenging official doctrines. Specific understandings of secularism varied greatly throughout my interviews, and I could even detect differences with respect to understandings of secularism as well as personal religious observance and identification within one group. While not always evident in the responses of the women I interviewed, it is important to distinguish conceptually between personal observance of religion and the political sphere of institutionalized religion.

The problem of categorization arises in a context where boundaries seem to be rather blurred. In her insightful study about women's activism and Islamism in Egypt, Azza Karam (1998) uses three different categories to distinguish Egyptian feminists: Islamist, Muslim and secular. She describes the latter as follows:

Secular feminists firmly believe in grounding their discourse outside the realm of any religion, whether Muslim or Christian, and placing it, instead, within the international human rights discourse. They do not 'waste their time' attempting to harmonize religious discourses with the concept and declarations pertinent to human rights. To them, religion is respected as a private matter for each individual, but it is totally rejected as a basis from which to formulate any agenda on women's emancipation. By so doing, they avoid being caught up in interminable debates on the position of women within religion. (Karam, 1998: 13)

Muslim feminists, on the other hand, argues Karam, 'try to steer a middle course between interpretations of socio-political and cultural realities according to Islam and a human rights discourse' (ibid.: 2). As my study is specifically concerned with secular-oriented women activists, I am not taking issue with Karam's definition and analysis of Islamist feminists. However, with regard to the categories 'secular' and 'Muslim', my own findings suggest that their boundaries might not be so clear-cut, and the categorization, in some ways, even misleading. As I will try to show in what follows, views and opinions about secularism and religion are extremely complex and variable even among members of the same group. Moreover, international conventions of human rights constitute only one reference point among many, in contrast to Karam's definition and my initial presuppositions.

Differences aside, all women interviewed were united in their opposition to the establishment of an Islamic state, the implementation of the *shari'a*, the existing Personal Status Law and an imposed dress-code, that is, compulsory veiling. They also shared a sense that religion should not be conflated with politics. Siham K., a member of Rabtat Al-Mar'a Al-'Arabiyya (the Alliance for Arab Women) told me:

I am one of the people who believes that Islam has to be separated from civil, political and economic rights and duties. It is an option that Egypt is a Muslim country. This should remain personal. The freedom of belief is integral. It should not interfere with women's rights. It cannot be part of the view of politics and the future. This is another story altogether. I want religion to be detached away from actual politics.

In their responses to my questions about secularism many women activists emphasized that women would have to pay a particularly high price if the Islamists were to succeed in their demands. Only few see religion *per se*, whether Islam or Christianity, as antithetical to feminism. Most distinguish between Islam and Islamism, frequently described as extremism, and assert that Islamists, particularly Islamist men, distort religious teachings as a way to gain power and authority. Hoda L., writer and activist in her late thirties, put it the following way:

I am a Muslim, Arab, Egyptian woman. When I say Muslim I mean a personal dogma and that is all! Those who demand an Islamic state use a wrong concept of Islam and interpretations based on verses related to a certain historical period. There are many types of Islam and trends in Islam, which are we talking about? How are we going to decide on women's rights? Islam is geographically and historically specific with some trends being progressive and others conservative.

Some women activists expressed their conviction that any interpretation of Islam poses an obstacle to women's equality and, like those women arguing the opposite, they point to specific verses and sayings to back up their argument. A few women expand their criticism of Islam to religion in general and contend that all religious teachings are inextricably linked to patriarchal values. Leila M., a young activist involved in women's health issues, says:

Whether Islam, Christianity or Judaism, it's all the same! In one way or another women are seen as inferior and religious practices are supposed to make sure it will stay like that.

Religions have been such a powerful tool in the hands of men all over the world. I think you really have to stretch yourself a lot to read anything positive into religion where women are concerned.

Religious affiliation enters the political struggle and the daily lives of those women whom I call 'secular women activists' in different ways. First of all, they include both Muslim and Coptic women. They were brought up in environments with different degrees of religious observance. Some activists pray, some fast and celebrate religious holidays; others do not. Some believe in the importance of reinterpreting religious texts as a means of attracting more Egyptian women into their struggle as well as to reveal the distortions of male interpretations. Others reject the idea of working within religious frameworks, as it could eventually backfire. What justifies the label 'secular' for a heterogeneous group of women who employ very different strategies is that religion is not seen as the only framework for analysis – whether in their own struggle or among Egyptian women in general.

The origin of values: doctrines or experiences?

A departure point for most secular women activists is the recognition that religion does not constitute the only source of values and axis of orientation in people's lives. As Aida Seif El-Dawla expresses it:

Women from both religious communities in Egypt, whether Muslims or Copts, and from the same social and educational class, speak a similar language, have similar values, abide by similar social norms and are hurt or perceive violation by similar events. When we say women from both religions, we mean the average religious woman who is a believer, who may be wearing the veil, may be practising her prayers and does not dispute religion as the organizer of the world. This does not mean, however, that those women use religion as a reference in every decision they take in their lives. It constitutes part of the ideology among other things, some of which are own experiences, others are social norms and similar experiences of friends and family, coloured and influenced by a culture that is a constellation of so many cultures and ideologies to the point that one can hardly say where one influence ends and where the other starts (Seif El-Dawla, 1996: 25).

Seif El-Dawla addresses religious observance as a feature of everyday life, which, in her view, represents only one aspect of the backdrop to women's lives and values. Because of the increased politicization of Islam within Egypt and within academic discourses, elements of religious observance, most notably wearing the veil, have come to represent a whole range of meanings which might actually overstate the weight of religion in women's everyday lives. Niveen B., a young activist from the group Al-

Bint Al-Ard (Daughter of Earth), recalls the role religion played in her own upbringing:

We were moderately religious at home. Islam played a neutral role. My mother, for instance, used to say it is important to pray and I did until the age of fifteen and then I did not want to any more. My mother tried once, twice and three times and then gave up. I put on a veil for six months at the age of fifteen. I put it on, because I felt I had done something wrong: a friend had kissed me on the cheek. Now I see it as trivial, but then it felt like a great mistake. Then I realized that I was fooling myself and after five or six months I could not go on and told my mother that I wanted to take it off. I did and went to Alex and swam in a bathing suit. My sister put on the veil after the age of fifty-five. She also used to wear a bathing suit. She is enlightened compared to others. She is more reasonable than religious. We had a not very religious upbringing but religion was there in the background all the time. It was never the prime motive though. We used morals rather than religious concepts. There was not the haram [forbidden in Islam] *concept, but* ʿeib [not socially acceptable]. *I never use the word* haram *with my daughter.*

Among the women activists I interviewed, many stated that their religious observance relates much more to cultural traditions and customs than religion. Fasting during Ramadan especially was perceived by many as a way to engage in a collective activity and they described Ramadan, and the particular lifestyle it imposes, as a cultural event. Sometimes religiosity and cultural practices merge, as described by Samia E., one of the younger members of Markaz Dirasat Al-Marʾa Al-Gedida (the New Woman's Research Centre):

I believe in Islam. I believe in God. I pray. I fast. I pray regularly. I read the Qurʾan. I drink, but I do not feel guilty about it. I don't eat pork. This is very important. In Qurʾan pork is forbidden, because it is supposed to be a dirty animal. I know that in the West pigs are clean, but it is not in my culture. Culture is stronger than any religion. My uncle, for example, is an atheist, but he is so conservative. These are cultural codes and not a matter of religion. Yes, Egyptians are somehow religious with their own double standard: we would drink and then fast during Ramadan. Religion is there in the background. I am being secular because it's rational behaviour. It is my common sense. Religion should not be the point of departure at a political or academic meeting. There are values already there in our culture that you should believe in, not because of a particular religion. Equality, respect, offering help to the others, not being aggressive, kindness, charity, honesty, frankness, these are all values of humanity which anyone can believe in regardless of religion. I also believe in not scandalizing or stigmatizing others, as the Islamists are doing.

According to Samia E., religion and custom constitute an intricate web not easy to disentangle. She refuses to submit to those who identify a 'good Muslim woman' with a particular dress-code or way of behaviour. Unveiled and often wearing mini-skirts, Samia E. complains: '*I have been a Muslim all my life. Why do they want me to be any different?*' In her view, education and morality should not be based on religion, but on universal human values. As for politics, whether in terms of women's activism or her involvement in other political issues and campaigns, Samia E. is generally very outspoken and does not refrain from criticizing attempts to frame political issues into religious frameworks. During a two-day workshop to discuss the launching of a 'women's media watch', Samia E. passionately spoke out when the discussion revolved around the question of whether Coptic women suffer from additional forms of discrimination, other than those endured by Muslim women, because of their religious minority status. Several speakers denied any discrimination against Copts and stressed the sameness between Coptic and Muslim women in terms of their rights, duties and problems. Samia E. took the microphone and asked: '*Come on, why are you talking all the time about Muslims or Christians? Suppose I want to be a third party? What are you doing then?*'

It requires familiarity with current debates to recognize how daring this comment was, especially in a context with people from varying political and religious backgrounds, merely united by their interest in the media. Was Samia E. referring to the possibility of being a non-believer or from another religious affiliation other than Christian or Muslim? It was not made clear, but many of the other participants looked puzzled enough. Later on Samia E. told me about the incident: '*I was furious. They are sidetracking the issues of the discrimination against Copts and they are also pretending that society was homogeneous. And why are they talking all the time of Muslims and Christians; now suppose I am a Jew. What are you going to do with me?*' The issue of discrimination against Copts arises frequently in connection to Samia E.'s discussion of secularism. Just like male intellectuals, such as the late Farag Foda, Samia E. is alarmed by sectarian leanings and feels troubled by the treatment of Copts within the national collectivity.

It comes as no surprise that Coptic women activists have a particular stake in debates about secularism. Nadia M., one of the oldest activists I interviewed and a self-proclaimed believer, defines her secularism in terms of a divergence from religious dogma articulated by the church. She views her faith as an integral part of her life, but rejects the idea that faith equals official doctrines or rulings by religious authorities: '*Religion as institutions are always trying to close the door on others. I look beyond the confines of parochial religion, accepting humanism, accepting pluralism, basing my decisions on the good for all.*' Nadia M. avoids the subject of discrimination against Copts in her account of secularism, and only hints at the issue of national unity in terms of her value of pluralism. Raga N., on the other hand, is more vehement about the relation between secularism and her Coptic religious affiliation:

Public figures in the Coptic community argue from a political religious context. It is not that I want to assert myself as a Copt, but if the whole society only sees you in this frame, you have two options: either you denounce it, or you say 'yes, so what'. But I never say 'I am Copt first', I say 'I am Egyptian.' When suddenly in the seventies a religious identity replaced the national identity, I still made the choice that I am Egyptian first and then a Copt. This is against the general trend though. I still feel that the only salvation of this country is to go back to the 1919 revolution slogan: 'Religion is for God, and the nation for its citizens.' I believe in a secular state where being Egyptian means to be a citizen. In an Islamic state citizenship is based upon a particular religious denomination. That automatically discriminates against non-Muslims.

Raga N. views herself as being part of two minority groups: women and Copts, and feels that second-class citizenship is conferred to both groups. She despises the exclusionary nature and claim to truth by any religion, an aspect she compares to fascism: '*I do not even like the word "tolerance", because it means that you just bear with something. In the religious context, it means to bear the other's belief. It means that these people are really wrong, but you tolerate them. It is a condescending attitude. I do not want tolerance, I want respect!*' Aside from her conviction that only a secular state could grant her equality, justice and respect, she also stresses that her secular orientation is an outcome of a conglomeration of value systems. Her religious upbringing was tied to an exposure to humanist values, mainly through her readings and her conversations with her father. Later on she developed a socialist orientation, which, as she recalls, was inspired by specific readings, but originated in her profound sense of justice. Raga N., like Nadia M. and Samia E., emphasizes the need to recognize the mosaic nature of the backdrop against which values are shaped and decisions made. Religion, in her view, might play more significant roles in other people's lives, but for Raga N. there are other significant frameworks.

Often, as in my own assumptions prior to fieldwork, these other frameworks are presumed to derive from comprehensive world-views and doctrines, such as socialism, or specific documents, such as the Universal Declaration of Human Rights. Many of the leftist-nationalist activists explained to me that they would still take a Marxist approach in their analyses. However, most emphasized that they had moved away from earlier certainties concerning the direct relationship between economic exploitation and women's liberation. Their own experiences within the political parties and with their 'progressive' husbands at home changed their outlooks in such a way that, today, they argue for the necessity of an independent women's struggle. Other women, who mainly refer to international conventions of human and women's rights, emphasize that they do not believe in cultural specificity with regard to basic human rights in general and women's rights in particular. However, a number of women I interviewed stressed that their values and concepts were not based on a specific doctrine or on the Universal Declaration of Human Rights, but emerged from various experiences of collective and individual struggle. As Hania K. told me:

Islamists solely use the text and this is their framework. Their judgement of the value system comes through the text. My frame of reference is based on certain abstract concepts, such as egalitarianism, humanism, human rights, pluralism, tolerance etc., which have come from my everyday experiences. Of course, these concepts did not come out of a void, but emerged from different schools of thought. However, I do not uphold a certain ideology, because it would reduce the forms of oppression and the complexity of reality. My values and concepts are as much part of my personal development as they grew out of collective struggle.

In this context Hania K. and some other activists complained about the tendency among western scholars who are doing research in Egypt to dismiss individual everyday experiences and the capacity to synthesize creatively from various value systems. Human agency is mainly framed in terms of collective ideologies – whether secular or religious – and very little space is given to individual improvisation and resistance. The individual level was mentioned in connection with women's own frames of reference, their relation to religion, but also concerning their concepts and values. Hania K. argues that one has to start building one's own framework based on specific realities: '*The reality I see today is characterized by the existence of different oppressed groups of people: women, Christians, low-income classes. My reality is filled with all kinds of inequalities. Solutions have to be found taking these inequalities into consideration.*'

Secularism in and of itself, according to Hania K., does not provide a remedy for these inequalities. She recalls her own experience with socialism, which, as she thinks today, worked in many ways as a blinker limiting her ability to see other viewpoints and prevented her from considering new concepts. Today, Hania K. denounces all forms of rigid doctrine and totalizing frameworks which she describes as part of the modernist project:

I am fed up with a lot of secular people I know. They live on old images and experiences, and they are not creating new concepts. They are not even giving themselves the opportunity, because they shut themselves off from new experiences, so they become rigid and insecure. They are fervently trying to hold on to something. These people are actually very close to the Islamist way of thinking. The opposite would be tolerance and open-mindedness.

Secularism, in Hania K.'s understanding, only provides a very broad umbrella under which a variety of discourses, practices and concepts may be accommodated, some reiterating old truths, others breaking with rigid paradigms. Her perception parallels my analysis throughout this book as I repeatedly point to the heterogeneous constitution of secular-oriented women's activism.

The secularist continuum

Rather than imagining bounded categories, it might be more productive to conceive of secular and religious positions and attitudes in terms of a continuum. The very dichotomy of religious versus secular seems rather counterproductive as it only feeds into Islamist conceptualizations of secularists 'being against religion'. However, it needs to be stressed that people's degree of religious observance cannot be conflated with degrees of institutional religion. Nor is personal religiosity an indicator for political attitudes, and vice versa. My respondents displayed a much greater range of positions and attitudes towards personal religiosity and observance than their political positions. All the women I interviewed support a secular state and are opposed to the implementation of the shari῾a.

As I have attempted to show, it is hardly possible to draw profiles about religious background, levels of observance, attitudes towards religion with regard to women's activism and the specific interpretation of secularism. One factor, which might account for variations in attitudes and practices among the women I interviewed, is age and generational affiliation. As I showed in the previous chapter, different entry points into the women's movement influence political convictions and the type of activism a woman engages in. Similarly, generational differences may be discerned concerning a woman's specific perspective on secularism.

This was apparent throughout my research, but became particularly noticeable with regard to Markaz Dirasat Al-Mar᾿a Al-Gedida (the New Woman's Research Centre), since the membership consists of two generations of activists: those who had been part of the student movement in the 1970s and are now in their forties, and the younger activists, in their late twenties and early thirties, who have joined the group in recent years. Overall, it appeared that the younger members were more observant of their respective religions than were their elder counterparts. In the case of Samia E., for example, it became particularly obvious that personal religious observance in and of itself is not a marker of political orientation. Even among the older women of the group, I could detect differences concerning their approach to religion, and their positions were far from unanimous. Some of the older members rejected the idea of engaging in the reinterpretation of religion in order to counter conservative male interpretations; others, however, advocated this approach. My findings, which indicated heterogeneity even on an intra-group level, diverge from Azza Karam's characterization of secular women activists:

At one end of the political spectrum is secular feminism represented by the Tajammu' Party and the New Woman Research Centre (NWRC). Both call for total equality between the sexes, attempt to ground their ideas on women's rights outside religious frameworks and unanimously perceive Islamism as enemy No. 1, and the state as already Islamist to all intents and purposes. As far as most secular feminists are concerned, their antagonism towards any discourse which involves Islam is paralleled only by their intense dislike and suspicion of what they perceive as a hegemonic Islam. (Karam, 1998: 234–5).

No doubt, unsurmountable differences exist between Islamists and secular women activists. However, as I have shown in my discussion of constructions of the 'West' (chapter 1) and will explore further in the context of political culture in Egypt (chapter 6), commonalities are also discernible. These similarities mainly revolve around the opposition to imperialism and the perceived threat of western cultural encroachment. Moreover, modernist paradigms adhering to clear demarcations between public and private spheres of women's lives can be found in either 'camp' which, in many ways, create a common discursive universe. What cannot be overemphasized is that at the same time as the very concept of secularism has been open to various constantly evolving interpretations, new discourses and concepts have emerged within this changing framework which cannot be simply characterized in terms of their opposition to religion or Islamism.

By way of conclusion, I would like to invoke Homi Bhaba's notion of 'subaltern secularism' mentioned earlier in the chapter. Bhaba insists on the separation of secularism from 'the unquestioned adherence to a kind of ethnocentric and eurocentric belief in the self proclaimed values of modernization' (1995: 6). If there is nothing inherently secular about either the 'West' or about Christianity, there is also nothing inherently progressive or democratic about secularism. It is only through careful historical and political contextualization that any meaningful association can be made. Egyptian secularists in the 1930s looked to European fascist regimes to find inspiration for what they saw as fit models for progress. Moreover, prevailing notions of secularism, based on liberal ideas about individualism, choice and egalitarianism, fail to take the specific concerns and plight of marginalized groups into consideration. Egyptian women activists, far from being passive victims, are engaged in the difficult task of subverting hegemonic discourses related to the state, Islamists and conservative male intellectuals.

5   From words to deeds: priorities and projects of contemporary activists

If individual experiences as well as broader political developments result in different entry points into the women's movement, questions about content and form of activism have to be asked. What do secular-oriented women activists in contemporary Egypt want? Do they all strive towards the same goals? How do they translate their priorities into action? What actions do they engage in? And how effective are they?

These were the questions on my mind when I interviewed women activists, read their publications and participated in their activities. On several occasions, when I actually put those questions forward, accounts of women activists' own goals and projects included references to the activities of other groups, often signalling, if not explicitly stating, criticism or disapproval. Some objected to the degree of research-oriented work and described it as being removed from 'real concerns and issues'. Others criticized service-oriented groups for their apolitical approach. In other words, there appear to be incommensurable differences among groups concerning the content and form of women's activism in Egypt today. Or, as I will try to inquire, could these incompatibilities actually be exaggerated by the women activists themselves? Is there a tendency to turn a blind eye to commonalities and grounds for alliance and stress differences instead?

In this chapter I shall first examine the stated goals and priorities of the various groups and individual activists I interviewed. I will link their perceptions of what constitute the most urgent issues and problems to conceptualizations of 'politics', which in turn links to notions about 'private' and 'public' spheres. In the last part of this chapter I shall consider the forms of action into which the perceived goals and priorities translate. A general presentation of the various activities of women activists is followed by a more detailed presentation of several projects, such as a credit programme, the FGM Task Force, the Media Watch, core building strategies and a project focusing on the problem of violence against women.

Political analyses: modernist and dependency discourses

Articulations of goals and priorities of any form of women's activism are generally based upon a specific analysis about gender relations and the position of women at a particular time and place. In the Egyptian context there is certainly no lack of literature concerning analyses of 'women's position in society', 'the status of women' or 'women's roles'(Abdel-Kader, 1973, 1987, El-Baz, 1992, 1997; Zulficar, 1995b). However, Nadia Farah's extensive literature review on material about women in Egypt,[1] covering a period of eighteen years (1975–93), reveals a gap between theoretically informed literature, mainly produced by foreign researchers, and empirically grounded work by either local researchers or development agencies. In Farah's assessment only very few manage to bridge the gap, thereby combining both theory and substantive data.

The bulk of the research generated touches upon a wide range of issues, such as economic development, labour-market participation, education, family planning, health, legal rights, political participation, women's position in the family and the impact of Islamist movements and discourses. Most of the literature, as Farah states, works within a modernization paradigm and stipulates that 'traditional culture', sometimes equated with religion, constitutes the main obstacle to women's liberation. The reification of Egyptian culture remains largely unchallenged in most of the works dealing with various aspects of women's position in society. The process of modernization, equated with rising education, entry into the labour force, political participation and industrialization, is presented as the means to achieve gender equality (Farah, 1994: 9). This approach is based on the distinction between a public and a private sphere and assumes that

the integration of women into the public sphere will lead automatically to changes in family relations. Modern education and work in the modern sector are assumed to give women economic independence, change their traditional cultural perceptions and enable them to renegotiate their relations within society and the family towards more equality and democracy. (ibid.)[2]

Another common framework in which situation analyses of Egyptian women are articulated is what has been called dependency discourse.[3] As pointed out by Hatem, this discourse characterized the works of a new

---

[1] Nadia Farah identified 450 titles, but only half of them were available in any of the consulted libraries in Cairo. Almost half of the literature was carried out by foreign researchers or Egyptian researchers residing and working abroad.
[2] For interesting similarities with Iran in this respect see Paidar (1995).
[3] For analyses of modernist and dependency discourses on women's issues see Hatem (1993); and Kandiyoti (1996); Paidar (1995: 8–14).

generation of Arab women trained in the social sciences. In these analyses, problems of rural and urban working-class women are analysed with reference to the general underdevelopment of society which is seen to be a result of the international division of labour under capitalism (Hatem, 1993: 43–4). Gender inequality, according to this view, can only be tackled if the more general problems of underdevelopment are addressed and successfully eliminated. Modernist and dependency discourses neither adequately challenge existing gender relations and forms of subordination of women within the family nor do they address linkages between so-called private and public spheres. Moreover, both approaches tend to gloss over differences and specificities among nation states and fail to consider the distinct national and international contexts in which women's issues have to be situated.

Scholars and researchers writing about women in Egypt regularly invoke several problems which, by and large, converge with the agendas of current women's activism: (1) the ongoing economic crisis, *infitah* (open door) policies, increased labour migration, and more recently the impact of structural adjustment programmes; (2) discriminatory practices within the labour market; (3) the impact of Islam on women's rights with a special focus on reactionary interpretations of religious texts and Islamists' call for women to return to the home; (4) restricted access to education and a high rate of illiteracy; (5) limited political participation; (6) discrimination on the level of both legal rights and their implementation; and (7) unsatisfactory health provisions, especially concerning women's reproductive health.

Unequal gender relations within the family are the focus of a separate body of literature, mainly written by western or western-trained researchers (Abu-Lughod, 1986, 1993a; Early, 1993; B. Ibrahim, 1982; Macleod, 1991; Rugh, 1979, 1985; Singerman, 1995; Watson, 1992; Wikan, 1980). This literature – mostly ethnographic studies – represents a very different genre from the more statistically oriented works of development agencies and independent local researchers. Accordingly, there is very little engagement between these different bodies of literature which, despite challenges by several scholars, might actually work to reinforce the conceptualization of a private sphere (family), clearly demarcated from a public sphere (education, work, state institutions etc.).

It should be clear that some of the underlying assumptions of foreign and local researchers and scholars concur with the prevailing paradigms of women activists. As I will show in what follows, the various goals and priorities of groups and individuals belonging to the women's movement are based on similar assumptions described by Farah above and mainly work within a modernist or dependency framework. However, in recent years some groups and individual activists have challenged prevailing discourses and paradigms and have managed to open new grounds for contestation.

Sharing common goals?

On the basis of a study carried out by Markaz Dirasat Al-Mara'a Al-Gedida (the New Woman's Research Centre) about the feminist move-ment in Egypt, Palestine, Sudan and Tunisia (Abdel Wahab Al-Afifi & Abdel Hadi (eds.), 1996), I carried out a content analysis of the stated goals of the various groups presented in the Egyptian section of the study. Despite my knowledge about the tensions and rifts within the movement, I realized that the stated goals were not as diverse as I had assumed. However, these goals, such as 'improving women's lives', working 'towards the promotion of women's situation in the society' or 'to help raise consciousness of women's issues and sensitize society to these issues', were often so general and vague that it became clear to me that differences occurred mainly at the level of operationalization of goals and their translation into activities.

It became apparent that it was difficult to evaluate the actual politics and specific outlook of each group based on their 'formal' platforms. One could detect different emphases, but most of the above-mentioned goals are too vague to be analysed in depth. Both the notion of improving women's lives and the issues of consciousness-raising can be open to very different interpretations and might vary significantly in terms of content and ways to achieve them. Differences between the various groups become slightly more evident with regard to the emphases of priorities. In the following section I will present the priorities and goals of women acti-vists as they were expressed throughout my research.

Is the personal really political?

Many of the women I interviewed found it difficult to identify a top prior-ity issue and many started sighing, as Iman L. did, when I posed the ques-tion: '*A priority? You must be joking! There are so many issues that are of equal importance. The point is that we don't know where to start. We have lots of goals and every goal is a priority issue.*' I encountered similar reactions on many occasions. However, when the individual activists actually started to speak about the many problems and goals, it often became obvious that they regarded certain issues as more important and more pressing than others. Many women formulated their goals and aims in terms similar to the situation analyses provided by scholars working from a women in

development (WID) perspective, which constituted a critique of the previously prevailing modernization theory. As Deniz Kandiyoti notes, this
literature

contested the notion that the benefits of modernization had trickled down to
women and even argued that women were, in places, disempowered by losing
access to some of their traditional avenues of livelihood and social participation.
The concept of disadvantage based on gender was firmly back on the agenda, but
remained tightly enmeshed in concerns about development. (1996: 11)

The WID approach has characteristically paid great attention to the
issues of underdevelopment and poverty. However, all the women
involved in the Egyptian women's movement in one way or another
acknowledge that within the wider framework of fighting the conditions
of underdevelopment, which affect society as a whole, there are issues of
particular relevance to women. Poverty, while affecting both women and
men, becomes a gender-specific issue in a situation where the 'feminiza-
tion of poverty' has been documented widely in relation to Third World
countries (Afshar and Agarwal (eds.), 1989; Boserup, 1989; Mies,
Bennholdt-Thomsen & von Werlhof (eds.), 1988; Sen & Groven, 1988;
Vickers, 1991).

Next to the alleviation of poverty another issue that ranks high on the
list of priorities is the problem of illiteracy. Siham B., a member of the
socialist party-affiliated Ittihad Al-Nissa'i Al-Taqadummi, says:

*It does not make sense to campaign for women's equality if some basic means of survival
do not exist. Many women here struggle for mere survival, to feed themselves and their
children. Poverty has to be addressed first, and poverty affects both men and women. I do
think that illiteracy is an important issue though, and that seems to be more prevalent
among women than among men. So, aside from fighting against poverty in general, we
need to provide focused services for women to tackle the problem of illiteracy.*

The link between improving the situation of women in Egypt and elimi-
nating illiteracy is widely acknowledged, not only among women activists
but also among NGOs, development agencies and government bodies.
For women activists, literacy is often conceptualized as more than the
skill of reading and writing: it is also viewed as a tool to spread ideas and
raise women's consciousness about their rights. Legal literacy, that is,
knowledge about existing laws and the ability to understand them, is
often mentioned in this context. Indeed, the notion of increasing
women's awareness about their legal rights is perceived as a priority issue
for many activists I interviewed. As one member of the liberal-oriented
Rabtat Al-Mar'a Al-'Arabiyya (the Alliance of Arab Women)[4] put it: '*We*

---

[4] The Alliance of Arab Women consists of mainly professional upper-middle-class and
upper-class women, most of whom are between fifty and sixty years old.

are interested in helping the Egyptian woman who is not fully educated. We want her to be educated, that is to be able to read and write. But we also want her to know her legal rights, so that she won't be cheated easily and that she could increase her income' (Amal M.).

While legal awareness constitutes one of the prevailing goals among women activists, a considerable part of women's *rights* activism in Egypt is channelled towards changing existing laws, to legalize what women activists conceive of as *'huquq al-mar'a'* (women's rights).[5] The law that continues to evoke most anger and opposition is the Personal Status Law:

> *I am against any set of legal stipulations that could say that women are inferior to men, such as the Personal Status Laws. The way I see it is that the Islamic* shari'a *emerged before the concept of a modern society. It was only kept because some men wanted to keep it. But it works against the attempt to modernize society. The* shari'a *might even promote the rights of women on some occasions, but the judges abuse that. I do not think that there are any women who are happy with any aspect of the Personal Status Code, particularly the divorce and custody laws. (Randa K., member of El-Nadim Centre for the Psychological Management and Rehabilitation of Victims of Violence)*

The majority of activists I interviewed concurred with the view that the Personal Status Law is a source of inequality and discrimination, but they vary in their demands between modification, reform and drastic change of the existing law. For many activists the aim to change the laws regulating marriage, divorce and child custody is the only aspect of their conceived goals that touches on women's 'private' lives. However, marriage and divorce are often conceptualized as public affairs and have emerged as signposts of modernization, therefore becoming more legitimate areas of discussion. The widespread perception that the Personal Status Law belongs to the past, that it is outdated and impeding the process of 'becoming a modern nation' is at the centre of arguments against it.

Only one young activist, Niveen B., expresses the view that there is a direct link between the discriminatory Personal Status Law and the prevailing social norms restricting and controlling the way young men and women meet each other and get married: '*What we actually have to fight against is the underlying system of patriarchy. This should be our main goal, because it affects all aspects of our lives: the existing laws, cultural values, norms that say what is proper and what is not, and so on.*' Her analysis remains exceptional though, as the vast majority of activists do not link laws promoting gender inequality to notions of patriarchy, which permeate not only legal stipulations and their implementations but also so-called cultural values.

This also holds true for the debate around the Nationality or

---

[5] See Karam (1998: 140–75) for a more detailed discussion on issues and campaigns related to women's legal rights in Egypt.

Citizenship Law, which is likewise considered to be discriminatory and therefore widely rejected in its current form. The law does not grant Egyptian women married to non-Egyptians the right to pass on Egyptian nationality to their children, while Egyptian men are granted this right. This is seen as the ultimate example of the confining of women to second-class citizenship and, like the Personal Status Law, many activists argue, the Nationality Law is unconstitutional and in conflict with the Convention on the Elimination of all Forms of Discrimination Against Women (CEDAW).[6]

Women activists are much more ambiguous in their assessment of labour laws and laws dealing with women's political rights. For some, the Labour Law and laws pertaining to political participation do not specifically reflect gender inequality, but their implementation is regarded as the main problem. Others maintain that the overall lack of democracy and an ongoing economic crisis result in the limited political participation among women and their discrimination at the workplace. However, some activists point to discriminatory elements within the laws and demand modifications, such as the re-establishment of the law allocating seats for women in parliament – a law which had been ruled unconstitutional in 1986 on the grounds that its stipulations opposed the principle of equality embraced by the Egyptian constitution (Karam, 1998: 152–3).

The increased political participation of women is certainly one of the priority issues. But groups and activists differ in their specific interpretation of this goal. For some, increasing the numbers of women representatives in the parliament and in decision-making positions is an end in and of itself. This view appears to concur with Connell's description of how liberal feminists in the West have approached the state: 'If men presently run the governments, armies and bureaucracies, the solution is more access, packing more and more women into the top level of the state until balance is achieved' (1990: 512). Despite the dangers connected to the attempt to categorize women's activism in Egypt in terms of its western counterparts, I think it is worth looking at the parallels between one strand within the Egyptian women's movement and liberal feminism in the West. Many of the activists supporting the idea of increasing the number of women candidates would recoil in horror if labelled liberal. Many subscribe to socialist ideas and recognize the state's implication in the class system. However, only a few challenge the gendered nature of the state and the way it is implicated in upholding patriarchy.

Those who do make it clear, however, that they are not content with a sheer increase in numbers of female politicians emphasize that they are

---

[6] See Mayer (1995) for a discussion on Egypt's reservations to the CEDAW treaty.

'*not willing to support and promote any woman candidate just because she is a woman*'. Instead, their goal is to increase feminist consciousness among the wider population. They also wish to see more women who are sympathetic to their cause entering positions of decision making within party structures and the state apparatus. But most important, in their view, is the challenge of the very political system and structures of power upon which the contemporary Egyptian state rests. This, in the view of members of Al-Mar'a Al-Gedida, for example, involves a total remodelling of traditional male-dominated, autocratic and hierarchical political structures.[7]

Another set of laws, which evokes different reactions among women activists, is the labour laws. According to many activists the Egyptian labour laws are much more progressive and woman-friendly than the respective laws in other developing countries and even in the West. They praise the generous paid maternity leave and unpaid childcare leave, as well as the stipulated provision for nursery facilities for companies employing over a hundred women. Nevertheless, most activists acknowledge the discrepancy between theory and practice and complain about the various forms of discrimination within the labour market, such as job advertisements exclusively for men, or the systematic rejection of female applicants after they have been interviewed (El-Baz, 1997: 156; Karam, 1998: 161–2). Equality in the workplace and equal wages, but also specific attention to working-class women's problems of exploitation and the double burden of paid work and unpaid housework, are among the most common issues mentioned. Sexual harassment in the workplace has not been discussed until quite recently, except in connection with the reasons why women veil: to protect themselves against verbal and physical harassment on the way to work and at the workplace itself. However, verbal and physical harassment in the workplace has lately been addressed in connection with different forms of violence against women.

The urgency of being aware of existing laws and of campaigning to change them in favour of gender equality appears to have increased among the younger generation of women activists as a result of their experiences at the International Women's Forum in Beijing in 1995. As Amal H., an activist in her late twenties working on several issue-related campaigns, told me:

---

[7] Markaz Dirasat Al-Mar'a Al-Gedida (the New Woman's Research Centre) registered as a non-profit company to circumvent control by the Ministry of Social Affairs. The group consists of two generations of activists, those who were active in the student movement in the 1970s and a younger generation of women who recently joined the group. Members of the leftist-oriented group are self-proclaimed feminists. I am going to discuss the group's history and current agenda in the following chapter.

I want to study law, because the number of lawyers in the field of human rights who are really committed to women's rights are very small. Also, when I attended the Beijing conference, I found out that all women in the world have similar problems to the ones we have here in Egypt. But many women have laws which support them, and they can work through these laws to promote their cause. Of course, I know that on many occasions it is not the laws, but the people who implement them, specifically lawyers, who discriminate against women. At least I could make an appeal if the law is on my side.

Not all activists are convinced that changing the laws is the ultimate goal. For members of Maʿan (Together) women's research centre, a Marxist feminist organization (also registered as a non-profit company to avoid constraints from the Ministry of Social Affairs), the exclusive focus on 'rights activism' ignores the underlying problems of exploitation under capitalism and imperialism. They reject short-term goals related to the alleviation of poverty, eradication of illiteracy and the modification of certain rights, but believe in the long-term goal of class struggle within Egypt and the struggle against imperialism on an international level. Being a relatively new organization (they started at the beginning of the 1990s), the more immediate and concrete goals relate to building cadres:

Our aim is to build a real movement. We want to discover the problems of women in different areas. We first have to build up a core within our own group, a core of people who are confident and have their own opinions, who can make choices and take decisions. This is a process which takes a long time as we first have to develop the ability to discuss topics. We also want to obtain a theoretical accumulation to deepen our ideas. Another aim is to deepen links with working-class women. You cannot talk about having a Marxist approach while you are mainly dealing with middle-class women in your life and not actually care about working-class women. (Leila I.)

The more immediate aim of building up a strong and democratic core is presented as a necessary step with regard to the long-term goal of creating a broad-based women's movement. Self-education becomes a priority for the members of Maʿan at this particular stage of their struggle. In a pamphlet produced by the group a few years ago it is stated that 'knowledge about our history, our rights as well as wider social, economic, cultural and political issues will help us to gain confidence and obtain the means to oppose dominant gender ideologies in society'.

The notion of patriarchy, as a system of male domination, does enter the discourse of members of Maʿan, and they do acknowledge women's specific problems within the wider struggle against class oppression and imperialist exploitation. But if mentioned, forms of male oppression and gender inequality are usually contextualized within the framework of capitalist exploitation. Maʿan perceives itself to be more radical than the Ittihad Al-Nissaʾi Al-Taqadummi (the Progressive Women's Union), which is affiliated with the socialist Tagammu party, as the latter does pursue short-term welfarist goals.

The Ittihad Al-Nissa'i Al-Taqadummi, and to a lesser extent Ma'an, locate the site of their struggle outside the home and the family. Most of the Progressive Women's Union's goals relate to women's access to education (in particular the aim to eradicate illiteracy) and political participation, including a contestation of the Law of Association (Law 32). They also address the rights of working women to equal pay, non-discrimination in employment and the establishment of day-care centres for the children of women workers in institutions employing a hundred women or more. Furthermore, the Ittihad Al-Nissa'i also expresses its demand for change to the existing nationality law. Just like many of the leftist-oriented but also liberal women's rights activists, such as members of Rabtat Al-Mar'a Al-'Arabiyya (the Alliance of Arab Women), the Ittihad Al-Nissa'i see their activism as primarily directed towards the public realm.

The focus on political economy has, of course, a long history in the various discourses of modernization, whether in its more leftist and socialist variants or conservative and nationalist versions. The underlying assumption that an improvement of conditions in the so-called public sphere will eventually erase inequalities within 'the private' does also involve another postulate, namely what exists within the realm of politics and what stands outside it.

One of the most astonishing discoveries throughout my own involvement in the Egyptian women's movement even prior to my research was that women's activism was not necessarily perceived as political work. This notion became even more pronounced throughout my fieldwork, when I encountered many situations in which politics was often defined exclusively with reference to party politics or being involved in a clandestine left-wing organization. In other words, politics is generally associated with those issues and struggles that are related to political economy and the national question. This is not to say that all women activists conceive of their work as being non-political. And there are also activists who challenge the limited definition of politics and the clearly demarcated division between 'the public' and 'the private'.

For Hind M., a writer and activist in the forties, who used to be an active member of the Arab Women's Solidarity Association (AWSA) before it was closed down by the Egyptian authorities, there is no question that the two are linked:

You should really start with the things closest to you. Class, imperialism and independence are important, but it is more logical to get rid of the daily oppression against our minds and bodies which is taking place in our homes. We always tend to look at the exter-

nal enemy and forget the enemy at home. This is blindness! We do not see things when they are so close. If I cannot make my husband fair, I cannot make my ruler fair. If I am beaten or abused by my husband, I am not going to go to the parliament and call for the elimination of class distinction. If there is justice at home, there are going to be no class distinctions. I am focusing on the patriarchal problem. It is very important to look at this, because the ruler is going to be another patriarch. Any outside invasion or any national problem, whatever it might be, cannot harm the country if patriarchy has been eliminated. No external enemy can be in control of a country where men and women are equal, because enemies play on distinction and segregation, like the one between religions or the ruler and the ruled. Home is the most basic point: if you have justice there, you have a healthy country. This is the most important criterion of progress.

Since the closing down of AWSA Al-Mar'a Al-Gedida has been at the forefront of challenges to conventional discourses on women's subordination in Egypt. Members of the group have also been engaged in the process of expanding the concept of politics. They have no doubt that what they are engaged in is politics and that the issues they raise are political. As they have systematically put previously taboo issues, such as women's reproductive rights and violence against women, on the agenda, they have pushed the limits of what can be talked about and struggled for. Their general goals include raising feminist consciousness, increasing awareness of legal rights and women's health, and the struggle against fundamentalism. These days their aims are more directly linked to the practical implementation and application of their research findings:

Now we are very much interested in creating support programmes within the various communities we have been dealing with. We have managed to raise certain issues, such as violence against women. Now we need to implement our findings. This is quite a challenge as we have reached a new phase in our activism. (Hania K.)

The problem of violence against women has been one of the most controversial issues as it touches precisely the core of what has been side-tracked for so long: forms of oppression within the home, within the family. It comes as no surprise then that not only conservative and progressive men, but also many women activists themselves dismiss this concern as a western imposition, not relevant to their own context. Others tend to relativize its significance by acknowledging the problem as such, but pointing to more pressing priorities such as poverty and illiteracy. Mona A., a human rights activist who works on feminist issues, has a different view and supports the research and the campaign around violence:

The issue of violence against women should be on top of the agenda. Whether it is on top of the list in the West is irrelevant. I do not care if the origin of the idea is western. We were not aware of the magnitude of the issue until we were forced to face it. It is not like it is just a western concern. The West did not put the problem here. Violence against women or circumcision, it always takes someone from the outside to see it. This holds especially true for a culture that holds the view that nobody should interfere with regard to women and the family. Women have to accept whatever happens within the families. The CNN documentary on circumcision did not mean that it did not exist before.[8] *People said it was a western attempt to defame the reputation of Egypt. The West came and focused on it. So what? We have ignored the issue for a long time and did not do anything about it.*

No doubt, then, significant differences exist among women activists in terms of what they want and aspire to. Yet the most significant differences exist only with respect to a small but increasing number of activists who are willing to develop feminist positions outside the framework of modernization or dependency paradigms. They reject well-established and historically rooted discourses about and approaches to women's rights within Egypt. It is these women, who include personal forms of oppression within the realm of the family and point to the links between the 'private' and the 'public', who might succeed in creating the new 'independent discourse' so much needed (Hatem, 1993). Neither modernization, national liberation nor dependency discourses, as Hatem contends, offer the tools to analyse the complexities of women's situation comprehensively nor do these approaches offer satisfactory solutions.

Attempts to translate goals into action

One has to be cautious not to assess and evaluate any form of activism in terms of its officially stated goals. It is the translation into concrete activities and projects that can actually bring about change and realize these goals. In this section I shall present various activities and projects and try to evaluate their impact on policy making and women's lives in Egypt.

Poverty-alleviation projects: charity or development?

Throughout the history of the Egyptian women's movement there has been a welfarist strand which engaged in charity work and small-scale income-generation projects. These schemes provided women of low-income strata with some form of extra income as they were engaging in traditional domestic work, such embroidery, sewing or cooking. Often income-generating projects were connected with literacy classes, which were considered part of longer-term strategies in the fight against poverty. This form of activism aiming at poverty alleviation continues to be widespread in contemporary Egypt, where groups as politically and ideologically different as the liberal Alliance of Arab Women and the

---

[8] During the International Conference on Population and Development in Cairo (1994) CNN filmed and broadcast the circumcision of a young girl. The documentary deeply embarrassed the Egyptian government and stirred up a great debate about the issue of FGM within Egypt.

party-affiliated leftist Progressive Women's Union organize various projects related to both income generation and illiteracy.

The very immediate and concrete approach to the aim of 'improving women's lives' and fighting poverty among women is often belittled as charity work. The critique usually makes reference to the underlying problems of poverty, namely unequal distribution of resources, capitalist exploitation, the *infitah* and most recently structural adjustment policies. The accusation of being conventional and conservative in their specific approaches and projects might be harsh in the light of the fact that most of the groups or individuals involved in these kinds of income-generating projects are simultaneously involved in other forms of activism and work from different angles simultaneously. The Alliance of Arab Women, for instance, has been organizing many legal rights awareness seminars for women of low income.

Nevertheless, the various criticisms levelled against income-generating projects that promote women's traditional roles cannot be totally dismissed. They concur with a shift in development thinking, moving away from short-term projects which cannot bring sustained improvement to more recent conceptualizations of long-term thinking and the notion of sustainment. It comes as no surprise then that the changes in the domain of professional development work have been reflected within women's activism. This has been particularly enhanced by the fact that several women who had been working within the field of development also became involved in the women's movement, thereby contributing their professional experiences to political activism. However, the intersection between local and international constituencies cannot be overemphasized, since the shift in development thinking, and particularly the focus on gender and development, has been promoted and enhanced by various international foreign funding agencies.

One of the most successful examples for a new approach to women and development is a credit loan programme based on the model of the Grameen bank in Bangladesh. The Egyptian project was designed by a group of women who had been involved in development work for several years and felt the need to create a project that would specifically target women and empower them. Through their professional work as development practitioners and programme implementers, the initiators of the project had several experiences with income-generating projects, such as a very successful project among the *zabaleen* (garbage collectors) living close to the Muqattam hills in Cairo. Initially they decided to transport the very project carried out among the *zabaleen* into the area of Manshiat Nasr, an urban squatter area in Cairo with a population of about ten thousand families. But soon they discovered that the community, in which they wanted to work outside their professional lives, had a very different character from the *zabaleen* community, as one of the founding members told me: '*It was a much more heterogeneous and mobile community than the one we had worked with before. So the project had to be adapted to correspond to the specific needs of Manshiat Nasr. We wanted to work through an NGO in the area, but there wasn't any. So we decided to establish an NGO.*'

After extensive community consultations over a period of months, the group decided to implement two programmes: a credit and technical assistance programme and a legal aid programme. In 1987, Gama'at Nuhud wa Tanmeyyat Al-Mar'a (Association for the Development and Enhancement of Women, or ADEW), was registered as a PVO (private voluntary organization), and it took another year and a half to design the programme in detail and to secure funds. The group created an office within Manshiat Nasr, trained young women from within the community to work as extension workers, appointed a project director from the area and established a decision-making body, a board, of which they became members.

The actual project has been successfully carried out for almost ten years now. The achievements of the project can be mainly based on its well-thought-out adaptation to the specific area and its long-term aims. Founding members of ADEW had recognized that women are often in the position of being the main providers of their households, for various reasons: death of husbands, divorce, unemployment or sickness of husbands.[9] The loan programme specifically targets women who are in charge of households and provides them with credit to set up a sustainable personal project, such as selling vegetables, shoe making or sewing. ADEW has been using the principle of 'group collateral' with the aim of increasing women's participation in the decision-making processes, to provide a support mechanism, create group solidarity and to ensure repayment through group pressure.

In a paper presented at a panel discussion on women-headed households during the ICPD in Cairo, one of the founding members describes the notion of group collateral as applied in ADEW as follows:

Before receiving a loan, women are only asked to form credit groups of three to five women building on existing support networks. In the groups, they discuss their proposed enterprise collectively and select a group leader. ADEW's community mobilizers work closely with the groups during the process, which could take up to three months, and help the women conduct simple feasibility studies for their activities. The specific terms of the loans, however, i.e. repayment schedules, size etc. are taken collectively by the members of the group. (El-Kholy, 1994)

[9] Estimates of women-headed hosueholds range between 20 and 30 per cent.

Once granted a loan, a woman is expected to pay back her debt on a monthly basis.[10] Extension workers, who promote the project throughout the community, also give advice to women starting their own projects. According to members of ADEW, almost all women granted a loan are able to pay the money back.

Next to the credit programme, ADEW also created a legal assistance programme that provides legal advice for women and aims at raising women's legal consciousness. The close attention paid to women's day-to-day problems induced ADEW to include the difficulty of obtaining identity cards on its agenda. Most illiterate low-income women lack such cards, yet public benefits depend on obtaining one. During the time of Sadat, a pension for widows was introduced ('Sadat's pension'), a small contribution to the income of widows that many women were not aware of. It is not only the lack of knowledge about their right to this pension, but also the necessity of producing an identity card, that prevents many poor widows from claiming their pensions.

In the future, as one member told me, '*ADEW wants to work on a different level and draw government's attention to difficulties in obtaining papers. We want to make it a national cause.*' The obstacles and difficulties involved in obtaining identity cards on the community level have enticed members of ADEW to start a national advocacy campaign to raise public consciousness about the problem and change government regulations on the issue.

Within the women's movement at large, ADEW is generally seen to be involved in the process of empowerment of women as opposed to mere welfare work. Some activists, however, dismiss ADEW's work as reformist and as '*too much related to the development discourse*'. This criticism seems to be based on the fact that many ADEW members are also professional development practitioners, who are often perceived to be careerist rather than political activists and representatives of international agendas rather than local ones. Such criticism appears rather unfair and based on clichés rather than on the actual agenda and activities of ADEW. The very initiative to set up the project was an attempt to take prevailing notions of development a step further and focus on the empowerment of women in women-headed households. Members of ADEW have been consistently targeting Egyptian researchers to take up the issue of women-headed households in order to provide the necessary background information to influence policy makers. Moreover, ADEW exerted great efforts to respond to the specific needs of a particular community, i.e. Manshiat

---

[10] The repayment rate has been maintained at an average of 96 per cent. ADEW only experienced major repayment difficulties in 1991, when prices went up sharply due to the implementation of the structural adjustment programme in Egypt (El-Kholy, 1994).

Nasr. Members of ADEW combine their specific grassroots project, which successfully improves women's lives and that of their families on a long-term basis, with their involvement in activities related to women's subordination on a national and international basis. They do think and act both on the level of the grassroots and on the level of national politics and international fora – a multiple form of engagement that is not the norm.

Legal awareness and legal rights campaigns

The various attempts to raise women's legal awareness have not really taken off in the case of ADEW, as several members acknowledged. The difficulty in raising legal awareness in a situation where women are primarily preoccupied in daily survival, and supporting their families and households, is not an easy task, as other activists had to recognize as well. However, since a group of women, the 'Group of Seven', produced a booklet in 1988, in which the main laws relating to women were compiled and explained, the aim of raising women's legal awareness has been translated into several projects. The booklet entitled *The Legal Rights of the Egyptian Woman: Between Theory and Practice* grew out of a self-initiated project; it involved research, seminars and discussions and became a model for several research studies and publications to follow (Bahiy Al-Din, 1994; Zulficar, 1995a, 1995b).[11]

The booklet and various later publications by individual researchers and lawyers have been used during campaigns, in which differences between the letter of laws and their implementation are criticized. They have also been presented in national and international fora to document women's legal status and to pressure the Egyptian government to change discriminatory laws. Moreover, the various studies about women's legal rights have constituted the main sources for legal awareness seminars organized by several women's rights organizations. The organization most closely associated with legal awareness programmes is the Alliance of Arab Women, which has been combining classes about legal rights with specific legal advice programmes provided by lawyers from within the organization. Several human rights centres such as the LRRC (Legal Rights and Research Centre), CIHRS (Cairo Institute for Human Rights Studies) and CHRLA (Centre for Human Rights and Legal Aid) address

---

[11] The group that published the booklet refers to itself by different names: 'the Group of Seven', 'the Group of Women Concerned with the Affairs of the Egyptian Woman' or 'the Communication Group for the Enhancement of the Status of Women in Egypt'. During my interviews most of the women who had been part of the project referred to themselves as 'the Group of Seven'; I therefore chose this particular name.

women's legal rights within the wider framework of human rights, but include programmes that specifically focus on women's issues. The New Woman's Research Centre organized several workshops and a regional conference around a number of the issues widely related to 'Women, Law and Development'.

It is difficult to measure the impact of these legal awareness projects as only a very limited number of women have been able to attend them. Moreover, several activists emphasized that the difference between stipulated laws and their actual implementation poses a great problem. Legal awareness often does not help a great deal in a male-dominated judicial system, which, according to many women activists, is generally not sympathetic to women.[12] Women's groups recognize the need to lift the ban on promoting women to the position of judges (Karam, 1998: 144), but also aspire to become more actively involved in the legal system as lawyers or legal advisers.

Campaigns to change existing laws are rare, even if this presents a prominent aim articulated by women activists. Several pressure groups were formed sporadically to address the Law of Association (Law 32), which is generally seen as restrictive of any form of political activism. Likewise, women activists have been campaigning to change the Nationality Law, which does not grant Egyptian women married to foreign men the right to pass on their nationality to their children. However, there have been no concerted efforts leading to a long-term campaign, partly because of the difficulties in overcoming differences among the various groups and activists. Another reason might be the apparent ambiguity of the state, which has given contradictory signals and discouraged activists from addressing issues so closely related to the authority of the state. Another problem might be the lack of specific and systematic institutional targeting on behalf of the women activists. Only sometimes decision-making bodies are clearly targeted, such as in the campaign around Law 32, which specifically targeted the Ministry of Social Affairs.

The campaign around the Personal Status Law, which marked the beginning of a new era for the Egyptian women's movement in the mid-1980s, resulted in some sort of compromise between the Islamists, the government and the women activists. The campaign has not been sustained in the 1990s, despite the overall feeling that the law reproduces gender inequalities and discriminates against women. However, one particular aspect of the Personal Status Law, namely the marriage contract, has been the subject of a specific project and campaign carried out by a

---

[12] See, for example, Chemais (1987).

group of women's rights activists. This project, based partly on research, and partly on a campaign – targeting both the wider public and the Ministry of Justice – resulted in the drafting of a new marriage contract, a standardized form which includes a list of possible demands, such as the right to work, the right to travel or the right to file a divorce. This standardized contract is intended to help women to articulate their rights and conditions of marriage without alienating their husbands and families. Even if the stipulations mentioned in the carefully devised document do not contradict the rights bestowed upon women in the *shari'a*, the new marriage contract has been the subject of much controversy.[13]

Azza Karam (1996) in an article titled 'An Apostate, A Proposed New Marriage Contract and Egyptian Women: Where To Now?' addresses conservative male interpretations of which rights are granted within Islam and which are not, highlighting the increasing difficulty of attempting to be an effective social force in an atmosphere in which voices promoting patriarchal values appear to have more weight than voices challenging them. Karam links the debate about the marriage contract to the case of Nasr Hamid Abou Zeid, a university lecturer at Cairo University in Islamic thought and philosophy, who had applied for a promotion in 1992.

Several members of the board responsible for promotions had accepted Abou Zeid's application, but it was refused by one member. Dr Abdel Sabour Shahin, head of the religious commission of the Egyptian ruling party, not only criticized Abou Zeid's writing for its lack of academic quality, but also accused him of propagating against Islam. In 1993 a group of lawyers, led by Semeida Abdel Samad, filed a charge of blasphemy against Abou Zeid, who repeatedly denied the charges brought against him. In 1996 the Court of Cassation (higher court) in Cairo judged that Abou Zeid was a *murtad* (apostate) and consequently must divorce his wife. Both Nasr Abou Zeid and his wife Ibtihal Younis left Egypt, and have been living abroad ever since.

Karam (1996) shows that certain voices have been marginalized in present-day Egypt, while conservative male interpretations and approaches have gained increased legitimacy. However, she emphasizes that Islamist positions are far from homogeneous, as there are Islamist women and men who acknowledge that women have been subject to oppression and have been robbed of the rights granted them within Islam.

---

[13] The Egyptian lawyer and activist Mona Zulficar and Hoda El-Sadda, activist and lecturer at Cairo University, have been particularly engaged in this campaign and in the drafting of the new marriage contract.

FGM Task Force: the struggle on many fronts

The increased political authority of conservative religious forces has been particularly obvious in the ups and downs of the campaign against female genital mutilation carried out by a group of Egyptian men and women.[14] While FGM was not been a priority issue for women activists in the past, it was put on the agenda of various groups and activists in preparation for the International Conference on Population and Development in Cairo in 1994. It was not until the screening of the circumcision of an Egyptian girl by CNN during the ICPD that the issue was brought to the forefront of discussion. An embarrassed government had to issue statements denouncing the practice at a time when the world was watching closely. Both the Minister of Health and the Minister of Population made promises to the international community, assuring the world that they would work towards legislation prohibiting the practice.

After the conference, as soon as the international audience moved their attention to other matters, the emphasis changed. Several Islamist constituencies, but most notably the official religious institution Al-Azhar, angered by several statements of the government prior to and during the ICPD, thought the time fit to reassert its increasing political authority within Egypt. As Aida Seif El-Dawla (1996) argues, Islamist organizations and Al-Azhar were outraged by the possibility that women activists could in any way be successful in their demands and feared a general development in which more comprehensive demands of women activists would be met:

So to forestall any hope that the demands made by women's organizations could be realised, a full and multi-party campaign was soon launched against the attempt to advocate the eradication of FGM. The tone in the campaign was fierce in its denunciation of the call for the eradication of FGM and waxed sentimental about the cultural meaning of the practice . . . FGM was pictured as a local tradition that constitutes part of our identity as Muslims, it represented part of our code of ethics and morals as opposed to the codes of ethics and morals that are being imposed by the West. (Seif El-Dawla, 1996: 26)

The fierce campaign of conservative religious forces found resonance within the government which felt pressured not to alienate the religious authorities any further. Soon the Minister of Health issued a decree

---

[14] The project has been set up under the auspices of Nahid Toubia, a Sudanese doctor and champion in the campaign against FGM. The Ford Foundation, especially Jocelyn De Jong, was also instrumental in setting up the FGM Task Force. It is co-ordinated by the Egyptian activist Mary Assaad, who addressed the problem of FGM long before it became a national issue after the 1994 ICPD. See Wassef (1998a) for a detailed analysis of past and present discourses and activism on FGM.

allowing circumcision to be carried out by medical doctors and prohibiting it only for non-medically trained people. Several women's groups, and also NGOs and individuals working on human rights or health issues, formed a pressure group campaigning against FGM and demanding the annulment of the decree legalizing the practice in hospitals.

The FGM Task Force was eventually successful in that the Minister of Health cancelled his decree. However, all members of the network are aware that the practice itself will not disappear through a mere change of laws, and have continued their campaign to reach Egyptians at the grassroots level, as well as religious authorities and government bodies. The campaign against FGM was fuelled by the 1995 Egyptian demographic and health survey which stated that 97 per cent of ever-married women are circumcised and 82 per cent still support the practice.[15] Meanwhile the attack of the religious authorities has become more violent, and, on several occasions, prominent figures among the religious authorities have declared the practice to be Islamic.

Despite or rather because of the 'Islamization' of FGM, the task force consciously decided not to preach the eradication of FGM through a debate centred on religion but stresses that 'FGM is a practice of culture, not religion'.[16] Resorting to arguments mainly based on women's health also proves problematic, as Nadia Wassef (1998a) so lucidly argues. The 'medicalization of FGM' does not question the rationale behind the operation as much as the medical dangers. The 'side effect' approach could be alien to many women who have not experienced medical complications, and it also tends to ignore aspects of sexual and mental health. Moreover, members of the medical profession tend to support the practice which could also be formulated in terms of human rights abuse. The approach based on human rights conventions has also been viewed as problematic by FGM Task Force members. Their main concern is that the Egyptian public by and large feels excluded from formulations and articulations of human rights conventions which, consequently, are generally being perceived as western products.

In contrast, the task force perceived a 'developmental gender approach' to be most suitable for the specific situation and context of their struggle: 'Development cannot be successful if one half of the country's population is subordinated and violated by the values and norms of the other half' (FGM Task Force, 1997a). More significantly even in this context, this particular approach questions the rationale upon which the practice of FGM is based. In this perspective, FGM is a means to reproduce gender

---

[15] Egyptian Demographic and Health Survey, p. 171; quoted in Wassef (forthcoming).
[16] See FGM Task Force (1997b: 3–4).

inequity, the discrimination of women and patriarchal power relations (Wassef, forthcoming). The campaign against FGM has recently been framed within the wider issue of violence against women, since activists increasingly recognize that the practice of FGM and the prevailing social attitudes underlying it are part of a broader phenomenon in which violence against women is being ignored, accepted or condoned by society at large. In the case of FGM, violence against girls is widely accepted as a tradition. Other forms of physical violence, such as wife battering or rape, are not condoned in the same manner, but have been treated as taboo issues. Only very recently have women activists managed to break the silence, provide concrete information and started to work on ways to combat different forms of violence.

Violence against women: fabricating dissent?

Several members of Al-Mar'a Al-Gedida had worked on FGM within the context of reproductive rights in preparation for the ICPD. The group decided to work on women and labour laws in preparation for the International Women's Forum in Beijing, but the issue was allocated to another group by the co-ordinating committee regulating the division of labour among Egyptian NGOs. In the beginning, 'women and violence' was not the group's first choice, and several members were not particularly enthusiastic, but attitudes changed in the process of their involvement: *'No one really wanted to work on violence, so we ended up taking it. But then it really took off and we all feel very committed to the issue, even after Beijing.'* The Centre for the Psychological Management and Rehabilitation of Victims of Violence (El-Nadim) was appointed as co-ordinator, and Al-Mar'a Al-Gedida joined with the organization ACT in designing a questionnaire and carrying out a survey on the issue of violence against women.

The three organizing groups spent their first meetings brainstorming about the concept of violence, tried to operationalize it and formulate appropriate questions. The women identified various forms of physical and psychological violence, which take place in the 'private' domain within the home, and in 'public' spheres, such as the street, the workplace, the police station, courts and so on. This conceptualization radically broke with previously accepted distinctions between structural forms of violence by the state and domestic violence by men. For the first time, the various forms of violence were tackled in a systematic way and linked analytically.

As the issues seemed to be too vast to address within one questionnaire, the participants of the project decided to limit their field study to three contexts in which violence takes place: at work, at home and in the street. Sample questionnaires were distributed to a small number of women, and were revised until the actual research took place. More than five hundred women and a hundred men of different class backgrounds and varying levels of education were included in the survey.[17] A report was written which was presented in the various preparatory meetings throughout Egypt before a final version was presented in Beijing. A young member of Al-Mar'a Al-Gedida recalls: '*We participated in the regional and national preparation meetings and consultations. This was the first time we really discussed our findings with women from the grassroots. I went to Alexandria with the report. Most of the women who came to hear us were veiled. The men were religious too. Some were trying to intimidate us, but many women reacted positively.*'

Others did not react so positively. Especially within conservative religious circles but also among the progressive left, the issue was seen to reflect western agendas, to overlook the real problems of Egyptian women and ignore cultural taboos and values. Some of the criticisms almost seemed to suggest that it was the women activists who created violence in contemporary Egypt. Nevertheless, the three groups that had engaged in the project were convinced that their research findings revealed that violence constitutes a real and urgent problem which needs to be addressed and combated. The committee had found that in all areas – at home, at work and in the street – women are subject to various forms of physical and psychological abuse and violence. Indeed, violence appeared to be part of many women's everyday lives. The fact that one of the organizing groups, El-Nadim, provides medical and psychological treatment and legal aid to victims of various forms of violence, ranging from torture at police stations to rape, provided evidence beyond the survey carried out in preparation for Beijing. The experiences of El-Nadim increased the level of awareness and sense of urgency among all the participants in the project.

Subsequently, the three groups decided to continue their efforts and activities and expand the campaign to include other groups and individuals interested in the issue. Six other organizations, among them a human rights centre, a legal advice group and a health organization, were invited to join in and to create a network. In several workshops, brainstorming sessions took place in which long-term goals were defined and responsibilities distributed. One of the members of Al-Mar'a Al-Gedida, who has been very much involved in the organizational dimension of the

---

[17] A summary of the findings can be found in National NGO Committee for Population and Development (1995): 35–41.

project, told me: '*The various participants coming from different organiza-tions have been divided into various working groups: we have a research group, a legal aid group, an education group, a training group, and a rehabilitation group. Each group is working out a plan of action right now.*' Raising public awareness through the wider NGO movement and the media was identified as one of the first steps in the service of the long-term goal of combating violence. The various participants in the project agreed that religious and cultural arguments which tend to either ignore or normalize violence need to be systematically countered, exposed and demystified. The process of establishing links and creating a network as well as setting agendas was intense at the time of my fieldwork and the project appeared to grow steadily. Violence had stopped being a taboo in wider circles of society, and even if the project's significance was still undermined by some, it had put the issue on the agendas of many local NGOs[18] and had shaken up several members of the state.

Consciousness-raising or talking shows?

If the aim to inform and raise consciousness about women's issues within society at large is inevitably linked to the battle against growing conserva-tive religious tendencies, where are these battles being fought? There are a number of different means used by women activists in contemporary Egypt ranging from seminars, conferences, the publication of studies and magazines and involvement with the media to more development-oriented tools such as the use of gender-training packages. In some of these areas consciousness-raising becomes more of an exercise in self-education among women activists themselves, while in other women acti-vists are exposed to a broader public.

Nadwat (seminars/workshops) and *mu'atamarat* (conferences) are among the most commonplace and visible activities of the Egyptian women's movement, a phenomenon which is sometimes used to discredit the women's movement as '*women who spend their time sitting and talking*'. Such a judgement appears unfair in light of the multitude of activities carried out by different groups and the actual significance of workshops and conferences. They can be productive fora to exchange ideas, discuss problems, present research findings, search for solutions to tackle specific problems and establish contacts which might result in networks. However, they can also be events in which old issues are re-hashed, differences turn into conflicts, where individuals might not listen to each other, and where the discussions might be far removed from the realities

---

[18] See, for example, Tadros (1998).

of the majority of Egyptian women. In brief, they could also be unproductive.

Throughout my research I attended numerous seminars and workshops organized by different groups relating to a variety of issues, such as the question how to implement findings after the ICPD and Beijing conferences, the elections and political participation of women, the representation of women in the media, reproductive health and violence against women. As in any other context, some of the events seemed worthwhile, others not. Aside from the noticeably huge number of such events which are quite time-consuming, I noticed a high level of repetition in discussions and research topics. Not enough effort seems to be channelled into networking and the building up of knowledge and alliances. This is not surprising in the light of the fact that the sense of competition and rivalry sometimes takes precedence over feelings of solidarity and common goals. Where constructive discussions took place and exciting research findings were exchanged, they often remained the exclusive knowledge of those who attended the event, and little attempt was made to spread the findings among a wider public. Another drawback was the occasionally hostile atmosphere during conferences and workshops, as the events were regularly used to reiterate certain positions rather than actually discuss them and listen carefully to other positions and the underlying arguments.

According to numerous women interviewed, the situation was quite different during both the ICPD and the Beijing conferences, particularly during the preparations for either event. Seif El-Dawla and Ibrahim (1995) describe the enthusiasm and the great level of co-operation and co-ordination among women's groups and NGOs in Egypt before the ICPD. During the preparations for the ICPD and later Beijing, the various committees, which had been formed to co-ordinate research on specific issues, presented their research findings to people in communities all over Egypt, from the Delta (northern or 'lower' Egypt) to the Said (southern or 'upper' Egypt). Productive and creative exchanges took place within the women's movement and the NGOs working on issues related to women but also between the activists from urban Cairo and the 'grassroots' all over Egypt.

Despite the widespread criticism towards the flurry of conferences and seminars and the tendency to 'talk in circles', they remain important tools for exchange and raising awareness about issues. Many activists stressed to me that conferences are not an end in themselves, but are part of a wider project including research and the implementation of research findings. This has been emphasized specifically with regard to the two big international conferences in Cairo and Beijing, but has also been mentioned in connection with regional or local conferences. Projects related to legal rights, poverty alleviation, the situation of working women, reproductive health, education, the media and violence all involved different levels of research, the presentation of research findings in seminars and conferences, discussion of possible strategies and implementation. The last step seems to be on the agenda of many groups in post-ICPD and post-Beijing times.

It is too early to assess how far the various research findings and recommendations put forward in both conferences and in the series of 'post-Beijing' events will actually be applied and implemented by Egyptian policy makers. It is also difficult to assess how far various issues and campaigns remain on the agendas of women activists and are not short-lived projects closely tied to international agendas and funding. This would have to be studied by researchers who follow. What can be said with regard to conferences and seminars prior to the preparation for either the ICPD or Beijing is that the most common outcome has been publications: booklets, pamphlets, articles and books.

Building cadres and the struggle against imperialism

Consciousness-raising and building women's confidence are among the goals of women activists who see imperialism as the main enemy and obstacle for a just society. The aim to fight imperialism and capitalism – both implying relations of exploitation – has been translated by activists from the Ma'an (Together) women's research centre into various activities which are meant '*to help build a strong core*', the basis for a broader movement that is envisioned as a long-term goal for the future. Ma'an is an independent organization, registered as a non-profit company, which combines Marxist and feminist analysis and is vehemently opposed to foreign funding.[19] The centre, which is located close to Cairo University and not too far from the city centre, attracts young women and men interested in politics, but also old-style leftist activists who seem to spend their free time going from one political or cultural event to the next. The events taking place at the centre usually take the form of discussions, seminars or lectures.

Ma'an, which, unlike most other groups, invites men to attend its events and also join its decision-making core, rejects the idea of being an exclusively women's organization and dismisses this idea as being related to 'western feminism'. Their specific Marxist approach to women's issues subordinates patriarchal relations of exploitation to injustices based on

---

[19] I shall discuss the debate about foreign funding and Ma'an's specific position in the following chapter.

class relations, international capitalist relations and bourgeois conspiracies. Like-minded men, that is, leftist political militants, are therefore viewed as important allies and partners in the struggle against the prevailing social system. However, the founding members of Maʿan stress that their analysis includes unequal gender relations, and they criticize leftist men who overlook or belittle women's specific problems.

Women and men are encouraged to participate actively in the various events organized by a group of core activists by preparing presentations, asking questions or suggesting topics for discussion. However, what might turn out to be a constructive dialogue often develops into a situation where dominant societal patterns end up being reproduced. In other words, men, especially the older generation of political activists, occasionally dominate discussions, often intimidating young women with their use of political jargon and their tone of voice. This also holds true for more politically experienced women activists, who had to fight their way within male-dominated political structures and who often 'talk over' the younger, politically inexperienced women.

That is not to suggest that young women interested in women's issues, seeking a platform and a network of support, do not gain confidence within Maʿan. Many do, and not just because they are taken under the wings of the older activists. For some it comes as quite a revelation that they are not alone in facing problems within their families, in their relationships, at university and at the workplace. Often Maʿan provides the only safe space in which they can talk freely without the fear of being judged or ostracized. Through readings and discussions they are made aware of many issues and connections to which they had not been exposed before. Seminars and lectures at the centre focus on a wide range of topics, such as the history of the Egyptian and Arab women's movement, approaches to women in Christianity, Judaism and Islam, problems of female workers, particularly women working in factories, approaches to gender in the social sciences and, most recently, discussions on love, sexuality and the family.

Often, seminars at Maʿan take the form of presenting different viewpoints or a particular idea being discussed from various angles. This can result in different outcomes, either alienating people or increasing their democratic consciousness. According to one of the older activists within the group, it is precisely one of the goals of discussions in Maʿan to transform shouting matches leading to hostility and anger into democratic discussions where different opinions are accepted and taken seriously. However, framing the multitude of attitudes and opinions, the prevailing Marxist ideology and particular political stand of the founding activists and core members still appears to be the yardstick with which truth is measured. That, of course, makes sense if one considers that the over-arching aim is slowly to build a strong movement which would share the same goals and same analysis.

A big turnover of both people attending events, and also people being actively involved in the core makes it a difficult task to expand beyond its own centre. However, activists in Ma'an reach out to women outside the group and seek contact particularly with female factory workers and university students. Several members of Ma'an, most of them from middle-class backgrounds, actually worked in factories, not just to carry out research, but also to engage in consciousness-raising and support work. The first magazine published by the centre a couple of years ago focused on issues related to women workers, their specific problems, forms of exploitation and forms of resistance.

It is difficult to measure the impact of Ma'an outside the centre itself. Its activities are extremely restricted due to very limited financial resources. Within those limitations there is a great level of commitment and creativity. Unfortunately, however, lots of energy and time seem to be devoted to solve intra-group conflicts and, even more sadly, to discredit groups and activists with different political views.

Gender training

If research and conferences present the more theoretical element of women's activism, occasionally overlapping with academic work, at other times with political militancy, the introduction of gender-training packages presents the link between the growing NGO and development sector and women's activism. Gender-training packages have been an increasingly important tool within the field of development, a process which has not gone unnoticed by Egyptian women activists. These packages are generally used to familiarize and sensitize social and health workers, NGO personnel and also government representatives on issues pertaining to 'gender'. They have been designed initially by foreign funding agencies, northern NGOs and academic institutions, and, as many activists argue, often fail to address the specific needs of Egypt. Recently there have been several attempts to 'Egyptianize' these packages in order to make them more suitable and relevant to the specific context in which they are employed.

One of the founding members of Al-Mar'a Al-Gedida established a private non-profit company in 1992 called ACT (Appropriate Communications Techniques). The aim of the organization is to provide tools for community workers to increase communication with 'the grassroots'. The notion of gender has recently been introduced as an important aspect of development work. As Karima A., the founder of ACT, says:

I have been working for six years, training women like health workers, nursery teachers and those working with the handicapped. I train them to make audio-visual aids and show them how to use these tools in creating awareness. We show them how to make puppets as visual aids, for example. In Upper Egypt, women get embarrassed when they have to convey certain information about health. The puppets help them in doing this, and they also attract the attention of the children. We show them how to document certain events using videos, pamphlets, bulletins, and tell them how to make feasibility studies and strategic planning for their projects. I also help them in defining their problems and objectives and setting up plans for group work. This aims at improving the situation of women in places where they work and in society in general. We do experiments on gender as a new issue in Egypt. We hold discussions with the various target groups and try to engage them into issues related to gender. There are many translations in Arabic of 'gender'. There is no specific term for it and that is why we tell them to call it what they want to call it. We had a workshop on 'Women and the Obstacles of Development' in 1994 and there will be a report on it. It was the work of a number of interested groups and led to a number of recommendations on women and violence, women and NGOs, work, creativity, the environment. Each group worked for six days and made a theatrical performance with reversed roles for women and men. They showed us how men would feel if the roles would be reversed.

The idea of performing a play with reversed gender roles is a unique way to illustrate aspects of gender in Egypt. As Karima A. points out, the Arabic terminology used when speaking about 'gender' varies greatly and is subject to much debate.[20] What becomes obvious, however, is that in most cases, and specifically with regard to development, gender signifies 'women', and gender issues, most of the time, means women's issues. Indeed, the two terms are often used interchangeably, while men and masculinities habitually escape from the focus.

Appropriating the world of letters

At the same time as gender-training packages and consciousness-raising at the grassroots have been points of convergence between development work and women's activism, women activists have been increasingly seeking allies and gaining influence within the media. Attempts to raise consciousness and change public opinions are revealed in several campaigns and activities related to the press, radio and television, but also cinema, theatre and literature. Several years ago, the 'Group of Seven'

---

[20] The Arabic translation of gender currently in use is *al-nau'* (kind), and occasionally the English 'gender' is retained in Arabic texts. Another translation being used *al-jins* (sex) might explain the negative connotation ascribed to gender by religious conservatives who associate the term with pre-marital or illegitimate sex, abortion and homosexuality.

(the Communication Group for the Enhancement of the Status of Women in Egypt) had recognized the importance of the media in their booklet about women's legal rights as a major platform where opinions and attitudes are being shaped, contested and changed. In the booklet the group of activists describes a positive development within the media as a new generation of women have entered the field. As journalists, authors, directors and screenwriters, these women are addressing problems of women in their professional work. However, as the group had cautioned:

These remain individual efforts whose impact on mainstream media representation of women is quite limited. In our view, one main reason for the failure of the mass media to give women their due and to provide them with a forum from which they can express their views is the reluctance of media leaders to provoke the anger of the religious fundamentalists who have come to exert a powerful influence on society. (Communication Group, 1992: 36)

A broad definition of 'the media' would include literature and relates to both the content and the production of books, more precisely the selection of what is published and what is not. Over the past decade more and more attention has been paid to 'Egyptian women's writing' by local and international media and scholarship. Even if the number of women writers has steadily increased, the publication of books had been, until a few years ago, controlled by men. A group of academic and professional Egyptian women from different Arab backgrounds living and working in Cairo decided to establish the first Arab women's publishing house (Nour) in 1993. Ever since its creation Nour has been successfully showing that a group of women can launch an enterprise previously monopolized by men, run it professionally and creatively. The publishing house has encouraged and supported women writers from all over the Arab world, has designed specific research projects carried out by qualified researchers who are being temporarily employed, and has organized the first Arab women's writings conference (Cairo, 1995).

Another entry into the 'world of letters' and a tool to spread ideas and research findings has been the publication of newsletters and magazines by several independent groups and committees belonging to political parties or human rights centres. The publications of human rights centres, such as *People's Rights – Women's Rights* (Legal Rights and Research Centre) and *Sawasiah* (Cairo Institute for Human Rights Studies), are very much concerned with women's issues. Many of the independent groups started their public activism by publishing a magazine or newsletter. Since 1984 Bint Al-Ard has published several issues of a magazine called *Bint Al-Ard*, tackling issues as diverse as working women and the call to return home, education and problems of illiteracy, political participation, cultural values, conditions among rural women, religious extremism, Coptic–Muslim relations, the Palestinians living under occupation, women's feelings and their psychological well-being. The group Al-Mar'a Al-Gedida started to issue their magazine a couple of years later. In the beginning, *Al-Mar'a Al-Gedida* addressed a number of different topics, but later each magazine was devoted to a specific issue, such as 'women and work', 'women and the media' and 'women and violence'. Many of these specific issues became part of wider research projects, sometimes followed with publications and projects aiming for concrete implementation, such as the most recent 'women and violence' project discussed above.

Over the past years, women activists have increasingly recognized the significance of the media in shaping views and attitudes about women, and also in constituting a platform where conservative religious interpretations become normalized. Their struggle with the media has been influenced by the experience that the media can serve as a tool to spread their ideas as well as discredit and attack them. It has also been informed by the realization that the Egyptian media itself does not present a homogeneous entity; it consists of different forms of media (newspapers, magazines, literature, television etc.) and contains different political, ideological and cultural tendencies.

Women's media watch: liberation of mind or increased censorship?

In 1993, a special issue of *Al-Mar'a Al-Gedida* on 'women and the media' was published as the group had continuously been confronted with the way the media shapes public opinion, particularly in matters concerning women. In large part the magazine is based on content analyses undertaken by members of the group, but feature articles are also written by other activists. The content analyses of prominent Egyptian newspapers and magazines, such as *Al-Ahram, Sabah Al-Khair* and *Hawaa,* for example, reveal clichéd depictions of women, focusing on fashion and beauty or issues concerning motherhood and domestic chores. At the end of the analyses it was recommended that women activists should try to encourage a different discourse on the press by writing articles themselves and simultaneously confronting officials within the media with the research findings and their implications. Furthermore, women of Al-Mar'a Al-Gedida emphasized the need to 'create an alternative women's journalism which will be able to know and understand the problems of Egyptian women, especially with regard to those women who have no chance to be heard or mentioned in the pages of current journals' (*Al-Mar'a Al-Gedida,* 1993: 11).

About a year later the group organized a workshop entitled Censorship and Women's Image in the Media at the British Council in Cairo, which attracted a diverse group of people. Three papers were presented,[21] which stimulated an animated discussion. The issue of presentations of violence against women in the media was particularly acute, as Egypt's media had been sensationalizing the story of a rape which took place in a notoriously crowded area of Cairo called Attaba. In the view of many activists this incident showed that *'this woman who was raped on the street was once again raped through the media'*. In the course of the discussion, the idea of a 'women's media watch' was suggested in order to monitor the media, provide counter-images and discourses and eventually change public opinion and attitudes.

Throughout the preparations for the International Women's Forum in Beijing, much work and effort was channelled into the issue of the media in the framework of a committee. The media committee conducted research and wrote papers on theoretical concepts underlying the issue of women in the media, the image of women in the cinema, the image of women in caricature and cartoon, and the image of women in the crime pages.[22] All the studies confirmed the notion that the media presents predominantly negative stereotypes of women. However, a preliminary survey conducted among 250 women of different educational backgrounds revealed that many women are generally unaware of the level of stereotyping of women on TV.

The committee took this discrepancy between their own analysis and the perception of women interviewed as an indication that conservative trends have become internalized by many media consumers, which only strengthened the view among participants in the media group that more concrete efforts need to be exerted to counter the negative impact of the media on public opinion. The media group recommended the establishment of a women's media watch that 'would monitor and ultimately combat all unacceptable images or ideas about women in the media as well as encourage and promote positive initiatives'. In the process of trying to translate this goal into a tangible project it soon became obvious, however, that the lack of definition of what constitutes 'unacceptable images of women' stirred up confusion and dissent among the various participants in the project.

---

[21] Radwan El-Kashif (film director): 'Censorship and Its Relation to the Image of Women in the Media'; Dr Hoda El-Sadda (professor of English literature and women's rights activist): 'The Image of Women in the Media' and Dr Aida Seif El-Dawla (psychiatrist and women's activist): 'Media and its Position on Violence against Women'.

[22] A summary of the various research findings and the recommendations of the media committee can be found in a 1995 booklet prepared by the National NGO Committee for Population and Development (Gender Equity Subcommittee) entitled *The Road from Cairo to Beijing* (pp. 23–34).

It was agreed upon that the media watch should be an independent organization with well-defined goals (monitoring and analysing the media; establishing a database, advocacy work, publication of a newsletter, setting up communication channels and advertising, film and programme production), it would need financial support, an executive administration and full-time employees. However, the media committee could not agree on several issues that remained controversial, such as the priorities and limits of the project. It was not resolved whether the main role and nature of the media watch should be defined as research work, the circulation of progressive ideas or whether it should be conceptualized as militant activism. The structure of a women's media watch was another point of contention: would the project be undertaken by a group of individual activists, by an independent organization, or by a federation of NGOs?

Despite a series of unresolved issues, the final report by the media committee presented to different constituencies within Egypt and at Beijing was well received and appeared not only to show detailed and in-depth research findings but also to provide concrete recommendations which could be implemented and used towards the launching of a women's media watch. Unfortunately, the attempt to implement the carefully researched findings and well-thought-out recommendations failed for several reasons which illustrate some of the pervasive problems within the movement and obstacles for the actual implementation of projects.

After the International Women's Forum in Beijing, conflicts arose around the question of how to proceed, who or what organization would co-ordinate the subsequent activities, and who would participate. These conflicts stalled any activities for some time, until Al-Mar'a Al-Gedida decided to appropriate the co-ordination and to organize a workshop in which they would invite several prominent women intellectuals, activists and artists to present the idea of the media watch. One member of Al-Mar'a Al-Gedida described the events in the following way:

Everybody attacked the idea and drifted away from the main issue, that is, the media watch. I think this happened because the way we introduced the project was not clear enough, it was too general and too vague. Sometimes the language used was too academic and some people did not really understand it. The idea was to have a kind of brainstorming. Well, we stormed and stormed and we were stormed. I remember two women were just screaming: 'What are you talking about, look at women in the countryside, poor women, not such an irrelevant issue as a media watch.'

While the vagueness and lack of clarity might account for some of the negative reactions, more significant, to my mind, is the constant phenomenon of pointing to poverty and harsh living conditions of rural and low-income urban women as being the only legitimate point of discussion and activism. Moreover, there appears to be a recurring dilemma about whom to invite and whom to exclude, as some people might obstruct any constructive discussion by questioning the very basis of any idea, now and then even challenging the very idea that women are subjected to specific forms of discrimination.

The problem of inclusion and exclusion, and the impossible task of reaching any common platform within a group of people sharing very different backgrounds and agendas, became painfully apparent in a two-day workshop organized jointly by Al-Mar'a Al-Gedida and the British Council in March 1996. It could have been a constructive opportunity and creative encounter, as the organizers had invited an Indian woman activist who had played a crucial role in establishing a women's media watch in India. The Indian activist presented the underlying goals and motivation for the Indian project, but also presented specific tools and methods used not only by the Indian Women's Media Watch, but by several groups all over the world. She emphasized the need to adopt specific goals and methods appropriate to the Egyptian context and encouraged a discussion among the participants of the workshop.

For the purpose of public relations the British Council had invited several mainstream media journalists, TV announcers and various public figures, in addition to a number of women activists. Not surprisingly, a representative of the mainstream press, known for his liberal outlook which sometimes translates into using women's bodies to sensationalize issues and attract the attention of readers, became defensive and questioned the whole project as presenting the basis for new forms of censorship.[23] Much time was spent in responding to his grievances, preventing a more in-depth exchange. But what became even more of an obstacle on the way to concretize the idea of a women's media watch was a dissension among the participants concerning the criteria and frames of reference for assessing and countering images of women. The point of contention surrounded the issue of images of women related to religion, specifically the question of whether to tackle women's images in the media from a secular or religious point of view and whether to include discrimination against Copts as a criterion for monitoring the media.

Members of Al-Mar'a Al-Gedida and other activists who had participated in the workshop expressed their disappointment with the discussions, but stressed that they learned a lot through the presentation of the Indian project and the overall experience of the workshop. Most women

---

[23] While this particular journalist appeared to be concerned about censorship in the widest sense, one aspect of his objections related to the depiction of women's bodies. The question of whether to oppose pornography or to condone it in the name of freedom of expression and freedom of the press constitutes a classic debate among western feminists.

agreed that a women's media watch can only come into being if it is initially built from a small core of activists who, at least, share some basic common assumptions and outlooks. An initial small-scale project could then expand and might be able to accommodate differences without destroying the project.

Until the end of my research no concrete efforts were undertaken to salvage the project, which might be partly explained by Al-Mar'a Al-Gedida's concentrated efforts to expand the 'violence against women' research, while no other group or individual activist has volunteered to continue the project. One might suspect that the difficulty on the level of implementation might be emblematic in a context where specific institutional frames seem to be lacking.

How to measure impact

It has not been an easy task to decide which projects to present and which to leave out among the number of diverse activities taking place. Any attempt to present a picture of the activities carried out by contemporary Egyptian women activists can only remain sketchy and incomplete, but I hope to have been able to outline some specific projects and the wider context in which they take place. It has been an even more difficult task to assess the activities of the women I interviewed as I am aware that one could all too easily misjudge the various efforts by simply looking at the outcome. But how can one evaluate success? How is it possible to assess the impact of women's activism?

What should have become obvious throughout this chapter is that it is not enough simply to consider the achievements and failures of the women's movement with reference to specific projects; one has to consider several other factors, such as government attitudes and policies, the institutional frameworks for policy making and implementation, Islamist discourses and campaigns as well as the impact of international organizations and agendas. Women's activism does not take place in a vacuum and should therefore not be assessed as if it did.

One overall problem seems to be the lack of specific institutional targets in many of the campaigns which, consequently, tend to become diffused. The translation from raising certain issues and suggesting ramifications to actual implementation is impeded by both the state's ambiguity and lack of commitment and the women activists' own failure adequately to retain momentum and display solidarity among themselves. Competition and rivalry – often revolving around the wish to guarantee funding and resources, but also in terms of claims to ideological and political truths – frequently block collective action. In some instances it seems a legitimate question to ask whether some activities remain short lived because they respond more to international agendas than local ones. However, it needs to be stressed that the two might not be mutually exclusive and might, if constructively used, feed into each other.

The way debates around the new marriage contract, FGM and violence against women developed make one point crystal clear: women activists are not just struggling against general obstacles to women's rights, they are also battling against the increased political authority of conservative religious forces and a state that is inevitably caught between the demands of Islamist groups and pressures by the international community. What also becomes obvious is that attempts to increase the political participation of women, another stated goal among many activists, work best on the level of women activists' own political participation. In other words, there is not much women activists can do to increase the number of women voters, as people have become politically apathetic in a system where the election outcomes are predetermined. Nor can they increase the small number of women in the parliament or other decision-making bodies. Perhaps they can help to raise the feminist consciousness of those women who are active within political parties and within the government. But certainly, they make an impact by remaining political actors, challenging prevailing discourses and policies and refusing to give in to conservative interpretations of either the law or religion.

Many women activists, perhaps a declining majority, are still holding on to modernist frameworks (I am tempted to write 'traditional modernist'), and defining their activism in the strict sense of 'rights activism'(rights to education, political participation, work etc.) within the public sphere. Others work from within a dependency paradigm focusing on issues pertaining to political economy while issues bearing on the 'private realm' of the family and home are ignored or only addressed marginally. Debates about the Personal Status Law might be considered an exception, but, as mentioned earlier, laws regulating marriage, divorce and custody have become public issues, rather than constituting a critique of what goes on between a woman and a man within a marriage or during a divorce. 'Politics' is often seen as something apart from 'women's issues' and is generally interpreted as the involvement in activities related to 'formal party politics' or clandestine organizations.

A new generation of women activists have been gradually, but consistently, challenging and unsettling some of the older notions and stipulations belonging to modernist and dependency discourses in which women's situation at home is seen to improve automatically if her public rights are increased. They have managed to rock the boat in which the well-pampered public–private dichotomy has sat comfortably for ages.

By addressing issues such as reproductive health and violence against women these activists have pointed to links between women's oppression at home and in the public realm. It is these women who, in the words of Mervat Hatem, could overcome 'old and tired concepts and roles that cannot be expected to deliver new solutions' (Hatem, 1993: 45).

The expression 'patriarchy' is only rarely used, as it is seen to be too closely linked with western feminism. However, women often make allusions to the multifarious ways in which women are subjected to male domination and oppression. Many activists seem to concur with western liberal feminists in the assumption that the increase in the number of women entering the male-dominated systems, such as those related to education, work and politics, brings a solution to inequality. This notion is not shared by activists critical of both liberal and socialist stipulations and, in their analysis, the various systems themselves need to be changed as they reflect hierarchical autocratic male conceptualizations of power.

In the light of these distinctions it is not surprising that women activists tend to emphasize differences among themselves; however, these divergences are generally perceived and articulated in rather different terms. In a critical reference to another group these differences might be expressed as 'those who sit and talk', 'those who do charity work' or 'those who have no links to the grassroots'. On another level groups identify themselves and each other in terms of their political affiliations and frames of reference for their struggle, their relation towards the state, their perception of and involvement in international movements and events, and their stand towards foreign funding. I shall focus on some of these debates in the following and final chapter, which specifically aims at shedding light on the underlying political culture in which many of the debates within the contemporary women's movement take place.

6   A mirror of political culture in Egypt: divisions and debates among women activists

In Egypt – as in many other post-colonial societies – contestations of identity and authenticity are part and parcel of complex processes of self-definition. Sometimes these contestations take an explicitly political form and are articulated as anti-imperialist positions. This is the case in the debate about foreign funding of local research and development activities, for example, which, in the view of some political actors, is a form of external meddling and interference. As mentioned earlier, the debates about foreign funding have to be set in the context of Egypt being the single largest recipient of aid from the United States after Israel. Moreover, foreign aid ranges from bilateral and multilateral projects to the funding of specific projects at 'the grassroots' by various international funding agencies. Perceptions about international organizations and the value given to international conferences must also be considered in the light of struggles for political independence and especially the rejection of increasing American influence.

However, at other times, debates about identity and authenticity are formulated less in political than in cultural terms. This tendency becomes noticeable in the controversy about the cultural frame of reference for Egyptian women's activism. In chapter 4 I addressed the role of religion as cultural marker with regard to authenticity and identity. At this point I shall concentrate mainly on the dispute about the universality versus specificity of women's rights and the 'culturalization' of many political debates.

I will start by narrating the history of Markaz Dirasat Al-Mar'a Al-Gedida (the New Woman's Research Centre) as a means of illustrating some of the tensions, problems and debates, and how these affect the women's movement. The various recollections and different positions of the founding members of Al-Mar'a Al-Gedida constitute the main resource for this narrative attempt. I shall also consider the positions of new members concerning discussions about more current activism and the organization of the group. Rather than attempt to document the actual events and conflicts, I would like to use this case as an illustration of the problems and rifts both within the women's movement and, more broadly, within contemporary Egyptian political culture. I will continue the chapter by exploring in greater detail the concerns surrounding foreign funding and debates about universality versus specificity by considering the positions of women activists from a broader spectrum of opinion.

The past contested: histories of Al-Mar'a Al-Gedida

Issues and debates among the 'old new women'

All founding members of Al-Mar'a Al-Gedida interviewed stressed that their initial motivation for meeting and discussing women's issues was related to '*the way the whole society developed*'. Most women activists came from the political left and had been, to varying degrees, involved in the student movement in the 1970s: '*In the beginning we were six or seven women. We were looking for change, for social justice. The whole thing of women's issues seemed to be part of a broad mosaic.*' The women stress that it was not particularly correct to speak just about women's issues at the time, but they initially came together and sought new ways to express their discontent with party politics and the omission of women's rights. Most of them were married to progressive men, and they had realized that on a personal level change does not necessarily follow from progressive political ideas. Nawal El-Saʿdawi's work was mentioned on several occasions as having influenced their thinking, but it did not provide satisfying answers to the numerous questions posed by the group of friends involved in political activism. Gradually they departed from their initial conviction that women's rights are best pursued in the context and organizations of the wider socialist struggle:

One of us said that we should question the whole notion of women's issues being part of a mosaic. We started a period of investigating this question. We studied and discussed the history of the women's movement and read a lot. This made us realize that fighting for justice and independence does not necessarily mean that women's issues will be solved. Algeria and Palestine were very valid examples. Algerian women were pushed back after the country gained independence. Palestinian women always had to struggle to have women's issues included in the political agendas of their organizations and parties. Male political activists always considered women's issues as secondary to the national struggle. We had informal contacts with Palestinian women. We were not organized as a group, but we met regularly at each others' homes. People started to ask us: 'What is it that you want to say? What is so different?' So we started to publish a newsletter in 1986. We got the material and we started to negotiate the name of the group. Because of Qasim Amin's book we chose Al-Mar'a Al-Gedida [the New Woman]. This was one of the only two times that we decided on something by voting. I was not so much in favour of this name, but, fair enough, the book symbolized many things for women. (Summaya D.)

Two founding members stressed that the idea of working on a magazine was triggered by another publication of the newly established group, Bint Al-Ard (Daughter of the Land) in Mansoura, after the Israeli invasion of Lebanon in 1982: '*We thought that this was a really interesting idea and we pursued it. And we were also trying to get to know this group, which was quite radical, but not very clear on the feminist question. So we started to make the first issue of our own magazine.*'

A number of issues emerge in the quotation from Summaya D., which still continue to be of relevance. I have already discussed the ongoing debate on the relationship between women's activism and wider political struggles, such as the struggle for national independence and struggle for social justice in chapter 2. In the previous chapter I explored notions about public and private spheres, and showed how women's public rights, such as access to education, political participation and work, have continued to gain legitimacy at the expense of women's rights in the so-called private sphere (the Personal Status Law regulating marriage, divorce and child custody, domestic violence and reproductive rights). But Summaya D. also addresses the issue of the organizational form and structure of women's groups and particularly the attempt to create independent and democratic structures. I will return to the debates concerning questions about the internal structure and processes of decision making. At this point, however, I shall explore different facets of ideological and political differences which also include the question of self-definition.

The emergence of the group Al-Mar'a Al-Gedida and the subsequent publication of their magazine need to be contextualized within the conjuncture both of political experiences related to the specific historical developments at the time and individual personal experiences of the founding members. The political experiences that gave birth to the attempt to establish an autonomous women's group are related to the disintegration of the student movement, the general crisis of the political left and the widespread disillusion with hierarchical male-dominated political structures. But the idea of an autonomous women's group did also develop in an atmosphere in which the pioneering activist Nawal El-Sa'dawi, and to some extent the members of Bint Al-Ard in Mansoura, had articulated their anger about women's oppression in a way that engaged people across the political spectrum. Most of the founding members did not only bring with them leftist revolutionary ideas, but also a disillusionment with the possibilities of working with leftist men, especially in the framework of traditional hierarchical party or organizational structures.

Some of the women who created 'the New Woman' had split off from existing socialist groups who, in their view, did not give adequate consideration to questions related to women's liberation. A few women stressed that their personal experiences with leftist 'progressive' men – fathers, brothers, friends and husbands – added to their conviction that a socialist ideology does not automatically involve a commitment to gender equality. Yet most of the founding members were still deeply entrenched in Marxist ideology, so that their feminism included socialism. In other words, most founding members of Al-Mar'a Al-Gedida did not abandon socialism, but abandoned the 'double militancy' of fighting for and against socialist organizations dominated by male activists. Tensions arose over the way in which socialism and feminism could be merged in terms of concrete approaches, goals and strategies.

One of the activists, who eventually left the group and established a new group called Ma'an (Together) in the beginning of the 1990s, maintains that the final schism and break-up of the group was rooted in the existence of different orientations:

From the very beginning, we were really divided into two orientations: one group was more interested in working-class women's problems; the other group was more engaged in their own personal problems, their identity, and their problems with their husbands. In other words, they were more concerned with self-expression. Women like me, who were more relaxed with themselves, wanted to be in interaction with wider problems. (Leila I.)

This view can be linked to the discussion in the previous chapter about diverging perceptions and definitions of 'the political' and 'the public' versus 'the private'. It is reflective of traditional leftist discourse which locates women's activism within the wider framework of class struggle at the same time as it dismisses concerns about women's subordination within the family, problems related to health (both physical and psychological), personal relationships and sexuality as liberal bourgeoisie concerns. Moreover, this view seems to suggest that it is only insecure women, those suffering from personal and psychological problems, who would relate to issues concerning women's self-expression. Debates among members of Al-Mar'a Al-Gedida about the definition of what women's activism and politics in general entail also took place on a wider scale and continue to be conducted within the women's movement at large and also among the political left, Islamist groups and within the government.

Opinions diverge concerning differences at the initial organizational stage, but most members agree that they were united on many issues and constituted a group of women who tried to find ways of approaching these issues that differed from the methods of those around them. This became particularly evident in the campaign around the Personal Status Law in 1985, which brought together activists from across the political spectrum. Even at that time, founding members of Al-Mar'a Al-Gedida felt that their agenda differed from that of most other activists. As Summaya D. put it:

Concerning the reformed Personal Status Laws, we believed that we should suggest an alternative that will grant equal rights to women. We thought that we could negotiate something. But we were in the absolute minority. Opposition even came from progressive women. Elites, if you want to use the word, middle-class and upper-class women. This is something that we have encountered until today: the accusation that what we are doing is alien, that it is outside of our culture. We have always heard something like this. Our interaction with, I do not like the word, 'grassroots' women is usually better than that with women from the elite. This situation has been playing a very important role in the development of our group. We are on trial all the time. In the beginning of our work, the accusations were very different from now though. First they told us that we were too radical. Then it was our agenda which did not reflect the reality of women's problems. They also told us that religion plays an important role in life and that we did not give religion sufficient consideration, because we were all outsiders. Today they say that we are all too western, or that we stress 'non-priorities'. These are the polite accusations. But our experience has proven that we are close to the right track. We are activists, and activists need to have a vision which has to be ahead of what exists. The reactions we have received from people who have worked with us show that we touch on important issues which are of concern for many women in Egypt, such as decision making, polygamy, violence etc. No, our language is not alien, and the things we talk about are real.

Whether articulated in terms of 'working outside the culture', 'being removed from religion' or being 'too western', these various accusations give evidence of the continuous contestation about legitimate cultural frames of reference for women's activism in particular and political activism in general. Linked to the controversy about cultural frames of reference is the debate about 'universality versus specificity' which occupies not only the Egyptian women's movement but also the human rights movement and general political discourse. Especially during the preparations for the International Women's Forum in Beijing (1995), but also earlier, during the International Conference for Population and Development (1994), women's and human rights activists discussed at length their positions on the question and content of cultural specificity, and the merits and perils of universalism. This debate occupies a significant space within contemporary Egyptian political culture, as I will try to show later in the chapter.

Going back to Summaya D.'s account of the history of Al-Mar'a Al-Gedida, it becomes obvious that her formula of merging socialism and feminism implies a reference to patriarchy:

Most people insist to address the issue of equal pay and women's right to work, even if many women do not even want to work. It has all to do with the make-up of political parties. A major part of them are men. They are the other half of this society. If you talk about oppressive relations between men and women, you will always evoke the anger of some men who are not sympathetic.

The founding members concur that many of their former colleagues, friends and comrades during the student movement started to feel threatened the moment Al-Mar'a Al-Gedida started to address the issue of male power and women's oppression. This experience is not unique as, outside of the frame of class and nationalist struggle, feminist agendas continue to pose threats to male power elites all over the world. In the West, the second-wave feminism of the 1960s was characterized by similar disillusionments with male-dominated political struggles. Within Al-Mar'a Al-Gedida there certainly existed differences concerning an emphasis on either patriarchy or class oppression, but even if some founding members construct these differences as insurmountable now, it appears that all members acknowledged the significance of a complex system of oppression related to imperialism, capitalism and patriarchy.

Another point that emerges is that inherent to many of the charges brought forth against the group are class-related tensions. Typically, most of the secular political activists in contemporary Egypt are part of an educated middle class, which might differ greatly in terms of income, but overall do enjoy certain privileges and move in intellectual circles. Curiously, many of those who are most outspoken in their allegations of elitism and being removed from 'the masses' are only connected to working-class Egyptians and 'the poor' through their rhetoric, while their activism, lifestyles, networks and friendships centre around the educated middle class. The tendency to denounce each other as elitist and not being grounded in 'the grassroots' cannot be easily dismissed and certainly reflects some of the gaps between the concerns of the majority of Egyptian women and the issues, debates and campaigns of the women's movement. However, what needs to be looked at more carefully is the way an apologetic populism simply functions to discredit different factions in the movement while not necessarily furthering any link with the so-called 'grassroots'. This is not to suggest that 'grassroots' activism does not exist, but what needs to be stressed is that those who are fiercest in accusing others of being removed from the concerns of 'the grassroots' are not necessarily any closer themselves. This tendency exists across the political spectrum and is as widespread among the political left and human rights organizations as among women activists.[1]

The various accusations directed against the group increased the tensions within it. As one woman recalls: '*Every accusation ended in an enor-*

---

[1] Heba El-Kholy (1998) addresses the gap between concern, problems and practices of poor Egyptian women and Egyptian women activists. See specifically 'Marriage Negotiations and Transactions' (chapter 6).

mous frustration which we took out on each other.' The women had initially decided to remain a closed group, but after the first magazine part of the group felt that they should open up. The only problem was that the criteria adapted for inclusion in effect excluded everyone except the original members themselves. Soon, the group of women felt that their activities should not be restricted to a magazine and to discussions only. Hania K. recalls: '*We felt that we have to go into communities. However, in the beginning, this idea was very marginal. We were all professionals. We were a small group of women and did not have natural access to grassroots.'*

Attempts to shift focus to work with the grassroots characterized Egypt's wider political culture during the late 1980s. This tendency, which coincided with a growing NGO sector, enticed the group to work on illiteracy, health consultation and education. These different experiences eventually led to a workshop on women and adult education. The most pressing question was how adult education could be conceptualized and delivered in a progressive way. Al-Mar'a Al-Gedida designed a joint workshop with the Arab Research Centre (Menial) in the mid-1980s, out of which came their first publication funded jointly by Al-Mar'a Al-Gedida and the Arab Research Centre and involved the donation of personal money.

Following the publication of the booklet about women and adult education, a severe crisis paralysed the group's activities for some time and led to the consequent split of the group in 1989. This rather sensitive episode is remembered in various ways by the women I interviewed, but all share a sense of pain and frustration when recounting the series of events and the causes leading to the finally unbridgeable schism. One of the members who supported the idea of expanding as an organization and to accept foreign funding, albeit under certain conditions and from particular donors, recalls:

Around the time of the discussion about funding, three of us started to work as individuals to engage in funded projects which were community based. I was in one of them, working as a doctor. For a while we did not realize what kind of split we were living. I was working in a childcare centre in Waeli,[2] and I also worked as a psychiatrist in Ain Shams University. This funny thing happened: we would go home and discuss how difficult it was to access local communities for our work with Al-Mar'a Al-Gedida. For a long time, it did not occur to me that my workplace actually gave me access to a local community. In one of the meetings I made the suggestion that we should use the various projects we were involved in professionally for our activism. Some members refused the idea to access local communities via our paid jobs, even if no one of us actually questioned the idea of our political work being strictly voluntary work. It did not follow from accepting

---

[2] Waeli is a low-income area in the north of Cairo. Aside from a core of two or three families which had settled a long time ago in the area, the majority of the population consists of rural migrants.

and receiving funding that members would get paid. Up till now, except for an administrative person, who is not a member, all work in the group is voluntary. We raised the issue in Al-Mar'a Al-Gedida on behalf of many people. Everyone followed. During this process grew the realization that we need an organization and financial support, so we started to apply for funding.

Those members who left the group stress the original ideological and political differences as decisive in the final crisis. For Leila I., who was the driving force behind the establishment of Ma'an in 1991, a couple of years after she and other members had left the original group, the crisis was a result of a political conflict over foreign funding and grassroots work. According to her account, she and some other activists refused the idea of foreign funding altogether and also opposed the '*mixing of professional working experiences with political militancy*'.

However, she acknowledges that the final clash was also related to the very structure of the organization: '*We were a shella, a group of friends, and we never managed to develop a system or structure that could accommodate differences. It could have happened in a democratic way if we had created the necessary mechanisms and tools, but we based everything on our solidarity as friends. There was also the problem that some of us did all the work while it was appropriated in the name of the whole group. This stirred up bad feelings too.*' Some activists reflect that, in retrospect, personal relationships among group members and individual definitions of self played a more prominent role in the intense confrontations than was recognized at the time. Founding members of Al-Mar'a Al-Gedida who continued to work in the group argue that the issue of foreign funding and the dissolution of the previously strict separation between grassroots political activism and professional work were only pretexts for some of the clashes, which were actually based on personal differences between friends. From my interviews with both members who left the group and those who carried on, it became obvious that there were multiple reasons for the clash and that women who eventually left the group had different reasons for doing so.

The controversy over keeping professional and voluntary work separate, as well as the question of whether to accept foreign funding, remain among the most vexed issues within the wider NGO movement. The major conflict within Al-Mar'a Al-Gedida took place in a context where there was both a rapid spread of NGOs in all kinds of sectors (such as public health, literacy, development, human rights and women's issues) and an increased influence of international organizations, especially UN and other donor agencies. The end of the eighties also marked the beginning of a period of increased professionalization of the voluntary sector.

Regrouping and new priorities

The clash within the group and the subsequent departure of four members involved intense and heated discussions among the remaining women, who were forced to confront controversial subjects and to articulate their positions. The group spent much effort in addressing previously ignored subjects, such as women's reproductive health and violence against women, but also worked on more traditional subjects such as labour laws, political participation and legal rights. While foreign funding had been accepted in principle, the women of Al-Mar'a Al-Gedida distinguish between 'good' and 'bad' donors and generally prefer to work with smaller, politically less controversial organizations such as the Dutch NOVIB and refuse to deal with funding agencies such as USAID.

Many of the founding members view the preparations for the ICPD as a turning-point in their efforts to create a feminist platform and to move from more research-oriented activism to project-oriented grassroots work. Before the ICPD, women's organizations had largely remained isolated from each other, except for a few instances of co-operation, which were limited to personal exchanges between women from different organizations or the exchange of publications. The *intifadah*, the Gulf war and the passing of privatization laws, among other things, brought the various organizations and groups together for a brief moment before they dispersed again to follow their own activities (Seif El-Dawla & Ibrahim, 1995: 115).[3] Hania K. sums up the period leading up to the ICPD as follows:

After the clash, we regrouped ourselves and tried to put some strategy into our work. Our main aim was to reach out and create a feminist platform. We began to work through human rights organizations and tried to put issues forward. We worked on this for two years, at the end of which we made a petition on the convention of all forms of discrimination.[4] Some were still hesitant to put down their names. For some time, we were mostly engaged in networking, which began to bear fruit during the preparations for the ICPD.

[3] Initially, Egyptian women activists were not very interested in the ICPD. During the first preparatory meeting the Egyptian delegation merely consisted of government representatives, and Egyptian NGOs were represented by an official from the Ministry of Social Affairs. After this meeting, the international community asked Egypt to involve NGOs directly, which resulted in the official nomination of five NGO representatives. One of these representatives was Aziza Hussein, head of the Egyptian Association for Family Planning and women's activist. She eventually became head of the Egyptian NGO forum and accepted all organizations as NGOs, even if they were only registered as non-profit organizations or civic companies rather than officially being registered as PVOs or NGOs in the Ministry of Social Affairs (El-Dawla & Ibrahim, 1995: 115).
[4] The UN Convention on the Elimination of all Forms of Discrimination against Women (CEDAW) was mandated by the United Nations in 1981. Egypt, like many other Muslim countries, has ratified the CEDAW with several reservations. For a detailed analysis see Mayer (1995).

We felt that this was a victory. Women began to organize themselves and raise new issues. This created more space. We created a platform in allowing to discuss various new issues and make them acceptable. In this platform you did not have any of the leftist organizations, except for one Nasserite activist representing the Arab Lawyers' Union. So this experience lacked certain elements and actors in the political scene.

In the period preceding the ICPD, Markaz Dirasat Al-Mar'a Al-Gedida[5] (the New Woman's Research Centre) concentrated on research that would give more evidence of *'Egyptian women's own perceptions of women's rights'*. In this process the group attacked the government's position on family planning and development, which, in their view, had been reduced to fertility control. The introduction of the notion of reproductive rights caused a great deal of controversy and much resentment among other women activists as it was perceived to be an issue imposed by the 'West'. However, activists from the group rejected this accusation, since they had based their attack on the concerns of women 'from the grassroots'. They also addressed the impact of privatization, structural adjustment and the new labour laws. Among many other projects, the group wrote a paper analysing the state and international agendas, and their dominant discourses, which, in the view of one member of the group, *'base their success story on women as cheap labour'*. In this paper the group addresses the informal and rural sector and also discusses the plight of women in domestic service.

During the actual conference the group was able to discuss with activists from all over the world the problem of governmental and international agendas compromising women's rights. The issue of national and international authorities neglecting or sidetracking women's issues was just one of many problems which were discussed for the first time within a larger forum. The preparations for the ICPD and the conference itself created space for many women activists to address previously taboo topics (abortion, violence, reproductive rights) or to discuss issues of common concern (equality before the law, political participation, structural adjustment, the Personal Status and Nationality laws) with women from different political orientations and backgrounds. As Seif El-Dawla and Ibrahim describe the time of preparation for the conference:

Women started to become interested in subjects which usually had not been part of their agendas. All over the country workshops were organized in which these issues were addressed and facts presented.[6] These encounters were very fruitful

---

[5] The group registered as Markaz Dirasat Al-Mar'a Al-Gedida (the New Woman's Research Centre) in the beginning of 1991, but continues to refer to itself as Al-Mar'a Al-Gedida.

[6] Once a group finished its research during the preparations for the ICPD, the co-ordinator of the gender task force organized meetings in different areas (focal points). The group

and exciting and gave hope for a re-emergence of a movement that was restricted
for so many years. Organizations met which had not known about each other
before. Agreements were found in areas where organizations thought they would
stand alone. At the same time, it became clear that there were some areas in which
no agreement could be found, like the analysis of the role of the state, the attitude
towards Islamists, the role of religion and political parties. Women did not try to
overcome these differences, but respected them. Before and during the conference, no one wanted to sell out these exciting and long missed encounters for a
consensus which would never have been obtained anyhow. (1995: 115)

The feelings of hope and success before and during the ICPD in Cairo
were soon shattered by a severe backlash triggered by the government, the
Islamists and certain actors within the NGO movement. Whereas the
organizing bodies for the ICPD had been very lenient and tolerant with
regard to the incorporation of all groups, even those not officially registered as NGOs, the government and the nominated organizing committee for the International Women's Forum in Beijing, headed by Hoda
Badran, put great emphasis on the legal definition of NGOs and on their
registration at the Ministry of Social Affairs. This approach had the consequence of excluding groups such as the New Woman's Research
Centre, which had circumvented the law of association by registering as
civic companies. The very location of the ICPD had also increased its
accessibility for activists and groups as they did not have to apply for
travel grants as was the case for Beijing. Moreover, the Egyptian government's public display of its commitment to gender equality was certainly
influenced by the wish to 'look good' in the eyes of international organizations and the world media.

While not being able to officially participate as an NGO, the group continued to be involved in the preparations for Beijing and ensured the
participation of individual members, especially those of the younger generation, who had joined the group shortly after the ICPD. Manal H., for
example, was working professionally with one of the older Al-Mar'a Al-
Gedida members and found out about the group and its problems from
her colleague:

*I was very sympathetic to their cause, and I felt that they were treated very unfairly in the
aftermath of the ICPD, because they were not officially registered as an NGO. When I
started to attend their meetings, I became fascinated with the organization. They were
working on a project about women and work, that is, the discrimination against women
doing menial work. I had never seen any kind of research like this in Egypt. My idea of*

that had done the research on a specific topic would present and discuss its findings, a
process which often led to modifications. In these encounters, Cairene women activists
encountered women from all over the country and, for some, these meetings and debates
with 'grassroots' women from the countryside and small towns were much more fruitful
and productive than the usual discussions among activists and scholars in Cairo.

an NGO was a bunch of old ladies sitting at a table drinking tea and doing charity work. When I started to go regularly, they had just started to work on a new project about women and violence in preparation for Beijing. I first did not know how to join them, but we were all brainstorming for the project and we formulated the questionnaire together.

The younger members stress that, despite the controversy about the International Women's Forum in Beijing, they were able to learn a lot about women's rights activism world-wide and gained great confidence for their own activism by participating in the preparations for Beijing. As mentioned in the previous chapter, most of the older members would have preferred to continue to work on labour rights in preparation for Beijing. However, this particular subject was allocated to another group by the Egyptian Preparatory Committee for the Beijing Forum, co-ordinated by Rabtat Al-Mar'a Al-'Arabiyya (the Alliance of Arab Women). Instead, Al-Mar'a Al-Gedida decided to work on violence, an issue '*not too many people wanted to touch*'.[7]

The Beijing conference was received with much less enthusiasm than the ICPD as the Egyptian NGO forum became much less supportive and co-operative and the government imposed greater restrictions and more conservative interpretations of the laws. Nevertheless, women of Al-Mar'a Al-Gedida view the gains of the ICPD as irreversible, since they feel that they have gained strength from working with the grassroots. In their view the ICPD helped to put issues forward, to research and discuss them. After the ICPD, efforts had to be diverted in that the existing researched material had to be translated into concrete programmes. However, as Seif El-Dawla and Ibrahim (1995) point out, partnership between NGOs and the government in implementing the ICPD plan of action often takes the form of NGOs carrying the burden of service provisions which the state fails to provide. Moreover, political compromises on the part of the government, like those related to FGM, reveal that the government's commitment to the empowerment of women diminished after the ICPD (ibid.: 116).

Generations and political culture: what kind of organization?

Throughout my interviews with current members of Al-Mar'a Al-Gedida, differences between the older and the younger generation were

---

[7] The Egyptian National NGO Committee for Population and Development (NCPD) decided to work towards implementation of the ICPD action programme in preparation for the Beijing conference. A sub-committee on gender equality was responsible for making sure that Beijing projects would be action oriented (NCPD, 1995: 7). Several women activists criticized the decision-making process related to the preparations for Beijing as they perceived it to be less democratic that the preparations for the ICPD.

pointed out to me on several occasions. Women of the older generation mainly relate the differences to distinct political backgrounds: '*The things we, the older generation, talk about grew out of our long political work and experience. Women of the new generation, on the other hand, have a basic instinct for justice. They are middle-class women with their heart on the right spot, they are democratic and do not have to deal with our initial questions when we worked politically.*' Another difference of the younger generation, as perceived by the founding members, is the greater affinity to religious discourse and practice, while the older generation feels more thoroughly secular.

Differences in attitude towards religion and political work in general are certainly linked to developments within Egyptian political culture. The student movement of the 1970s provided the background and arena for the founding members' initial political involvement. Politics, at that time, was full of promise for a brighter future. Political militancy was widely accepted and many parents supported their children in their struggles. Progressive leftist ideas shaped the secular outlook of these women, despite their recognition of differences within the older generation with respect to attitude towards religion.

Today, with leftist organizations increasingly losing appeal to Egypt's youth, the most visible movement is the Islamist one. In this context, young women who are not attracted to Islamist movements generally lack models for political involvement. They might be well educated and trained in work related to development, but often lack a political consciousness or framework. The overall shift towards greater religious observance and practice is reflected in younger women's stronger affiliation with religion. Personal trajectories appear to weigh heavily in the variety of reasons why members of the new generation joined a women's organization. As pointed out in chapter 3, younger women activists in contemporary Egypt were often initially motivated by personal forms of oppression which then led to a wider political consciousness.

Internal differences concerning decision making, organizational structure and leadership may also be found across the generational divide. The group is non-hierarchical in the sense that there is no organizational rationale for hierarchy, but both young and old members told me that some hierarchical relationships do exist. Some of the founding members think that '*some people are more committed than others. It is partly a matter of time allocation, but also where people live.*' Hoda A., one of the activists of the older generation, describes the decision-making process and internal structure of Markaz Dirasat Al-Mar'a Al-Gedida as follows:

If there is something that needs a decision, we discuss it. Our budget, all our programmes, all the issues we tackle are decided collectively. The same process takes place for deciding who goes to which event, like conferences abroad, for instance. But we do not vote, we have to reach an agreement, there has to be a consensus. If the disagreement is strong, we suspend the matter. If it is very urgent, we have to discuss it up to a point that we come to an agreement. People take charge of certain activities and report back to the group. Everybody is afraid of hierarchy. The lack of hierarchy, on the other hand, is an attractive thing. It allows for transaction and transparency. No one dares to represent the group without approval from the others. That does not mean that things go smoothly: there are some people who are more committed than others. The more dangerous thing is that some people feel more that it's their group than others. For me, if I walk into Al-Mar'a Al-Gedida, I feel it's my home. If I think something urgent is up, I call for a meeting, but until now, the members of the new generation would call us, the older generation, to tell us that we need a meeting. There is an underlying assumption that the older generation has more decision-making power, that it has more rights. (Hoda A.)

Most of the younger members recognize a difference in authority between the older and younger generation, but no woman perceived this to be a problem reflecting anti-democratic tendencies in the group. Rather, younger members generally feel that political experience and age grant the older members a certain degree of authority. Instead of complaints concerning hidden hierarchies, some of the younger members expressed their dissatisfaction with the constant process of consensus making, which they perceive as a bar to getting things done. Manar R. told me that the value of democratic decision making grew out of the political experiences of the women of the older generation, but does not necessarily constitute a priority for her: '*Sometimes I would prefer greater hierarchy and clarity of who is responsible for what. We spend so much time trying to take decisions that it can get very frustrating.*' Manar R. and Ola N., for instance, would prefer '*more control and less attempts for consensus making*'. However, both agree with the general ideals of the group and feel it provides the only forum where they can discuss ideas freely. Another new member, Siham E., on the other hand, very much appreciates the '*system of horizontal responsibilities in which there is no boss. They taught me the true meaning of democracy. This is why I could not work with any other group now.*'

After Beijing the group decided to stop new membership and take some time to reorganize itself and re-evaluate its strategies and organizational structure. Various members believe that there is a crisis and a need to discuss certain concepts, such as the cultural frame of the struggle (particularly the group's attitude towards religious approaches to women's rights), responsibilities, job descriptions, alliances and the simultaneous involvement in several organizations at the same time. A point of tension has emerged in recent years as some members have become part of or even established other groups, which also work on women's issues. In this context the issue of 'representativity' has been raised, that is, the question whether members who represent other organizations in national or international fora can simultaneously represent the New Woman's Research Centre.

What should have become clear in this rather detailed narrative is that the issues and debates within Al-Mar'a Al-Gedida did not take place in a political void. They mark shifts in social and political developments over the past decade, such as the general crisis of the political left, the consistent build-up of Islamist constituencies and an increased influence of international organizations and funding agencies. As much as there were personal aspects and individual misgivings responsible for some of the conflicts witnessed by the group, we find that tensions, controversies and issues reflect concerns of the broader political culture in Egypt. The emergence of new forms of organizations without the existence of widely accepted models for democratic structures involves a long process of experimentation and innovation. This process, as can be seen in the case of Al-Mar'a Al-Gedida, requires long-term commitment and may involve painful experiences. But it is also through these often painful experiences and political processes that long-established forms of authoritarian decision making and hierarchical organizational structures can be challenged and new ways of organizing envisioned.

Ma'an: together yet apart

Parallel to the developments and changes within Al-Mar'a Al-Gedida, a new group started to emerge around the very issues that had led to the split. Political disappointment, economic hardships and personal problems delayed the establishment of Markaz Dirasat Al-Mar'a Ma'an (the women's research centre 'Ma'an', meaning 'together') for a few years. In the early 1990s, one of the activists who had left Al-Mar'a Al-Gedida started to recruit men and women interested in a centre which would engage in gender-related research from a Marxist feminist perspective, would be strictly based on voluntary work and, most importantly, would not accept any foreign funding.

A relative and supporter provided an apartment with a library and slowly friends and politically like-minded people started to meet on a regular basis to discuss their visions, strategies and priorities for research and for grassroots work. As in the early days of Al-Mar'a Al-Gedida, the new group started by discussing the history of the Egyptian women's movement:

We had lots of young activists who would dismiss early activists like Hoda Sha'rawi as bourgeois. They had no idea about their role in the 1919 revolution. We organized a seminar on our history, because it is important to know it and be proud of it. They have to understand and realize why they are different from the earlier movement. Our initial discussions were very important for the seminars which followed, like the one on women and ideology. Here we looked at Marxist, feminist and Islamist ideologies. What makes it difficult is that some people joined us later and we cannot start from scratch every time. So we try to discuss with new people on an individual basis. (Leila I.)

In addition to a series of seminars and workshops, the centre is involved in several grassroots projects among female workers in various factories and among university students. As Ma'an does not accept any financial support from foreign donors, all the work is carried out on a voluntary basis and very few financial means are available to conduct any projects. Most members are struggling economically themselves, which makes it very difficult to sustain regular work and meetings: '*This is the contradiction of the group. We are all volunteers in a country where people have to work more than nine hours a day. People are penniless for most of the time, so they become really tense.*' The financially more stable members tend to contribute financially to pay the ongoing expenses, and membership fees vary according to financial means. One magazine addressing the problems of Egyptian working-class women was published on a very low budget by asking friends to help in designing and publishing it. A second issue about women and poverty was in the making towards the end of my research.

Ma'an remains one of the few strongholds of opposition against foreign funding in an environment in which, despite constant criticism of people who are funded, competition over funding is routine. Even those who criticize Ma'an's attitude over foreign funding, its effectiveness and general politics often acknowledge the integrity, commitment and effort of a group of people trying to work in a self-sufficient manner. For many other activists, especially those of the left, there is a big gap between rhetoric and practice. One often finds those who were too late in the rush for funding accusing others of having sold out by becoming dependent on foreign aid. This is a problem that plagues more constituencies than just the women's movement: it is a widespread phenomenon among political activists in the human rights movement, and among researchers of various political orientations.

Foreign funding: Egypt's post-colonial dilemma

While the heat of the discussions about foreign funding seems to have subsided in the light of widespread acceptance of it (especially since the preparations for both the International Conference on Population and Development in Cairo and the International Women's Forum in Beijing), it is still one of the 'hot topics' and among the main weapons for denunciation within the women's and the wider NGO movement. The ongoing controversy about foreign funding is symptomatic of contradictions inherent in post-colonial Egypt. This is mainly because the national struggle for total independence from imperialist powers is paralleled by new economic dependencies, often interpreted as neo-colonial configurations. This dilemma is certainly not unique to Egypt and poses an ongoing problem for many post-colonial societies. However, Egypt's obvious economic dependence on American financial aid in light of the USA's support for Israel makes it a particularly pressing issue.

Throughout my research I detected many nuances in this debate, which does not only take place between those who accept foreign funding and those who do not. What have increasingly become a matter of discussion are questions concerning whom to accept as a 'good donor', whom to reject as corrupt or 'politically incorrect', how much funding to accept, how to allocate funds and last but not least, how to justify accepting funds. Yet, Salwa F., a younger member of Rabtat Al-Mar'a Al-'Arabiyya, does not believe in the distinction between 'good' and 'bad' funders and rejects what she perceives to be a great level of hypocrisy involved:

The whole issue of foreign funding is really creating lots of problems. I very much respect the few groups who have declared from the beginning that they don't want foreign funding. The problem is that they are not very active, because of the very lack of funds. At least they have a clear position until now. But what I do not like are all the groups that are accepting funding and accusing others of accepting funding, because of the particular source. I find this ridiculous. One cannot judge whether the Dutch are better than the Germans, or the British better than the Americans. This is stupid for me, and it is consuming lots of energy. I do not think that this is going to get us anywhere. If you have accepted any funding, you do not have the legitimacy of accusing anyone else of accepting it. Inside one funding organization you could have different kinds of people: some could be part of intelligence agencies [and] others not, some could be more sensitive to our concerns and others are not. In other words, even within particular organizations there are differences and one cannot label them easily 'good' or 'bad'. All this is not very healthy.

As a woman activist who also works as a professional in a funding agency (UNICEF) Salwa F. is in direct daily contact with 'both sides'. However, she makes her position clear: '*Of course, the ideal situation would be no foreign funding at all, because most of the agencies have their requirements and their conditions.*' One of the frequent examples given to illustrate that funders are insensitive to local needs and impose their agendas unreflectively are the gender-training packages provided by western organizations. Many of those who are using these packages to train researchers and development workers call for the creation of locally relevant packages, because the packages used today '*are based on the western feminist movement and its problems. They are imposed on us without considering our specific context and history*' (Mona S.).

Unlike Salwa F., most of the other women I interviewed make distinctions between donor organizations. Those organizations based in countries perceived to be politically 'less threatening', 'less imperialist' and 'more progressive' in their politics towards the Third World are labelled as 'good'. Another feature of a 'good' funding agency as opposed to a 'bad' one is the level of freedom or control they impose on the receiving organization. In other words, those funding agencies that seem to respond more directly to the needs of Egyptian organizations without trying to impose their own agenda are much more acceptable to most activists.[8]

Even if the age of an activist is not the only variable in a particular woman's attitude towards funding, it is obvious that there are generational differences. While the middle generation (those who grew out of the leftist student movement in the 1970s) still have a great deal of trouble justifying the acceptance of foreign funding (and some still refuse), the older and younger generation do seem to have less trouble with the issue. Many of the younger activists seem to be more pragmatically oriented than their older counterparts. There might be several explanations for this difference, the most obvious being the difference in formative experiences and the transformation of the general political atmosphere between the 1970s and 1990s. Another factor is certainly the deterioration of the economic situation in Egypt, which forces everyone to be more pragmatic.

Also crucial with regard to the increase of pragmatic views towards funding is the general professionalization of advocacy-related work. This tendency has been on the rise in the 1990s and started to become the main model for any sort of activism. Human rights organizations, for instance, have mushroomed in recent years, and increasingly demand skilled researchers, professional lawyers and social workers. Another example can be found in the field of health care, where a number of politically active female medical doctors have been addressing women's reproductive rights, thereby combining their professional insights with women's activism.

Parallel to an increased sense of pragmatism towards foreign funding, an inclination to consider capital from within Egypt for funding purposes has also emerged. Especially among some of the older, less radical activists, there has been a move to take advantage of local resources as potential alternatives to foreign funders:

---

[8] On the scale of 'good' and 'bad' USAID ranges on the far side of 'bad'. The Ford Foundation has improved its reputation in recent years and moved to the centre of the scale, together with UN-related organizations such as UNICEF. The German GTZ is doing a bit better in its position towards 'good', while the Norwegian, Dutch and Danish funding agencies are certainly doing best.

First I refused to take money from others, but later I realized that funds are important. Until now, only a few organizations have the capability of collecting money from the community. We now developed the idea of a big fund-raising event to be held by the end of this year. Our NGO is serving women and therefore the community at large. People with money need to be convinced by the urgency of our work. I think we don't have the legitimacy if we only collect money from foreign donors. It's our own community which should give us the legitimacy. Until now, we have membership dues and donations from Egyptians, especially from the business sector. But I constantly have to go to people, show them our agenda and ask them to contribute financially. They should understand that this is a huge agenda which needs lots of effort and support. (Bahiga H.)

This particular activist's attitude to funding and her attempts to obtain sufficient funds from 'within the community' need to be contextualized in the specific social milieu of the membership of the Alliance of Arab Women, to which Bahiga H. belongs. Some of the members, who are generally older than the activists who grew out of the student movement, belong to the generation that initially became involved in activism through their engagement in social welfare and charity work. Most members are part of the upper-middle or upper class, and are not only well educated but also well connected. In comparison to groups such as Ma'an or Al-Mar'a Al-Gedida, women from 'the Alliance' have much greater access to Egyptian financial resources. Many other activists would rather rely on local funding, but are themselves struggling to make ends meet. The majority of women activists feel uncomfortable about asking people involved in big business for funding, as businessmen (and women) are generally perceived as corrupt and greedy, and the epitome of exploitative capitalism. However, some women feel that it is time to try to look for alternatives to foreign funding and to overcome the widespread antipathies towards local business. Layla H., a scholar and activist in her late thirties, says: '*Why should they be more corrupt and exploitative than foreign organizations which are based on capitalist principles too? Besides, they are not all corrupt. We just have all these stereotypes about businessmen. What we have to do is engage in some research about our business community and also try to raise their consciousness. At least they are Egyptian.*'

One of the latest twists in the debate about funding is related to the attempts by a Canadian–Egyptian group (CIAD) to create a network among women's organizations and groups from the whole political spectrum. A group of Canadian-based Egyptians decided to allocate funds to women's organizations to help them create a network by providing a physical space, computer facilities, a database etc. Some activists expressed their objection to this project: '*A network comprising all women's groups needs to grow out of local initiative rather than being fund-driven.*' Paradoxically, some of those activists who are generally most outspoken against foreign funding have been at the forefront in the CIAD project. In response to my question whether this involvement would not present a contradiction to her general principles, Nadia N., from the Ittihad Al-Nissa'i Al-Taqadummi (Union of Progressive Women, affiliated with the socialist Tagammu party), responded:

Our organization focuses on removing illiteracy and teaching women. If I can, through the CIAD project, increase the opportunities for girls to learn reading and writing and even computer literacy, then why not? We seek to benefit from this new project, but we stick to our strategies and our agenda. This is a new experience to combine social and political work. I discovered that we should know much more details about social work and even about charity, because our society is very deteriorated. In our party we formed a commission to face unemployment and to find a solution to this problem. Young people do not come to us any more to understand the cause but to search for work. If we can find them jobs through social work, then, why not?

The significance of Nadia N.'s words cannot be overemphasized as they present a radical break in her own and her party's previous position on social welfare work and charity. The socialist Tagammu party has traditionally been extremely suspicious of social welfare work and has generally dismissed it as a bourgeois response to social injustice. The more revolutionary outlook of 'changing the system instead of feeding a few poor' seems to have been replaced by a more reformist and pragmatic approach. One is inclined to doubt that this change of heart is simply related to the deterioration of the economic situation and the increase in poverty and unemployment. Other factors have to play a role as it is obvious that people have been facing economic hardships and deprivations throughout the history of revolutionary leftist politics. What seems to be a more likely reason for this radical shift is the decreased appeal of the leftist party to Egypt's youth and the general sense of crisis within the party after the disintegration of the Soviet Union. But even more significant is the realization that Islamist groups gain increasing support among the general population because they manage to deliver goods and services where the government fails to do so.

Concerning the controversial CIAD project, one of the reasons given for accepting money by people generally opposed to foreign funding is the 'origin' of the donors. Siham H., member of the women's secretariat of the Nasserite party, denies allegations that the project imposes an idea from outside. She also appeals to greater international solidarity and co-operation among Arabs to counter Zionist conspiracies:

The idea of network co-ordination between the various women's organizations has existed for a long time. It started as a national initiative on the International Women's Day in 1985. The committee consists of women from all political orientations; it has a programme and a vision for the problems of the nation and the problems of women. So

CIAD did not actually impose this idea on us, but offered financial assistance to support the structure and the mechanisms for our network. We need to establish a data bank; we also need to get computers and access to the Internet. All that needs financial support. The idea of funding from CIAD was also accepted because they are originally Arab. Just as I accepted to talk to you, Nadje Al-Ali, because you are of Arab origin – which helps to avoid divisions and obstacles between us – I accept funding from CIAD. The group was established by Egyptian emigrants, who obtained Canadian nationality. Our enemy is the Zionist movement all over the world which is supported by Jewish money. Why shouldn't we, the Arabs, not obtain help from Arabs all over the world?

Throughout my research this was the only positive reference made to intra-Arab financial assistance, since it is usually connected with 'Gulf money', which for many presents yet another undesirable and corrupting form of foreign influence. Saudi Arabia is especially disliked for its increasing control over the Arab media, perceived as promoting both conservative values and the Saudi regime. CIAD, on the other hand, is perceived to be a lobbying body that supports and promotes Egyptian interests on a transnational level, but also seen as a step towards the weakening of Zionist lobbying.

International conferences: transnationalism or western hegemony?

Issues of 'globalization', 'transnationalism' and the 'internationalization' of Egyptian women's activism, at least as far as the process of funding is concerned, have become more obvious in the process of preparations for both the ICPD and the UN International Women's Forum. However, for a few activists the widespread practice of accepting funding in order to attend international conferences has only increased the level of rivalry within the movement as the competition over travel funds has been fierce. A few activists describe allocated travel grants as evidence for the misuse of foreign funding and the level of corruption among donors themselves. Connections, in this view, are more important than qualifications.

Only a minority remains extremely critical and cynical, while reservations and doubt are more prevalent, even among those who welcome the idea of international forums. The notion of 'trendiness' was mentioned a lot with regard to the funding of the International Women's Forum in Beijing: *'Another fashion came along: Beijing. So everyone only funded Beijing. Nothing happened outside of Beijing. This has triggered a quantitative trend in research where everyone is quoting everyone else. There is no vigorous research, no analysis. Both international conferences have occupied the whole scene and funding arena.'*

Others do value the potential of international organizations, but express their disappointment with the notion of 'transnationalism'. 'International agendas', in their view, are dominated by western concerns and do not necessarily reflect the actual agenda of women from the Third World. Amal T., a medical doctor and activist who attended both the ICPD and the Beijing conference, believes that the international dimension of these conferences generally work at the expense of the concerns of Egyptian women:

I believe that the two conferences were international conferences. They are not local conferences, so they reflect the problems of all countries which participated. We must agree that different countries have different cultures and different problems. We talked about female genital mutilation, for example, but this problem is only confined to certain countries and doesn't exist in other cultures. Now, when we come to the implementation, then, of course, every country will see its own problems and will try to implement the recommendations in that specific context. So, my main criticism is related to touching on certain sensitive issues that do not represent big problems here in Egypt. What we have to do is Egyptianize the recommendations and implement what is relevant for our own problems.

However, many women stressed the importance of both conferences. Overall, the ICPD in Cairo – both the conference itself and the preparations for it – is considered more of a positive and enriching experience than Beijing. As mentioned earlier, one of the reasons for the success of the ICPD was that its very location made the competition for travel grants redundant and allowed a greater number of organizations and activists to participate. Aside from gaining confidence and raising new issues, many activists view the ICPD as particularly helpful in acquainting local groups with one another: '*We all had so many misconceptions about local NGOs and these were cleared up before and during the conference.*' Unfortunately, the overall positive experience of the ICPD was not repeated to the same extent during and before the International Women's Forum in Beijing. Competition over travel grants, lack of co-ordination in the period of preparation, the government's ambiguous position towards the conference, and controversial policies of inclusion and exclusion of the official NGO steering committee were all factors that led to tensions and conflicts within the women's movement.

Among all women interviewed, the harshest criticism towards Beijing was articulated by Leila I., the founder of the Marxist–feminist group Ma'an:

Beijing was part of a certain chain of conferences, which aimed at reconstructing the world agenda according to the needs of the World Bank. It was mainly their discussion and it had nothing to do with what women really need. Why should we go there and give them the appearance of democracy? They do not represent our agenda! If we would go as an opposition group we would have to be part of a strong movement. As long as this movement does not exist we should focus our efforts in creating it at home. People just went to Beijing to intermingle. And the show went on.

It becomes obvious that, for Leila I., the World Bank symbolizes the epitome of imperialism and capitalist exploitation. In her view the International Women's Forum in Beijing was yet another manifestation of imperialism and the way it manages to lure people into its all-encompassing net. In the name of women's rights and democracy, women from all over the world were being seduced to go along instead of challenging the 'real agenda', that is the expansion of western capitalist control. In her analysis, there is no distinction between the governmental and non-governmental agendas of participants, nor does she attribute agency to women activists from all over the world, as she describes them as passive victims of a World Bank conspiracy. She does not acknowledge the fact, for instance, that numerous panels in Beijing actually discussed and criticized structural adjustment policies in different parts of the Third World. However, Leila I. stresses that her strong objections to international conferences like the one in Beijing are not related to the notion of western corruption and foreign values. She considers herself an internationalist: '*Imperialism does not mean the West but certain economic relations.*' A self-declared Marxist, she opposes the idea of 'the clashes between cultures', and believes in international class struggle.

Even those who appreciated the experience of Beijing and found it enriching for themselves and their activism disclose their uneasiness about some aspects of the conference. What was generally appreciated was that Beijing showed that '*the West is not one thing as has always been argued by people whose main interest is not women's issues*'. Variations in attitudes, policies and forms of activism were not only found among activists from different western countries but also within the framework of one particular country. Most apparent were differences between government agendas and those of women activists belonging to non-governmental movements. This, of course, was not unique to western countries, and many Egyptian activists heavily criticized the official Egyptian delegation for its lack of actual involvement in women's issues in Egypt.

One of the most empowering aspects of Beijing, as perceived by Egyptian women activists, was the realization that '*women's organizations from South Asia and Africa working with peasant women face very similar problems as we have. They also have issues like violence and reproductive rights on their agendas which are falsely classified as "western" among many Egyptians.*' In the context of other Third World countries, the notion of transnationalism became more meaningful and enabled some Egyptian activists to counter accusations of imitating the West as they can point to feminist activism across the globe.

However, the actual final document produced as a result of the conference is frequently talked about with suspicion. Various activists question its relevance and describe it critically as not '*representing their realities*'. Often reservations about international declarations are not directly linked to '*concrete facts on the ground*', but rather arise out of doubts about values and principles and their universal relevance. The question about the universal validity of international declarations and their underlying principles presents another provocative and unsettling issue among women activists. Like the debate about foreign funding, no consensus may be found among the various groups and activists and there is a great variety of opinions. In the following section I will attempt to outline some of the main arguments and points of contention in this debate.

Universality of women's rights or cultural specificity: a false dichotomy?

The question of cultural specificity with regard to human rights in general and women's rights in particular is not only invoked by some Islamists[9] (and at times the government),[10] who view some items of the Universal Declaration of Human Rights as opposing Islamic values, but it is raised by many intellectuals and activists across generations and the political spectrum. Among Egyptian women activists the issue of universality versus specificity has constituted one of the main debates over the past years. Like the controversy about foreign funding, the debate is partly triggered by the growing presence of international organizations in Egypt and the increased involvement of Egyptian organizations in international forums. Discussions about the universality or specificity of women's rights are also aspects of processes of decolonization in which Egyptian political actors try to define their own agendas and aims.

An important factor leading to an increased aversion to claims of universality is the relatively new tendency of western governments, particularly the United States, to appropriate human rights discourse and to proclaim themselves the sole and legitimate proponents of it. This phenomenon has created a confusion between the notion of the internationalization of human rights on the one hand, read as the imposition of the

---

[9] As Kevin Dwyer (1991) and Sami Zubaida (1994) make clear, there is no specific Islamic position on the human rights debate.

[10] Ann Elizabeth Mayer examines some of the reservations of the Egyptian government with regard to CEDAW in the frame of a more general pattern of hypocrisy among male politicians assuring women's equality in principle yet resisting or even openly opposing its implementation (Mayer, 1995: 104–32).

moral imperative of the United States, and the universal validity of human rights. Paradoxically, the very governments that are frequently portrayed as defenders of women's rights, such as those of Thatcher, Reagan and Kohl, have often resisted women's struggles for equality within their own countries.[11] Nevertheless, in the official rhetoric and policies human and women's rights feature high on western agendas, often using a patronizing and superior tone which alienates many political actors in post-colonial countries. Furthermore, as Zubaida points out:

Triumphalist 'uniqueness of the West' arguments present human rights, constitutionalism and democracy as if they are somehow inherent in Western history and culture, and their establishment as a matter of unfolding of this history. By the same token, they are alien grafts on non-Western histories and cultures, and are soon rejected. The arguments of modern Islamic politics are consistent with this view of fundamental cultural difference and reject these Western-Christian concepts as part of the baggage of cultural 'crusader' imperialism. (1994: 7)

In Egypt, a number of women activists express their anger with the way universalism is used to reach political ends by western constituencies: *'The West has already achieved the spread of its culture everywhere, and now it is trying to universalize its values. We should not cling to their principles, which we did not create ourselves. Instead we should try to provide alternatives and reach the same level of development as they did.'* The surprising distinction between culture and values might be related to a conceptualization of culture being related to 'matters of consumption' while values are seen to denote moral and ethical bases for behaviour. However, most women interviewed equate culture and values and many express their concern with *'the cultural expansionism of the West'*. This judgement can be often heard in contemporary Egypt, but also constitutes a wider criticism voiced against the international human rights movement: 'that human rights concerns as currently articulated in international conventions are the direct product of one cultural tradition – the western tradition growing out of enlightenment – and thus do not respond to the concerns of other traditions' (Dwyer, 1991: 206).

While most women share a dislike for what they perceive as a patronizing appropriation of moral superiority by the West, activists differ greatly in their views on the universal definition of women's rights and on the question of cultural specificity. Criticisms of universality are repeatedly expressed in reference to 'our culture', thereby adopting, to some extent, the rhetoric of conservative and Islamist forces. It is these forces that continuously and successfully use the argument of 'our indigenous culture'

[11] R. W. Connell's (1990) analysis of the role of the state with regard to feminist reforms and sexual politics reveals the often reactionary and conservative nature of western states.

versus 'western culture' every time gender relations and women's rights are addressed. Yet, curiously enough, 'their culture' does not seem to be at stake when it comes to economic relations, education, work patterns and even models for marriage (Abu-Lughod, 1998b; Narayan, 1997). The 'culturalization' of political issues has become so naturalized in contemporary Egypt that it seems very difficult to doubt the legitimacy of this practice and question its grounds.

However, the very act of framing political issues in cultural terms is not enhanced only by Islamist and conservative forces within Egypt. Western feminists' claims to universality can be intimidating at times, and occasionally add fuel to the culture argument. Several Egyptian women activists gave accounts of incidents in which western feminists accused them of violating human rights principles, because they did not recognize the need to struggle for lesbian rights: '*Universality should not be used to force me to do things that really do not apply to my culture and is not part of its priorities.*' Once again, what might be framed as a political choice is presented in terms of culture; an argument that seems particularly compelling when put by someone '*outside one's culture*'.

Encounters with western feminists repeatedly put Egyptian women activists in a dilemma. While they might be arguing in the very same vein at home against a particular form of discrimination, such as FGM, for example, abroad, in an international forum, when some western feminists are outraged about 'the barbarism' practised in Egypt, activists often feel offended by their tone and its implicit racism. So it could happen that a woman, extremely outspoken against FGM within Egypt, might find herself defending the practice during a confrontation with certain western feminists. This is usually experienced as being extremely unsettling and disturbing. For Randa S. this entails a catch-22 situation in which one is torn between arguing despite one's convictions and arguing in a way that confirms negative stereotypes:

I feel that when a western feminist makes a negative statement about my own culture, I should make a positive statement to counter it. Living across two cultures is very difficult. There is the danger of playing up to western expectations. But sometimes it might just appear like it, because you might be really just saying what you feel and believe in. It is a real dilemma. It reminds me of Edward Said's notion of the eclipse of the two worlds in Culture and Imperialism. *As an 'intellectual of the divide' you have to acquire two tongues. The position of the mediator is never comfortable. You are always in the position of the potential betrayer, translator, double agent. It carries lots of responsibilities and it's full of tensions, but it's also very creative.*

Edward Said himself cautions against rigid, often chauvinistic and xenophobic constructions of cultures 'seeking to become independent of imperialism' (1993: 258). However, his particular positioning as a male scholar of Palestinian origin in the United States, difficult as it surely is, permits for a wider discursive horizon and an easier departure from cultural essentialisms than is possible for secular-oriented Egyptian women activists today. The stigma of 'betrayal' weighs heavily on any woman who carries the burdens of the colonial legacy when struggling against contemporary forms of patriarchal oppression (Ahmed, 1982: 122).

Most of the women I interviewed stressed cultural specificity and relativism, but, except for stating that lesbianism was a not an issue, often failed to concretize what is actually specific about Egyptian culture with regard to women's issues. Salwa F., however, illustrated her interpretation of cultural specificity in the following way:

The issue of FGM in Egypt is one example for specificity. Most of the women's rights activists think that it's bad. Some think it should be stopped immediately. I personally believe that if this will be stopped there won't be any improvement of women's position. There won't be an important change. The issue needs to be addressed in a wider context, not just as a barbaric act. Westerners get very emotional about the issue, but when I talk to a woman in Assiut, she might not even remember it, or say that it hurt more to get her appendix removed. There are actually families who stopped doing it. We do not know why, because they were not subject to any campaigns. We do not take the time to look for the reasons, and we do not take time to believe that women change rationally. There are many factors involved in women's position. The economic situation is much more determining than culture and tradition. It will take years and lots of education to change the general awareness about women's position. There is a rationale for everything that is done, even for the poor and uneducated, but we do not take our time to understand this rationale.

The argument for cultural relativism sometimes takes the form of promoting traditional values or religious imperatives, but in the context of secular-oriented women activists it seems to be more related to the rejection of an imposition from outside, as well as the realization that daily realities demand different priorities. As Hoda W. put it: '*International organizations are not willing to listen to us or any culturally specific voice. This is commonly implicit in the rhetoric of universal documents.*' Another significant element seems to be a certain level of respect and pride in 'the culture', so that cultural specificity is accepted as a concept '*only if I know it will add by giving me more protection and rights. What I should reject from my culture is the discrimination implicit against me. I want to bring out the best in my cultural heritage or what is specific about it.*' Here, as expressed by many women other than Hoda W., cultural specificity becomes more than a tool in the attempt to demarcate oneself from the 'West'. It is also employed positively to affirm one's own culture, somehow homogenized and defined as a monolithic entity, thereby discarding cultural differences within Egypt among different social classes, generations, rural and urban people and so forth.

Despite the strong weight and naturalization of 'our culture' in Egyptian political discourse, it might be time to question its validity and usefulness. Various feminists from other post-colonial countries and from minority groups within western countries, also burdened by the experiences of colonialism and the ongoing struggles with imperialism, provide useful analytical tools to examine critically the notion of culture as employed in the debates about international women's rights (Abu-Lughod, 1998a; Afkhami (ed.), 1995; Kandiyoti, 1995; Narayan, 1997; Saghal, 1992; Spivak, 1987). Kandiyoti, for example, makes the point that 'privileged sites of cultural distinctiveness and identity are, quite consistently, the family, gender relations, and women's status' (1995: 20).

In the Egyptian context, Lila Abu-Lughod (1991, 1998b) has played a pioneering role in unsettling the concept culture. In her earlier work (1991), Abu-Lughod pointed to the notion of culture as having been largely responsible for anthropology's conspicuous 'othering'. Essentialist notions of 'culture' do not only homogenize and simplify more complex realities, but they are also part of the kind of stereotyping that accounts for racism, sexism and other forms of discrimination. Her subsequent writings reflect concerns with 'the particular', which she always manages to relate back to wider national and global processes. Her overall critique of modernity involves the attempt to unsettle prevailing dichotomies such as traditional versus modern or indigenous versus western. In her most recent work Abu-Lughod (1998b) finds inspiration in the writings of Bhaba (1994), Chatterjee (1993) and Said (1993), as well as other post-colonial writers. She develops an innovative approach which permits her to re-evaluate the colonial encounter in Egypt in view of its 'complex processes of borrowing, translating, and creating new mixtures' (Abu-Lughod, 1998b: 412). Most interestingly and at odds with conventional analyses, Abu-Lughod uncovers similarities between secular modernists and Islamists concerning concepts of marriage and family. Her approach also allows her to re-examine the history of the Egyptian women's movement without ascribing the bounded categories of either westernism or authenticity.

Although the recourse to culture has remained largely unchallenged among women activists in Egypt, only a few activists paint a 'black and white picture' on the issue, acknowledging instead the multiple aspects and diverse effects of cultural specificity. If notions of universality can be used by political regimes to establish or expand their sphere of influence, those of cultural specificity can also be misused to obstruct women's rights struggles. This oppressive aspect of cultural specificity has parallels in the multiculturalism debate in the West, where the recognition of cultural diversity does not only entail the accommodation of differences, but also leads to the emergence of homogenizing and exclusionary tendencies (Kandiyoti, 1995; Saghal & Yuval-Davis, 1992). As Sahgal and Yuval-Davis argue: 'In the multiculturalist discourse, minority communities are defined by a stereotypical notion of their "culture", which is increasingly being collapsed into matters of religious identity' (1992: 15). Women are often at the centre of cultural exclusions sanctioned under the name of multiculturalism. Various fundamentalist movements in England, for example, have been particularly successful in legitimizing a series of women's abuses and forms of oppression by making claims to cultural difference and are often backed by the government's multiculturalist policies.

Some Egyptian women activists explicitly say that the notion of cultural specificity is used as a tool by men to reinforce their power over women, and question the whole notion altogether. In the same vein, they question the critical appraisal of traditions, because, as Randa K. says, '*our tradition encourages men's superiority over women. We should have in the back of our minds the goals of equality and gender non-discrimination whilst reviewing and redefining our cultural heritage.*' Leila I., for example, questions that a specific meaning of equality exists and says: '*I am very clear that there are certain things in our traditions which are against women's rights and we should fight them. FGM, for example, is part of tradition not religion. Some people try to give it a religious cover. The whole history of it shows that it is meant to control women's virginity which stems from an outlook based on a view of women's inferiority.*' Her opinion reveals a rare distinction between the increased influence of foreign organizations and forums, which she rigorously rejects (as revealed in her categorical refusal to accept foreign funding), and the notion of universally valid values and rights. Many of her politically like-minded colleagues from the left demonstrate a much more selective approach to what is universal and what is not – an inclination deeply despised by Raga N.:

Amazingly they scream here about western theories concerning women's issues, but they have adopted other western theories, like Marxism. Or those concerning political structures. The problem with the Arab world is that we have been eclectic. We take some elements from western theory, which do not clash with our culture, but we disregard elements that clash with traditional beliefs and values, which, of course, have concrete constituted political and economic interests. We scream: 'Our values!' when it clashes with power positions, but when it is beneficial to the same group, they adopt it, despite it being western.

Raga N.'s impassioned critique gives evidence to the fact that traditions are invoked in a politically selective manner: far from representing continuity with the past, traditions are being actively constructed by political constituencies. Ideas and values of western thought are borrowed when it seems fit, and ferociously combated and perceived as western values when the struggle for women's rights is on the agenda. This is precisely the argument brought forth by Abu-Lughod (1998b) when she uncovers the selective appropriation and repudiation of western modernist values and ideals by Islamists. Condemning feminist ideas as western (and therefore corrupt), they have nevertheless incorporated western modernist values. The ideals of companionship in marriage, the nuclear family, women's education and work are part of Islamist stipulations in which they have 'conveniently forgotten' that these values do not represent anything traditional (ibid.: 411–12).

Another conviction articulated by Raga N. is that the assumed clash between certain values and rights, especially those related to women, is more symptomatic of problems, crises and power struggles within Egypt than a conflict between Egypt and the 'West'. Some women activists relate the conflict between global principles and their cultural heritage to the general crisis of Arab political systems, which do not allow for democratic relations and the treatment of human beings as citizens who have certain human and political rights. Others state that cultural specificity is constantly being made legitimate by the Islamic *shari'a*, and cannot be easily abandoned even if it works against universally valid values and rights. A few activists, such as Raga N., deny the argument that human rights and the development of its universal recognition emanated from western culture. They point to the contributions of '*all cultures and religions in shaping and fighting for humanity*' and also draw attention to the fact that '*the West has only very recently started to pay attention to human rights*'. In a similar vein, Zubaida argues that there was nothing culturally specific about the institutionalization of human rights in the West, which took place after a series of religious wars and persecutions. Instead, human rights were a pragmatic response to the ongoing suffering among the various populations and a means to achieve social peace and stability (1994: 7). Here one might add that anti-colonial and anti-imperialist struggles are 'rights' struggles themselves and could be viewed within the broader context of human rights.

One argument being made by some women, such as Summaya D., for example, is that the accusation of being 'too western' is only used by the elite and not by women from the poorer strata: '*I do not think that we are the ones being alienated from the people. Even in the research work on women and violence we did for Beijing, we did not make an analysis, but we just wrote down what women were saying. It might be shocking for the Cairene community, but these were voices of women themselves.*' Furthermore, as Summaya D. told me: '*If we talk with western feminists outside of Egypt, they consider us conservative. Oppression is not a matter of the West only; it is part of the whole*

world. Human rights conventions have been reformulated by the struggle of people over the world.'
The argument that values of equality and justice are imposed on Egyptians by the West is also refuted by Raga N. who gives an account of her own value formation:

> *My value system comes from a combination of things. It is not one thing. I am not denying that part of my ethics come from my religious upbringing. All religions raise certain values. My ethics also come from my instinctive belief in the equality of people. This has shaped my socialist orientation. Without equality and justice we cannot have a fair society. My father was also a strong believer in equality and justice. This was reinforced through my readings, especially reading Marx. I could never understand the bully-boy or -girl mentality. I do not hate them as much as I pity them. There are some innate kind of values without which humanity would have vanished a long time ago. I hate force. I respect reason. I hate any kind of order and directives. I was born with this. This is related to my own sense of karama [self-worth] which was very much installed into me by my father.*

Even if Raga N.'s account does not make clear whether she perceives her values more as an innate part of her personality or the outcome of her education, she makes clear that values grow in different contexts and cannot be categorized simply into 'western' as opposed to 'Egyptian'. It is not only women like Raga N. who reject the claim that equality and justice are western impositions. Many Muslim scholars as well as some Islamists have been eager to show Islam's compatibility with notions of human rights, equality and justice. The complexity of the debate and the varying positions of different constituencies make it impossible then to draw sharp lines between those arguing for universalism and those for specificity.

Women activists find themselves in another dilemma: conservative forces within Egypt accuse them of adopting western agendas at the same time as western organizations and governments are trying to establish an absolute authority over issues related to women's and human rights. Caught in the middle, many activists express their anger at the perception that they are without agency and creative imagination. Whether in terms of women's or human rights activism, women activists feel that international development agencies and feminist organizations, western governments and also western academia are implicated in denying Egyptian women the ability to shape their own value systems and political ideas. A similar impasse faces women activists in the question of secularism which I explored in chapter 4. Yet there can be little doubt that whether with respect to interpretations of secularism or concerning women's issues, Egyptian women actively engage in struggles over meaning, power and change.

Conclusion: 'standing on shifting ground'

One of the main aims of the focus on secular-oriented groups in this work was balancing the increased interest in Islamist constituencies evident in much of the recent writings in Middle East scholarship by providing a fuller picture of contemporary political actors in Egypt. The heterogeneity of secular women activists constituted a consistent theme and was tackled from various angles, as I will briefly summarize in this conclusion.

Throughout this book I have tried to show that any analysis of the tensions and controversies within the contemporary Egyptian women's movement needs to address the wider political culture in which these debates take place. The emergence and evolution of the groups Al-Mar'a Al-Gedida and Ma'an, for example, illustrates quite vividly some unresolved issues, particularly the more general conundrums and tensions in the political left in Egypt. The crisis of the left after the disintegration of the Soviet Union and the increased appeal of Islamist groups among the popular classes has evoked a variety of responses, and often puts women activists on the defensive.

The growing influence of Islamist constituencies has certainly left its mark on Egyptian political culture, where the discursive framework is dominated by Islamist agendas. At a point when the political left no longer seems to provide a viable alternative, many issues formerly taken up by the left, such as social justice and national independence, have been incorporated into Islamist rhetoric. Moreover, Abu-Lughod (1998b) suggests, some Islamists have appropriated modernist conceptualizations of women's roles in society, marriage relations and the family, thereby competing with both conservative modernists and progressive political activists over these issues. Debates about identity and authenticity are certainly promoted by Islamists these days and influence the ways in which other political actors, such as secular women activists, address these issues.

Having emphasized some overlap in the frames of reference of the secular women's movement and the broader political culture of Egypt in the last chapter, it is important to stress that there are nonetheless

216

significant differences between political constituencies in which women activists occupy a specific place. Some activists subscribe to modernization and dependency frameworks, often trying to find new ways to attract supporters by engaging in welfare work. Others, who have moved on, question prevailing frames of analysis and forms of activism altogether. Caught between the pronouncements of Islamists, the government and nationalist voices and interests, they are constantly under attack, and often attack one another in their attempts to gain legitimacy and secure resources. Nevertheless, some activists are challenging these simplistic discourses by constructing new terms of reference and by looking for new forms of organization. The lack of models for non-hierarchical democratic structures often causes conflicts and tensions and poses yet another challenge for women activists. Those committed to democratic decision making experience many setbacks in the search for innovative ways to organize themselves. It is in the context of this endeavour that some women activists are emerging as a force of democratization in contemporary Egypt.

My presentation of recollections about the history of Al-Mar'a Al-Gedida and Ma'an in the last chapter also revealed the personalized aspect of many of the tensions within the movement. Problems are not just about political differences and ideologies, but also develop between activists who started out as friends. As I illustrated through life-stories in chapter 3, these friendships can be a source of both strength and conflict. Often 'the personal' and 'the political' become intertwined in ways where personal disagreements and problems might provoke tensions in the political sphere. This is particularly dangerous as women activists are still in the process of finding democratic structures and ways of organizing that will accommodate difference and absorb conflict, but also allow for a continuation of activities.

Women's activism and the state

The varied backgrounds to contemporary women's activism are simultaneously embedded in particular historical conjunctures and diverse personal experiences and motivations. I argued in chapter 3 that political orientations, goals, agendas and forms of engagement are all affected by general political trends and historical events. In conjunction with personal experiences of gender oppression, these historical particularities do not determine political action, but they do shape possibilities and frame choices. The 'formative experiences' that prompted individual engagement in women's activism constitute reference points and sources of ideas and action in one way or another, even if these experiences were lived heterogeneously.

Historically, the Egyptian state and its policies have played a key role in shaping gender relations. In chapter 2 I explored the changing and ambiguous relationship between the Egyptian women's movement and the state. Borrowing Connell's conceptualization of 'gender regimes' (1990), I attempted to illustrate the ways in which the changing Egyptian regimes – under Nasser, Sadat and Mubarak – have been actively engaged in constructing gender through their policies and legal provisions.

In this context it became obvious that women have been simultaneously described as modern citizens with equal rights and responsibilities and as bearers of cultural authenticity, thereby safeguarding 'traditions' and 'the authentic culture'. Tensions inherent in this contradiction significantly shape and influence feminist politics as they have to work both against and through the state, depending on the specific nature of the state and its policies. In present-day Egypt, ambiguities and contradictions continue to characterize state policies. On the one hand, the Mubarak regime has been increasingly pressured, due to the ongoing confrontation with Islamists, to legislate and implement more conservative laws and policies on women and the family, and to minimize its support for women's political participation. On the other hand, transnational apparatuses, i.e. international agencies and bodies, have increased their influence during the past decade, heightening the sense of obligation for the Egyptian state to adhere to UN conventions concerning women's rights.

I have argued that the ambiguities apparent in the Egyptian post-colonial state, its historically specific policies, its internal divisions and its links to international constituencies are all factors circumscribing women activists' shifting relations to the state. Not only do different groups within the movement adopt different strategies towards the state and have different relations with it, but women activists are also affected in different ways: they are recipients of both supportive and oppressive state policies at the same time as they try to influence them. Consequently, women's groups are part of Egypt's civil society – which in and of itself varies greatly in terms of its independence from the state – even if they only represent a small segment of it.

In chapter 2 I agreed with Suad Joseph's assertion that overall neglect of women's activism in discussions about Middle Eastern civil societies reflects the more general tendency to conceptualize 'the public domain' in terms of male engagement and activity (Joseph, 1993). However, as I have shown in the course of this book, women are actively engaged in contestations with the state about the shaping of gender policies. To varying degrees, women activists engage in grassroots activism and aspire to find non-hierarchical ways of organizing, thereby engaging in the process of democratization. Like other political actors within Egypt's civil society, they recurrently fight over resources in the process of expanding their platforms of action. Women activists often adopt Islamist frames of reference, sometimes strategically, other times unwittingly. Nevertheless, some secular women activists do challenge Islamist constituencies in their attempts to dominate discursive frameworks and activities within civil society and courageously express their positions publicly.

International agendas

A critical factor in shaping the political context for the women's movement, particularly in recent years, has been the influence of international institutions, such as UN organizations and international funding bodies. There is little doubt that the aims and goals of international institutions and agencies have been instrumental in shaping current state policies and the agenda of contemporary women's activism. The question that needs to be asked, however, is how far women's groups and activists manage to lobby and obtain support for local agendas, which may or may not overlap with international priorities. Certainly, local players, such as Egyptian women activists, do not merely adopt international agendas but selectively appropriate global issues and reinterpret them to suit their own needs and priorities.

The impact of international agendas on women's activism in Egypt has been multifold, entailing both positive and negative consequences. The sense of competition over foreign funding is certainly one of the negative effects of the increased presence of international donor organizations, as it often leads to rivalry and corruption and heightens divisions among women activists. In some instances projects and campaigns are short lived because they were more a response to 'available funding' than to pressing local issues and agendas. The professionalization of the previously voluntary welfare sector and political activism constitutes a more complex side-effect. On the one hand, it has created a situation where careerism could override political goals, which in turn augments the danger of rivalry. On the other hand, the professionalization of activities related to health care, reproductive rights, legal issues and development entails greater specialization and expertise which has been reflected positively in the quality of various projects and publications of contemporary activists.

Despite the fact that the struggle over resources presents an impediment to collective action and solidarity and might also give leverage to foreign donor organizations to impose their agendas, it has been put to use productively and effectively by some groups and individuals to pursue their own goals and priorities. Both Egyptian women activists and international donor organizations play a role in determining the effectiveness and usefulness of foreign funding. Those women's groups and networks that have researched a specific issue adequately, have formulated clear aims and provided an organizational structure to ensure the actual implementation of their proposed projects appear to have a good chance of putting allocated funds to good use. The donor organizations' policies of allocating and controlling funding as well their general sensitivity towards local needs and 'ways of doing things' also seem to make a difference in terms of the actual impact of their resources.

Anxieties about foreign funding spelt out in the previous chapter suggest that it has come to symbolize all that is wrong with contemporary Egypt. Foreign funding is perceived as a form of external interference which demonstrates Egypt's lack of independence. What is at stake in these debates is much more than the meddling of foreign donors in local agendas concerning women's issues; what are often behind the fierceness of arguments are conflicting interests and power struggles. Anti-imperialist positions are often overshadowed by harsh material realities, such as the ongoing economic crisis, which partly account for ambiguities and conflicts in the complex process of post-colonial state-building.

Similarly, I considered perceptions about international organizations and the value given to international conferences in the light of struggles for political independence, especially from American influence. However, I have come to the conclusion that the impact of international conferences, most notably the International Conference on Population and Development (Cairo, 1994) and to some extent the International Women's Forum (Beijing, 1995), cannot be overemphasized. Although women activists criticized the influence of western agencies and organizations, or the large scale of these international events, most acknowledged that the encounter with women activists from all over the world constituted a great learning experience and inspiration. The preparations for the ICPD in Cairo were appreciated as an opportunity to communicate with women activists and NGOs nation-wide. Despite the complaint about attempts by western constituencies to dominate discussions and shape agendas, both international conferences revealed to many that 'international' does not equal 'western'. The issues raised by African and South Asian feminists in particular appear to have left a deep impression on Egyptian participants who, often for the first time, recognized similarities and common concerns which had frequently been attacked as 'too western' by critics within Egypt.

UN institutions and resolutions, international conferences and donor organizations, governmental and non-governmental agencies and the international media have increasingly gained access to and influence over present-day Egypt – whatever the specific results might be. Therefore, any analysis of the women's movement has to take this international and transnational dimension into account and examine the level of what I have identified as semi-independent/semi-directed mobilization. Without doubt some western agencies, most notably USAID among many others, attempt to influence the agendas and activities of local political actors. It would be a fallacy, however, to characterize Egyptian women activists as mere recipients of foreign funding and willing collaborators of western schemes and conspiracies. The women I interviewed make choices, select, argue, negotiate and challenge international agendas. Some embrace opportunities and concentrate on making careers, others manage to pursue their goals and interests without undue compromises. In other words, local actors have agency and can selectively appropriate broader agendas to suit their own particular goals.

The issue of heterogeneity

My analysis of perceptions of the history of the Egyptian women's movement by contemporary activists (chapter 2) revealed a range of positions and opinions reflecting the multiplicity of current tendencies. I also explored various levels of dependence and autonomy of women's groups in relation to the state. The variety of 'entry points' into women's activism, disclosed in the life-stories of ten women activists in chapter 3, added a biographical dimension to the more general analysis of varied historical and political trajectories.

The notion of heterogeneity also constituted an axis of analysis in relation to contemporary women activists' understandings of secularism and the ways it manifests itself in their political activism (chapter 4). It has been my ambition to challenge undifferentiated portrayals of secular activists, especially in the light of more nuanced analyses of Islamist tendencies in contemporary Egypt. In current Egyptian political culture as well as in many academic analyses 'secular' has almost become a residual category, and is largely employed to gloss over the actual concerns, interests and goals of those thus labelled. I have stressed that under the label 'secular' one is bound to detect a range of political orientations and positions which cannot easily be subsumed under a single homogeneous category. This becomes particularly relevant in a context where 'secular' is increasingly used to describe those who are not Islamist, thereby reifying a dichotomy skilfully manipulated by Islamists themselves.

In chapter 5 I examined in greater detail significant differences among women activists in terms of their goals and aspirations and the ways in which they translate these into specific projects and campaigns. On the level of general officially stated goals, I detected a great deal of similarity among the various groups analysed. However, my analysis of more specific aims and perceived priorities revealed greater differences. Starting from the definition of 'politics' itself (which is often not equated with women's activism but linked exclusively to political economy), to notions about what women's activism entails, my respondents displayed rather varied positions. Among the priorities mentioned were the fight against poverty, the eradication of illiteracy, raising awareness concerning legal rights, campaigning to change existing laws (such as the Personal Status Law or the Nationality Law) and increasing women's political participation. These stated priorities are translated into concrete projects, some of which I described in chapter 5, and which account for the varied forms of engagements in women's activism.

On several occasions throughout this book I highlighted the fact that a small yet growing number of activists are developing feminist positions outside the prevailing frameworks of modernization or dependency paradigms. In this process, they challenge and reject well-established and historically rooted discourses about and approaches to women's subordination in Egypt. These activists include personal forms of oppression within the realm of the family, thereby pointing to the links between the 'private' and the 'public'. I suggested in agreement with Mervat Hatem (1993) that it is these women who might succeed in creating a new 'independent discourse' which offers the tools to analyse comprehensively the complexities of women's situation and propose more satisfactory solutions.

Legitimizing strategies

As in so many other contexts, the harshest accusations and denunciations take place between activists who once held shared positions but diverged over time. Being corrupt, bourgeois, too westernized and removed from the grassroots are among the most common allegations made. Unfortunately, these debates entail a greater competition over models of 'right thinking' than constructive exchanges to find common ground and platforms for action. One example is the accusation of being removed from 'the grassroots' which often serves as an easy weapon to discredit a particular group or activist, but does not necessarily mean that the accusers are themselves involved in such activity. This is not to suggest that the gap between urban middle-class women's activism and rural or lower-class women's needs and interests should not be bridged. Quite the contrary. And there are certainly groups and individuals who, especially after the ICPD and the UN conference in Beijing, make greater efforts to become actively and concretely involved in the concerns and problems of low-income and rural Egyptian women. However, the emphasis on 'speaking for someone else', usually for the less privileged, reveals the strong element of populism in Egyptian politics and reveals the continually felt need to justify and legitimize women activists' political engagement.

In the context of the women's movement it becomes obvious that the predominantly middle-class background of activists makes them easy prey for charges of elitism, usually topped with accusations of 'westernism'. Aside from political and human concerns (often based on socialist ideals), I suspect that speaking and struggling on behalf of the less privileged presents a strategy, even if unconsciously so, to proclaim one's own Egyptianness. The legacy of elitism attached to the history of the Egyptian women's movement has never been overcome and continues to elicit defensive attitudes among present-day activists. One might pose the question of whether women activists might not gain in the future not only by listening more carefully to the experiences at the 'grassroots' but also acknowledging their own. Personal forms of oppression and problems related to being a 'middle-class woman' might be seen as legitimate aspects of their struggles if a greater emphasis is placed on what individual women and groups of women actually experience. Moreover, one might argue that the way most privileged women activists behave, as though they had no problems at all, presents a rather maternalistic attitude towards their less privileged sisters. This would not be to displace high-priority issues, such as poverty and education, for example, but to add a more personal level of consciousness, thereby broadening and, one might argue, deepening the basis of their activism.

The reification of culture and colonial difference[1]

Linked to the allegation of being elitist are common accusations of being 'too westernized' and not being 'representative' of Egyptian culture. Women activists employ a variety of strategies to counter these attempts at dismissing their views and politics, thereby frequently engaging in a 'culturalization' of political issues. By asserting their allegiance to 'their culture' many women activists not only endorse the very rhetoric used against them by Islamists and conservative nationalist constituencies in Egypt, but also reify the notion of an unchanging homogeneous Egyptian culture. Paradoxically, the same activists who point to poor or rural women as being different and needing to be spoken for subsume rural and

---

[1] This term is borrowed from Partha Chatterjee who coined it in *The Nation and its Fragments: Colonial and Postcolonial Histories* (1993).

urban, lower and middle class under the label 'my culture' when put on the defensive by Islamist, conservative nationalist and western critics alike.

In chapter 6 I expressed my conviction that, despite widespread resort to 'indigenous culture' in Egyptian political discourse, the usefulness and validity of this concept needs to be challenged. As many scholars have argued in various other post-colonial settings, cultures and traditions, far from presenting static and bounded entities, are subject to change and are never unaffected by cultural encounters and exchanges whatever form these might take. Even without the encounter with a different culture, tensions and power struggles between different social forces and political actors account for transformation and change over a period of time. Traditions all over the world are not only open to reform, transformation and modification, but they are also actively reinvented to fit the ideals of those holding power in the present: 'What appears in the East in the guise of traditionalism is normally an apologetic or a radically reformist discourse whose terms of articulation and criteria for validation are by no means traditional – traditions do not validate themselves, they are idioms' (Al-Azmeh, 1993: 40). The language of 'authenticity' postulates a cultural identity that, according to Aziz Al-Azmeh, is 'self-identical, essentially in continuity over time, and positing itself in essential distinction from other historical subjects' (ibid.: 42).

Another reason for denouncing the rigid portrayal of an unchanging 'authentic culture' and its values as opposed to 'western culture' is that, ironically, this dichotomy was initially constructed by the colonizers to assert essential difference between themselves and the colonized. This 'essential difference' was not seen as an enrichment or source of knowledge for the colonizers, it was articulated instead in terms of a 'superiority of western culture' and a 'barbarism of indigenous culture'. In other words, it constituted a representation of the 'other' as inferior and radically different and, as Partha Chatterjee stresses, 'hence incorrigibly inferior' (1993: 33).

The colonial construction of difference did not only involve a eurocentric patronizing distortion of what the cultures of the colonized were all about, but it also indulged in boorish self-aggrandizement. The idealized construction of a western culture committed to values of equality, liberty and humanism stood in harsh contrast to the actual practices of 'western civilizations'. As the Indian feminist Uma Narayan forcibly argues: 'This self-perception was untroubled by the fact that Western powers were engaged in slavery and colonization, or that they had resisted granting political and civil rights even to a large number of Western subjects, including women' (1997: 15).

Conceptions of gender, particularly values and practices related to women, had been central to the assertion of essential difference and superiority by the colonizers. During the struggle for independence, and in the aftermath of colonialism, nationalist rhetoric and policies have continued to highlight differences in terms of cultural values and norms, especially those related to women. The argument developed by Partha Chatterjee (1993) that Indian nationalism distinguished between the 'outer' or material domain of the state and the 'inner' or spiritual one rings a bell in the Egyptian context. According to Chatterjee:

> The 'spiritual' or 'inner' aspects of culture, such as language or religion or the elements of personal and family life, were of course premised upon a difference between the cultures of the colonizer and the colonized. The more nationalism engaged in its contest with the colonial power in the outer domain of politics, the more it insisted on displaying the marks of 'essential' cultural difference so as to keep out the colonizer from that inner domain of national life and to proclaim its sovereignty over it. But in the outer domain of the state, the supposedly 'material' domain of law, administration, economy, and statecraft, nationalism fought relentlessly to erase the marks of colonial difference. Difference could not be justified in that domain. In this, it seemed to be reasserting precisely the claims to universality of the modern regime of power. (ibid.: 26)

In post-colonial Egypt nationalist elites and reformers adhered to notions of western modernity in the context of economic, political and social concerns all related to the 'outer' sphere. Women's right to vote and access to education and work were among the stipulations of Egyptian reformists and modernizers. Within the so-called 'inner' sphere of society, such norms and values related to women's 'proper' roles and behaviour, their duties and rights within the home and family and their relationships to men, an essential difference from western culture was and continues to be upheld.

It comes as no surprise therefore that even Egyptian women activists engage in the reification of essential cultural difference, since the prospect of an accusation of betrayal weighs heavily on anyone seeming to collude with the former colonial or the current imperialist powers. No doubt the ongoing feelings of threat from and disapproval of 'western culture' are based on concrete grounds in the light of the fact that political manipulation continues to shape post-colonial Egypt. However, it might be more constructive and effective in the long run for Egyptian women activists to argue that what differentiates them from others, both within and outside the national fabric, is not their degree of 'cultural authenticity' but their specific political analyses and approaches, their ethical values and visions for the future.

The burden of colonial experiences and ongoing struggles with imperialism are shared by many feminists world-wide who, nevertheless, often challenge an essentialized notion of culture as it glosses over the complexities and dynamics of cultural contexts. The Indian feminist Uma Narayan very eloquently puts it the following way:

We need to move away from a picture of national and cultural contexts as sealed rooms, impervious to change, with a homogeneous space 'inside' them, inhabited by 'authentic insiders' who all share a uniform and consistent account of their institutions and values. Third-World national and cultural contexts are as pervaded by plurality, dissension, and change as are their 'Western' counterparts. Both are often replete with unreflective and self-congratulatory views of their 'culture' and 'values' that disempower and marginalize the interests and concerns of many members of the national community, including women. (1997: 33)

In her view Third World feminists cannot be labelled 'outsiders' to the nation and culture, partly because they are generally familiar with and affected by the practices, institutions and policies they criticize. But they are also active citizens whose political struggles and campaigns are often crucial to raising awareness and concern with respect to issues affecting women (ibid.). Narayan articulates, to my mind, a possible and plausible way out of the dilemma facing women activists in many post-colonial countries:

I would argue that attempts to dismiss Third-World feminist views and politics as 'westernization' should be combated, in part by calling attention to the selective and self-serving deployments of the term, and in part by insisting that our contestations are no less rooted in our experiences within 'our cultures', no less 'representative' of our complex and changing realities, than the views of our compatriots who do not share our perspectives. Third-World feminists urgently need to call attention to the facts of change within their contexts, so that our agendas are not delegitimized by appeals to 'unchanging traditions'. (ibid.: 30–1).

This approach suggested by Narayan would involve the unsettling of both Egyptian nationalist and Islamist rhetoric as well as ongoing western claims to moral and cultural superiority. Just as the colonizers' rhetoric about their cultural values hardly matched their practices and politics, European and American governments today can barely be described as being fully committed to gender transformation. Indeed, in many western contexts feminist activism is marginalized and considered to be anti-communitarian.[2]

That the accusation of being 'too western' is used very selectively became obvious in my analysis of constructions of the 'West' and occidentalism in chapter 1, where I developed the argument that, historically, Egyptian intellectuals were selective in their appropriations and repudiations of European ideas about the nation state. It has become obvious to

---

[2] See Kaplan (1992) for examples of allegations brought against European feminists within their respective societies.

me that this process of selectivity continues to shape Egyptian political discourses and rhetoric up to the present. This process is not only visible among Islamist and conservative nationalist forces in Egypt today, but is, even if to a lesser extent, also noticeable among some women activists who display a great degree of selectivity with respect to the question of what is culturally legitimate in terms of women's struggle for equality and emancipation.

The internalization and naturalization of points of reference, which linger on from earlier colonial encounters, consequently limits the discursive space and platform of action for women activists. A small yet growing number of women has courageously and insistently started to unsettle the dichotomy set up by the 'colonial difference' by incorporating women's issues in the 'inner' or 'private' spheres of society (such as violence against women) and also by pointing to the very mechanisms through which parts of western modernity are being appropriated and others rejected and condemned. Consequently, contestations about modernity and its linked discourses of modernization and dependency represent another vantage point from which to consider Egyptian women's activism.

Modernity: the path to emancipation?

The idea that modernization is the framework in which to achieve progress and emancipation has been challenged from various perspectives. Numerous post-modernist critiques have pointed to the dehumanizing aspects of modernization projects of which colonialism presented only one example. Linked to the attempt to reveal atrocities and violations carried out in the name of modernity, there have been systematic and valuable efforts to unsettle universalist discourses and eurocentric scholarship. Within Egypt, challenges to modernity are mainly articulated within Islamist frameworks, which are depicted as presenting the only viable alternative to modernist fallacies.

Egyptian women activists, by and large, do not participate in discussions about the implications of modernity. For the majority, even those who are extremely critical of 'westernization', the process of modernization is accepted as the implicit background for promoting women's equality. Education, economic independence and nuclear families, for example, are seen as aspects of modern life that help to improve the situation of women. In line with my argument about 'cultural difference', the 'modern' is predominantly invoked in relation to the 'outer' or 'public' sphere of social life, while 'traditions' are employed to explain women's position in the 'inner' or 'private' sphere of society, such as the family.

Some women did, however, question the notion of modernity altogether, and pointed to the ways in which local modernizers imposed all-
encompassing and hegemonic discourses on women and minority
groups. These activists have, in most cases, been disillusioned with totalizing frameworks, such as Marxism, for example, and the ways in which
their voices had been subordinated to 'larger truths'. Inherent in their
criticism of hegemonic discourses, which do not allow for different
vantage points, is the rejection of male perspectives as being privileged
and rendered normative. In the same vein they reject the dichotomy of
modern versus traditional, which they see as distorting the complex patterns of traditions, change and innovation and the political developments
they are embedded in.

There is a sense of treading on very slippery ground when entering into
a discussion about modernity and its relation to the West. The question
that arises here revolves around the relation between modernization and
westernization. Are these two processes inextricably linked or do they
have to be analysed as separate developments? In other words, is modern
history characterized by the globalization of western order (Al-Azmeh,
1993: 39), or can we talk about local manifestations of modernity (Abu-
Lughod, 1998b; Miller (ed.), 1995; Sayyid, 1997). It is my contention
that the answer lies somewhere in between these often competing stipulations and, rather than 'either/or' positions, the issue at hand contains
complexity and ambiguity.

In my view one has to distinguish between the way in which certain
ideas and values, such as those associated with the Enlightenment, originally came into being, and the manner in which these ideas developed
and manifested themselves. Here I would like to reiterate Sami Zubaida's
(1994) position that neither the Enlightenment nor notions of liberalism,
rationality, democracy or human rights are inherently western notions.
This is to say that even if these notions have been articulated as foundations and principles of western culture, they actually developed in the
course of bitter and bloody struggles over a long period of time.
Moreover, ideals connected to the Enlightenment and modernity in
general have been far from consistent with the actual practices and politics of western civilizations.

In the past, western powers possessed the economic, military and political might to impose their visions and practices and, perhaps as importantly, the firm belief that their values, ideas and practices constituted the
only possible vantage point. Everything and everyone else was characterized in terms of distance from or proximity to this 'ideal and model
culture'. The United States' grip on economic, military and political
power after the end of the cold war makes the world appear even more

uni-polar than before. But however threatening this presence might be, the 'West' has lost its claim to the sole ownership of modernity. Widespread and expanding transnational movements of capital and people have been paralleled by internal critiques of western versions of modernity and eurocentrism. Displacements, diasporic communities and multiculturalism have to be inscribed in contemporary cartographies in which borders have increasingly been blurred.[3]

If we, as Uma Narayan so eloquently suggested, stop thinking of cultures as 'sealed rooms' it might be easier to conceive of 'travelling modernities' which are in a constant state of transformation and flux. This notion underlies much of the literature that explores 'local modernities' in contexts as diverse as Brazil (Rabinow, 1992), Trinidad (Miller, 1994), Cameroon (Rowlands, 1995) and Russia (Humphrey, 1995), for example. Different kinds of modernity might even coexist within the boundaries of one nation, as Abu-Lughod's analysis of intent, content and reception of American and Egyptian soap operas in Egypt shows (chapter 1). Her work gives evidence to the existence of a 'modernity of poverty' in rural Egypt and among lower-class Egyptians which differs decisively from the modernity of urban middle-class and elite professionals found in metropolitan Cairo. My own research findings among Egyptian women activists parallel Abu-Lughod's in that they showed me how a sense of being modern and/or being traditional is very much linked to patterns of consumption and consumer desires. Some authors, such as Daniel Miller, go as far as to suggest that 'the condition of consumption' represents one possible idiom for larger problems of modernity (Miller (ed.), 1995: 2).[4]

The common conflation of modern and western is paralleled by another misleading equation, namely that of secular and western. In chapter 4, I challenged eurocentric and orientalist conceptualizations that construct Muslim societies as inherently distinct from western societies with respect to their relation to secularism, because of some supposed essential differences between Islam and Christianity. Such a position, I argued, ignores not only the historical developments of secularism and its political contexts but also omits the multifarious and changing manifestations of secularism within western societies (which are

[3] Brah (1996) provides an innovative and illuminating approach to the theme of 'difference' and concepts of culture, identity and nation in the context of increased population movements and diasporic communities.

[4] Making reference to Jürgen Habermas, Miller states that to be a consumer is to possess consciousness that one is living through objects and images *not* of one's own creation (Habermas, quoted in Miller (ed.), 1995: 1; my italics). Forms of consumption also become significant in terms of diversity between peoples and cultures in post-colonial times.

still predominantly Christian but not exclusively so) and Muslim societies. It has been my contention that the question of whether Christianity
is more compatible with secularism than Islam is deeply entangled in
orientalist, colonialist and eurocentric positions, and that it works to reify
religious essences while ignoring social, political and historical realities.
Moreover, the focus on Islamism as an alternative to a western modernity
ignores the continuance and resurgence of religious movements in the
Christian and Jewish world.

Politics without essentialism?

Much recent post-colonial literature oscillates between attempts to stress
commonalities and points of connection between the cultures of the colonized and the colonizers and the celebration of and respect for difference.
Debates about difference and commonality have also been central to contemporary feminist writings, where the unitary category 'woman' – associated with the western white middle class – has been widely challenged
and disrupted. In the light of the recognition that significant differences
exist between women (with respect to ethnicity, class, religious affiliation
and sexual orientation), feminists had to reconceptualize the very subject
of their politics. The dilemma for feminist politics has been articulated by
Kandiyoti (1995: 19–20), who argues that, paradoxically, post-modern,
post-colonial and feminist critiques of modernity and universality have
complicated approaches to cultural difference and legal and ethical
grounds for women's rights by challenging universalist discourses. The
challenge to accommodate diversity without losing any ground for political action has become extremely difficult in the light of the conjuncture of
post-modernist critiques of universalism and post-colonial struggles for
'authenticity'.

A fault line almost inevitably takes shape for anyone simultaneously
committed to a politics of resistance, liberation and independence and a
rejection of essentialist notions of culture, identity and the subject of
emancipation. This conflict cannot be easily resolved and probably constitutes one of the greatest challenges for post-colonial and feminist
thinkers today. There are, however, several strategies available to ease the
tension and bridge over seemingly contradictory endeavours. A starting-
point might be a rethinking of the concept of 'difference', separating it
from the kind of essentialism and boundedness that characterized the
notion of 'colonial difference'. In the context of 'black' and 'white' feminisms, Avtar Brah, for example, argues that these should not be seen as
essentially fixed, oppositional categories, but rather as 'historically contingent fields of contestation within discursive and material practices'

(1996: 95). She points to the interconnectedness of markers of 'difference', such as gender, class, race and sexuality, and stresses the importance of paying attention to the interrelationships between various forms of social differentiation (ibid.: 95–6).

A suggestion along the lines of separating difference from an immanent essentialism has been made by Iris Young in her study called *Justice and the Politics of Difference* (1990). While specifically exploring notions of multiculturalism, individualism and communitarianism, her conceptualization of difference might also be of use in post-colonial and feminist debates:

> Difference now comes to mean not otherness, exclusive opposition, but specificity, variation, heterogeneity. Difference names relations of similarity and dissimilarity that can be reduced to neither coextensive identity or nonoverlapping otherness . . . Difference no longer implies that groups lie outside one another. To say that there are differences among groups does not imply that there are not overlapping experiences, or that two groups have nothing in common. (Young, 1990: 169–71)

On one level, Young's approach to 'difference' can be applied to my analysis of heterogeneity among Egyptian women's groups and activists. It allows for a recognition of particularities and diversities within the secular women's movement, but also leaves space for a common ground from which a politics of solidarity can emerge. On another level the above conceptualization of difference can be translated to characterize the mechanisms of separation, interaction and translation between and within cultures. 'Egyptian culture' undoubtedly contains values, norms and practices distinct from western cultures. At the same time, Egyptian culture has been in contact with western cultures and selectively appropriated certain values and practices. Certainly, neither western culture nor Egyptian culture constitutes an internally homogeneous entity.

Women's experiences and the specific cultures in which these are embedded differ not only cross-culturally, but also within the framework of one society. Within Egypt, for example, diverse social experiences and conditions distinguish educated middle-class women from women of less privileged background. Despite often radically different social conditions, privileged and less privileged women might share some forms of gender oppression, such as those reflected in the Personal Status Law. Likewise, there might exist similar experiences and commonalities between Egyptian and western women, which leads to some degree of overlap between the issues addressed by Egyptian feminists and those addressed by western feminists. For example, Egyptian women may or may not be exposed to the same level of violence against women related to rape and wife battering as in the West. However, Egyptian women do experience various manifestations of violence against women, such as wife battery, FGM, verbal and physical harassment.

My appeal against essentialism in relation to difference does not fully resolve the dilemma of trying not to lose 'the ground' while shaking it. Any reconceptualization of difference, however promising and corrective it might be, does not actually help to eradicate 'difference' as it is constituted and exploited in countless concrete inequalities and injustices which exist all over the world. Indeed, the failure to acknowledge unequal relations between nations, sexes and classes would 'play straight into the hands of the Oppressor' and lead to a 'premature Utopianism' (Eagleton, 1990: 23–4). A political commitment to resist inequalities consequently asks for a critical adherence to some form of narrative with essentialist elements. The notion of 'strategic essentialism' as developed by Gayatri Spivak (1987) might provide a provisional framework from which specific political struggles can be articulated and fought. Bart Moore-Gilbert argues that one of the advantages of strategically seeking shelter in essentialism is that it 'offers the possibility of alliances in a "war of positions" in a way that cultural particularism is reluctant to do'(1997: 202).

The adherence to 'strategic essentialism' can only avoid the pitfalls of prevailing notions of 'essential difference' if it is used with the awareness that it merely constitutes a political means but does not present an 'absolute truth'. Political coalitions between secular Egyptian women activists could be based around a strategic adherence to essentials, not only those related to being a woman and Egyptian – but also essentials pertaining to particular positions, such as promoting secularism and social justice. The category of 'Third World feminist' might, under certain circumstances, also constitute a strategic means to forge alliances with feminists from other non-western societies and counter western feminists' ability to dominate the setting of agendas. And even the notion of 'feminist identity' could be invoked in very specific contexts where strategic alliances with certain western feminists might be viable. Yet whatever 'essentialist shelter' one might have sought, the ultimate goal should not be left out of sight, namely to change the values, discourses and practices through which markers of difference signify markers of inequality.

Bibliography

Abdallah, Ahmed (1985) *The Student Movement and National Politics in Egypt.*
London: Al-Saqi Books
(1994) 'A Case of Compounded Identities', *Al-Ahram Weekly,* 10–17
November
Abdallah, Ahmed (ed.) (1995) *Al-Wa'y Al-Qanuni li Al-Mar'a Al-Misriyya* (The
Legal Awareness of Egyptian Women). Cairo: AMIDEAST and the Arab
Lawyers' Union
Abdel Wahab Al-Afifi, Nadia and Abdel Hadi, Amal (eds.) (1996) *The Feminist
Movement in the Arab World: Interventions and Studies from Four Countries
(Egypt–Palestine–Sudan–Tunisia).* The New Woman's Research and Study
Centre. Cairo: Dar El-Mostaqbal Al-Arabi
Abdel-Kader, Soha (1973) *The Status of Egyptian Women: 1900–1973.* Cairo:
Social Research Center, American University in Cairo
(1987) *Egyptian Women in a Changing Society, 1899–1987.* Boulder and
London: Lynne Rienner Publishers
(1992) *The Situation Analysis of Women in Egypt.* Central Agency for
Population, Mobilization and Statistics. Cairo: CAPMAS and UNICEF
Abrams, Philip (1982) *Historical Sociology.* Ithaca: Cornell University Press
Abu-Lughod, Lila (1986) *Veiled Sentiments: Honor and Poetry in a Bedouin Society.*
Berkeley and Los Angeles: University of California Press
(1990) 'Anthropology's Orient: The Boundaries of Theory on the Arab World',
in Hisham Shirabi (ed.), *Theory, Politics and the Arab World: Critical Responses.*
London and New York: Routledge
(1991) 'Writing against Culture', in R. G. Fox (ed.), *Recapturing Anthropology:
Working in the Present.* Santa Fe: School of American Research Press
(1993a) *Writing Women's Worlds: Bedouin Stories.* Berkeley: University of
California Press
(1993b) 'Finding a Place for Islam: Egyptian Television Serials and the
National Interests', *Public Culture* 5 (3): 493–513
(1995a) 'The Objects of Soap Opera: Egyptian Television and the Cultural
Politics of Modernity', in Miller (ed.), *Worlds Apart*
(1995b) 'Before Post-colonialism', *The Women's Review of Books* 12 (6): 13–14
(1997) 'The Interpretation of Culture(s) after Television', *Representations*
(University of California Press) Summer (59): 109–34
(1998a) 'Feminist Longings and Post-colonial Conditions', in Abu-Lughod
(ed.), *Remaking Women*
(1998b) 'The Marriage of Islamism and Feminism in Egypt: Selective

Repudiation as a Dynamic of Post-colonial Cultural Politics', in Abu-Lughod (ed.), *Remaking Women*

Abu-Lughod, Lila (ed.) (1998) *Remaking Women: Feminism and Modernity in the Middle East.* Princeton: Princeton University Press

Afkhami, Mahnaz (ed.) (1995) *Faith and Freedom: Women's Human Rights in the Muslim World.* London and New York: I. B. Tauris

Afshar, Haleh (1985) 'Women, State and Ideology in Iran', *Third World Quarterly* 7 (2), April: 256–78

Afshar, Haleh (ed.) (1996) *Women and Politics in the Third World.* London and New York: Routledge

Afshar, Haleh and Agarwal, Bina (eds.) (1989) *Women, Poverty and Ideology in Asia: Contradictory Pressures, Uneasy Resolutions.* Basingstoke and London: Macmillan

Ahmad, Ajaz (1992) *In Theory: Classes, Nations, Literatures.* London: Verso
(1995) 'The Politics of Literary Post-coloniality', *Race and Class* 36 (3): 1–20

Ahmed, Akbar S. and Donnan, Hastings (eds.) (1994) *Islam, Globalization and Postmodernity.* London and New York: Routledge

Ahmed, Leila (1982) 'Feminism and Feminist Movements in the Middle East. Preliminary Explorations in Turkey, Egypt, Algeria and the People's Republic of Yemen', in Al-Hibri (ed.), *Women and Islam*
(1992) *Women and Gender and Islam.* New Haven and London: Yale University Press

Al-Ali, Nadje (1994) *Gender Writing – Writing Gender: The Representation of Women in a Selection of Modern Egyptian Literature.* Cairo: American University in Cairo Press
(1997) 'Feminism and Contemporary Debates in Egypt', in Chatty and Rabo (eds.), *Organizing Women*
(forthcoming) '"We are not Feminists"': Egyptian Women Activists on Feminism', in Cynthia Nelson and Shahnaz Rouse (eds.), *Globalization and the Indigenization of Knowledge: Comparative Perspectives.* University Press of Florida

Al-Ali, Nadje and El-Kholy, Heba (1999) 'Inside/Out: The "Native" and the "Halfie" Unsettled', in *Emerging Voices – Cairo Papers in Social Sciences.* Cairo: American University in Cairo Press

Al-'Azm, Sadik J. (1981) 'Orientalism and Orientalism in Reverse', *Khamsin* 8: 5–26

Al-Azmeh, Aziz (1993) *Islams and Modernities.* London and New York: Verso

Al-Bishri, Tareq (1980) *Al-Muslimun wa 'l'Aqbat fi Itar Al-Jama'a Al-Wataniyya* (Muslims and Copts in the Framework of National Collectivity). Cairo: GEBO

Al-Hibri, Azizah (ed.) (1982) *Women and Islam.* Oxford and New York: Pergamon Press

Al-Mar'a Al-Gedida (1986) *Al-Mar'a Al-Gedida* (The New Woman) 2, July
(1988) *Al-Mar'a Al-Gedida* (The New Woman) 3, June

Al-Masri, Sana' (1989) *Khalf Al-Hihab: Mawqif Al-Jama'at Al-Islamyiya min Qadiyyat Al-Mar'a* (Behind the Veil: The Position of Islamist Groups on the Woman's Issue). Cairo: Dar El-Sina

Al-Naquib, Khaldoun H. (1991) *Al-Dawla Al-Tasallutiyya . . .* (The Authoritarian State in the Contemporary Arab East). Beirut: CAUS

Al-Sabaki, Amal Kamel Bayoumi (1987) *Al-Haraka Al-Nissa'iyya fi Misr bayn Al-Thawratayn 1919–1953* (The Women's Movement in Egypt between the Two Revolutions 1919–1953). Cairo: Hay'at Al-Kitab Al-Amaa

Al-Sayyid, Mustapha Kamil (1993) 'A Civil Society in Egypt', *Middle East Journal* 47 (2): 228–42

Alexander, M. Jacqui and Mohanty, Chandra Talpade (1997) *Feminist Genealogies, Colonial Legacies, Democratic Futures.* New York and London: Routledge

Altorki, Soraya and El-Solh, Camillia (eds.) (1988) *Arab Women in the Field: Studying your own Society.* Syracuse: Syracuse University Press

Amin, Hussein A. (1987) *Hawla'l-da'wa ila Tatbiq al-Shari'a* (Discussion about the Demand to Implement the *Shari'a*), 2nd edn. Cairo: Madbouli

Amin, Qasim (1899) *Tahrir Al-Mar'a* (The Emancipation of Women). Cairo: n.p.

   (1900) *Al-Mar'a Al-Jedida* (The New Woman). Cairo: n.p.

Amin, Samir (1978) *The Arab Nation: Nationalism and Class Struggles* (trans.). London: Zed Press

Anderson, Benedict (1983) *Imagined Communities: Reflections on the Origin and Spread of Nationalism.* London: Verso

Anderson, Lisa (1986) *The State and Social Transformation in Tunisia and Libya, 1830–1980.* Princeton: Princeton University Press

   (1987) 'The State in the Middle East and North Africa', *Comparative Politics* 20 (1), October: 1–18

Antonius, Rachad (1994) 'Human Rights and Cultural Specificity: Some Reflections', *Human Rights: Egypt and the Arab World*, PSS 17 (4): 15–23

Arends, Inge (ed.) (1996) *Women and Development in the Middle East: Perspectives of Arab NGOs and Project Participants.* Amsterdam: MERA

Armbrust, Walter (1996) *Mass Culture and Modernism in Egypt.* Cambridge Studies in Social and Cultural Anthropology. Cambridge: Cambridge University Press

Atiya, Nayra (1982) *Khul-Khal: Five Egyptian Women Tell their Stories.* New York and Syracuse: Syracuse University Press

Ayubi, Nazih (1991) *The State and Public Policies in Egypt since Sadat.* Political Studies of the Middle East. Reading: Ithaca Press

   (1995) *Over-stating the Arab State: Politics and Society in the Middle East.* London and New York: I. B. Tauris

Badie, Bertrand (1986) *Les deux états: pouvoir et société en occident et en terre d'Islam* (The Two States: Power and Society in the West and in the Islamic World). Paris: Fayard

Badr, Siham (1968) *Frauensbildung und Frauenbewegung in Ägypten.* Wuppertal, n.p.

Badran, Margot (1988) 'Dual Liberation: Feminism and Nationalism in Egypt, 1870–1925', *Feminist Issues* Spring 8 (1): 15–34

   (1991) 'Competing Agenda: Feminists, Islam and the State in 19th and 20th Century Egypt', in Kandiyoti (ed.), *Women, Islam and the State*

   (1993) 'Independent Women: More than a Century of Feminism in Egypt', in Tucker (ed.), *Arab Women*

236   Bibliography

(1994) 'Gender Activism: Feminists and Islamists in Egypt', in Moghadam (ed.), *Identity Politics and Women*

(1995) *Feminists, Islam, and Nation: Gender and the Making of Modern Egypt.* Princeton: Princeton University Press

Badran, Margot and Cooke, Miriam (eds.) (1990) *Opening the Gates: A Century of Arab Feminist Writing.* London: Virago

Bahiy Al-Din, Amira (1994) 'Al-Tamyeez Did Al-Mar'a Fi Qanun Al-Uqubat: Dirassa Awwaliyya' (Discrimination against Women in the Criminal Code: A Preliminary Study), unpublished paper

(1995) 'Wad'e Al-Mar'a Al-Qanuni fi Qanun Al-Ahwal Al-Shakhsiyya' (The Legal Position of Women in the Personal Status Law), in Abdallah (ed.) *Al-Wa'y Al-Qanuni*

Baker, Raymond William (1978) *Egypt's Uncertain Revolution under Nasser and Sadat.* Cambridge, Mass. and London: Harvard University Press

(1990) *Sadat and After: Struggles for Egypt's Political Soul.* London: I. B. Tauris

Baron, Beth (1981) 'Unveiling in Early Twentieth Century Egypt: Practical and Symbolic Considerations', *Middle Eastern Studies* 3: 370–86

(1993) 'The Construction of National Honour in Egypt', *Gender and History* 5 (2): 244–55

(1994) *The Women's Awakening in Egypt: Culture, Society and the Press.* New Haven and London: Yale University Press

(1997) 'Nationalist Iconography: Egypt as a Woman', in Jankowski and Gershoni (eds.), *Rethinking Nationalism*

Barrett, Michèle and Philips, Anne (eds.) (1992) *Destabilizing Theory: Contemporary Feminist Debates.* Cambridge: Polity Press

Basu, Amrita (ed.) (1995) *The Challenge of Local Feminisms: Women's Movements in Global Perspective.* Boulder, San Francisco and Oxford: Westview Press

Beattie, Kirk J. (1994) *Egypt during the Nasser Years: Ideology, Politics, and Civil Society.* Boulder, San Francisco and Oxford: Westview Press

Beck, Louis and Keddie, Nikki (eds.) (1978) *Women in the Muslim World.* Cambridge, Mass. and London: Harvard University Press

Beinin, Joel (1987) 'The Communist Movement and Nationalist Political Discourse in Nasirist Egypt', *Middle East Journal* 41 (4) Autumn: 568–84

(1993) 'The Egyptian Regime and the Left: Between Islamism and Secularism', *MERIP*, November–December: 25

Beinin, Joel and Stork, Joe (eds.) (1997) *Political Islam: Essays from Middle East Report.* Berkeley and Los Angeles: University of California Press

Berger, P. and Luckmann, T. (1967) *The Social Construction of Reality: A Treatise in the Sociology of Knowledge.* London: Cox & Wyman Ltd

Berque, Jacques (1972) *Egypt: Imperialism and Revolution.* London: Faber

Bhaba, Homi (1990) *Nation and Narration.* New York: Routledge

(1994) *The Location of Culture.* London and New York: Routledge

(1995) 'On Subaltern Secularism', *WAF – Women against Fundamentalism* 6: 5–7

Bibars, Iman (1987) 'Women's Political Interest Groups in Egypt', unpublished Master's thesis presented to the Economics and Political Science Department, American University in Cairo

(1999) 'Om Saber, Shadia and My Self: The Power Relationship between the

Researcher and the Researched', in *Emerging Voices – Cairo Papers in Social Science*. Cairo: American University in Cairo Press

Bill, James A. and Springborg, Robert (1990) *Politics in the Middle East*, 3rd edn. New York: HarperCollins

Binder, Leonard (1980) 'The Failure of the Egyptian Left', *Asian and African Studies* 14: 20–34

Bint Al-Ard (1987) *Bint Al-Ard* (Daughter of Land) 3, July

(1993) *Bint Al-Ard* (Daughter of Land) 8, January

Boserup, Ester (1989) *Woman's Role in Economic Development*, 2nd edn. London: Earthscan Publications

Botman, Salma (1987) 'Women's Participation in Radical Egyptian Politics 1939–1952', in *Women in the Middle East – Khamsin*. London and New York: Zed Books

Bouatta, Cherifa and Cherifati-Merabtine, Doria (1994) 'The Social Representation of Women in Algeria's Islamist Movement', in Moghadam (ed.), *Identity Politics and Women*

Bowen, Donna Lee and Evelyn Early (eds.) (1993) *Everyday Life in the Muslim Middle East*. Bloomington: Indiana University Press

Brah, Avtar (1996) *Cartographies of Diaspora: Contesting Identities*. London and New York: Routledge

Burke, Edmund (ed.) (1993) *Struggle and Survival in the Modern Middle East*. Bloomington: Indiana University Press

Butler, Judith (1993) *Bodies that Matter*. London and New York: Routledge

Butler, Judith and Scott, Joan W. (eds.) (1992) *Feminists Theorize the Political*. New York and London: Routledge

Calhoun, Craig (ed.) (1994) *Social Theory and the Politics of Identity*. Oxford and Cambridge, Mass.: Blackwell

Carrier, James (ed.) (1995) *Occidentalism: Images of the West*. Oxford: Clarendon Press

Carroll, W. K. (1992) *Organizing Dissent: Contemporary Social Movements in Theory and Practice*. Toronto: Garamond Press

Carter, B. L. (1986) *The Copts in Egyptian Politics (1918–1952)*. Cairo: American University in Cairo Press

Chambers, Iain and Curti, Lidia (eds.) (1996) *The Post-colonial Question: Common Skies, Divided Horizons*. London and New York: Routledge

Chapman, Audrey and Haggag Youssef, Nadia (1977) 'Egypt: From Seclusion to Limited Participation', in Giele and Smock (eds.), *Women: Role and Status in Eight Countries*

Charles, Nikki and Hughes-Freeland, F. (eds.) (1996) *Practising Feminism: Identity, Difference, Power*. London and New York: Routledge

Chatterjee, Partha (1986) *Nationalist Thought and the Colonial World: A Derivative Discourse*. London: Zed/UN University

(1989) 'The Nationalist Resolution in the Women's Question', in Sangari and Vaid (eds.), *Recasting Women*

(1993) *The Nation and its Fragments: Colonial and Postcolonial Histories*. Princeton: Princeton University Press

Chatty, Dawn and Rabo, Annika (1997) 'Formal and Informal Groups in the Middle East', in Chatty and Rabo (eds.), *Organizing Women*

Chatty, Dawn and Rabo, Annika (eds.) (1997) *Organizing Women: Formal and Informal Groups in the Middle East.* Oxford and New York: Berg

Chemais, Amina (1987) 'Obstacles Hindering Moslem Women from Obtaining a Divorce in Egypt' (monograph). Egypt: UNICEF

Chhachhi, Amrita (1991) 'Forced Identities: The State, Communalism, Fundamentalism and Women in India', in Kandiyoti (ed.), *Women, Islam and the State*

Clifford, James and Marcus, George (eds.) (1986) *Writing Culture.* Berkeley: University of California Press

Cohen, A. (ed.) (1974) *Urban Ethnicity.* London: Tavistock Publishers

Cole, Juan Ricardo (1981) 'Feminism, Class and Islam in Turn-of-the-century Egypt', *International Journal of Middle East Studies* 13: 387–407

Cole, Juan Ricardo (ed.) (1992) *Comparing Muslim Societies: Knowledge and the State in a World Civilization.* Ann Arbor: University of Michigan Press

Communication Group for the Enhancement of the Status of Women in Egypt (1992) *Legal Rights of Egyptian Women in Theory and Practice.* Cairo: Dar El-Kutub

Connell, Robert W. (1990) 'The State, Gender and Sexual Politics: Theory and Appraisal', *Theory and Society* 9 (5), October: 507–45

Coury, Ralph M. (1982) 'Who "Invented" Egyptian Arab Nationalism?', part 1, *International Journal of Middle East Studies*, 14, part 1: 249–81; part 2: 459–79

Crone, Patricia (1980) *Slaves on Horses: The Evolution of the Islamic Polity.* Cambridge: Cambridge University Press

Crone, Patricia and Hinds, Martin (1986) *God's Caliph: Religious Authority in the First Centuries of Islam.* Cambridge: Cambridge University Press

Dallmayr, Fred (1990) *Beyond Orientalism: Essays on Cross-cultural Encounter.* Albany: State University of New York Press

Derrida, Jacques (1981) *Positions.* Chicago: University of Chicago Press

Dirlik, A. (1992) 'The Postcolonial Aura: Third World Criticism in the Age of Global Capitalism', *Critical Inquiry*, Winter 1992

Dominguez, Virginia R. (1994) 'Differentiating Women/Bodies of Knowledge', *American Anthropologist* 1: 127–30

Dube, Leela, Leacock, Eleanor and Ardner, Shirley (eds.) (1986) *Visibility and Power: Essays on Women in Society and Development.* Oxford and New York: Oxford University Press

Durkheim, Emile (1954) *The Elementary Forms of Religious Life.* New York: Free Press

(1960) 'The Dualism of Human Nature and its Social Conditions', in K. H. Wolff (ed.), *Emile Durkheim 1858–1917.* Columbus: Ohio University Press

Dwyer, Kevin (1991) *Arab Voices: The Human Rights Debate in the Middle East.* London and New York: Routledge

Eagleton, Terry (1990) 'Nationalism: Irony and Commitment', in Terry Eagleton (ed.), *Nationalism, Colonialism and Literature.* Minnesota: University of Minnesota Press

Early, Evelyn (1985) 'Catharsis and Creation: The Everyday Narratives of Baladi Women of Cairo', *Anthropological Quarterly* 58 (4): 172–81

(1993) *Baladi Women of Cairo: Playing with an Egg and a Stone.* Boulder and London: Lynne Rienner Publishers

Eickelman, Dale F. (1989) *The Middle East: An Anthropological Approach*, 2nd edn. Englewoods Cliffs: Prentice Hall

(1997) 'Muslim Politics: The Prospects for Democracy in North Africa and the Middle East', in Entelis (ed.), *Islam, Democracy, and the State*

Eisenstein, Zillah R. (ed.) (1979) *Capitalist Patriarchy and the Case for Socialist Feminism.* New York and London: Monthly Review Press

El-Baz, Shahida (1992) 'Makanat Al-Mar'a Al-Misriyah fi Al-Mugtama'a' (The Status of the Egyptian Woman in Society), *Al-Ahram* daily, Cairo, 14 March

(1997) 'The Impact of Social and Economic Factors on Women's Group Formation in Egypt', in Chatty and Rabo (eds.), *Organizing Women*

El-Feki, Moustafa (1991) *Copts in Egyptian Politics.* Cairo: General Egyptian Book Organization

El-Gawhary, Karim (1994) 'An Interview with Heba Ra'uf Ezzat', *MERIP*, November–December: 26–7

El-Guindy, Fadwa (1981) 'Veiling Infitah with Muslim Ethic: Egypt's Contemporary Islamic Movement', *Social Problems* 28 (4): 465–85

(1983) 'Veiled Activism: Egyptian Women in the Contemporary Islamic Movement', *Peuples Méditerranéens* 22–3, January–June: 79–89

El-Kholy, Heba (1994) Unpublished paper given at a panel discussion on women-headed households, International Conference on Population and Development, Cairo

(1997) '"The Education of a Girl is a Treasure": Gender and Politics in Low-income Cairo', occasional paper. Cairo: Population Council, Regional Office for West Asia and North Africa

(1998) 'Defiance and Compliance: Negotiating Gender in Low-income Cairo', unpublished Ph.D. dissertation, School of Oriental and African Studies, London

El-Messiri, Sawsan (1978) *Ibn Al-Balad: A Concept of Egyptian Identity.* Leiden: E. J. Brill

El-Sa'dawi, Nawal (1971) *Al-Mar'a wa Al-Jins* (Woman and Sex). Cairo: n.p.

(1988) 'The Political Challenges Facing Arab Women at the End of the 20th Century', in Toubia (ed.), *Women of the Arab World*

(1993) 'Women's Resistance in the Arab World and in Egypt', in Haleh Afshar (ed.), *Women in the Middle East.* London: Macmillan

El-Sadda, Hoda (1996) 'From Arabic into English: The Politics of Translation in a Post-colonial Context', unpublished paper given at seminar in Cairo University

El-Solh, Camillia F. and Mabro, Judy (eds.) (1994) *Muslim Women's Choices: Religious Belief and Social Reality.* Oxford: Berg

Elias, Norbert (1978) *The Civilising Process.* Oxford: Blackwell

Entelis, John P. (ed.) (1997) *Islam, Democracy, and the State in North Africa.* Bloomington and Indianapolis: Indiana University Press

Erlich, Haggai (1989) *Students and University in 20th Century Egyptian Politics.* London: Frank Cass

Esposito, John L. (1992) *The Islamic Threat: Myth or Reality.* Oxford and New York: Oxford University Press

Faludi, Susan (1992) *Backlash: The Undeclared War against Women.* London: Vintage

Fanon, Frantz (1952) *Black Skin, White Mask* (trans. Charles Lam Markman). London: McGibbon & Kee
(1961) *The Wretched of the Earth* (trans. Constance Farrington). Harmonsworth: Penguin
Farah, Nadia R. (1986) *Religious Strife in Egypt: Crisis and Ideological Conflict in the Seventies.* New York, London, Paris, Montreux and Tokyo: Gordon & Breach Science Publishers
(1994) 'Women in Egypt: A Literature Review', unpublished paper. Cairo: UNICEF
Ferguson, Margaret and Wicke, Jennifer (eds.) (1994) *Feminism and Postmodernism.* Durham, N.C. and London: Duke University Press
Fernea, Elizabeth and Bezirgan, Basima Qattan (eds.) (1977) *Middle Eastern Women Speak.* Austin: University of Texas Press
FGM Task Force (1997a) 'Outlook and Activity Guidelines'. Cairo (September)
(1997b) 'FGM Task Force: Position Paper'. Cairo (December)
Flores, Alexander (1988) 'Egypt: A New Secularism?', *MERIP*, July–August: 27–30
(1993) 'Secularism, Integralism and Political Islam: The Egyptian Debate', *MERIP*, July–August: 32–8
Fluehr-Lobban, Carolyn (1988) 'The Political Mobilization of Women in the Arab World', in Jane Smith (ed.), *Women in Contemporary Muslim Societies.* London: Associated University Press
Foda, Farag A. (1986) *Al-Haqqiqa Al-Gha'iba* (The Absent Truth). Cairo and Paris: Dar Al-Fikr
(1987) *Hiwar Haula-l-'Almaniyyah* (Dialogue about Secularism). Cairo: Al-Mahrousa
Forster, Peter G. (1972) 'Secularization in the English Context: Some Conceptual and Empirical Problems', *Sociological Review* 20 (2): 153–68
Fox, R. G. (ed.) (1990) *Nationalist Ideologies and the Production of National Cultures.* Arlington: American Anthropological Association
Fraser, Nancy and Nicholson, Linda J. (1990) 'Social Criticism without Philosophy: An Encounter between Feminism and Postmodernism', in Nicholson (ed.), *Feminism/Postmodernism*
Friedman, Jonathan (1994) *Cultural Identity and Global Process.* London: Sage Publications
Gallagher, Nancy (1989) 'Islam v. Secularism in Cairo: An Account of the Dar Al-Hikma Debate', *Middle Eastern Studies* 25 (2), April: 208–15
Geertz, Clifford (1988) *Works and Lives: The Anthropologist as Author.* Stanford: Stanford University Press
Gellner, Ernest (1983a) *Muslim Society.* Cambridge: Cambridge University Press
(1983b) *Nations and Nationalism.* Oxford: Basil Blackwell
(1991) 'Tribalism and the State in the Middle East', in Philip S. Khoury and Joseph Kostiner (eds.), *Tribes and State Formation in the Middle East.* London and New York: I. B. Tauris
(1994) 'Foreword', in Ahmed and Donnan (eds.), *Islam, Globalization and Postmodernity*
Gerholm, Thomas and Lithman, Yngve G. (eds.) (1990) *The New Islamic Presence in Western Europe.* London: Mansell

Ghoussoub, Mai (1985) 'Feminism – or the Eternal Masculine – in the Arab World', *New Left Review* 161: 3–18

Giddens, Anthony (1979) *Central Problems in Social Theory: Action, Structure and Contradiction in Social Analysis.* Basingstoke and London: Macmillan
(1984) *The Constitution of Society.* Berkeley: University of California Press

Giele, J. and Smock, A. (eds.) (1977) *Women: Role and Status in Eight Countries.* New York: John Wiley & Sons

Gluck, Sherna Berger and Patai, Daphne (eds.) (1991) *Women's Words: The Feminist Practice of Oral History.* London and New York: Routledge

Göle, Nilüfer (1997) 'Secularism and Islamism in Turkey: The Making of Elites and Counter-elites', *Middle East Journal* 51 (1), Winter: 46–58

Graham-Brown, Sarah (1981) 'Feminism in Egypt: A Conversation with Nawal Sadaawi', *MERIP Report* 95: 24–7

Graham-Brown, Sarah, Hill, Enid and Kamal Eldin, Amany (1985) 'After Jehan's Law: A New Battle over Women's Rights', *The Middle East* 129: 17–21

Gramsci, Antonio (1978) *Selections from Political Writings 1921–1926* (trans.). London: Lawrence & Wishart

Griffin, Christine (1996) 'Experiencing Power: Dimensions of Gender, "Race" and Class', in Charles and Hughes-Freeland (eds.), *Practising Feminism*

Haddad, Yvonne (1984) 'Islam, Women and Revolution in Twentieth-century Arab Thought', *The Muslim World* 74: 160

Hale, Sondra (1991) 'Feminist Method, Process, and Self-criticism: Interviewing Sudanese Women', in Gluck and Patai (eds.) *Women's Words*

Hall, Stuart (1992) *Modernity and its Futures.* Cambridge: Open University Press
(1996a) 'When was the 'Postcolonial'? Thinking at the Limit', in Chambers and Curti (eds.), *The Post-colonial Question*
(1996b) 'Introduction: Who Needs 'Identity'?', in Hall and du Gay (eds.), *Questions of Cultural Identity*

Hall, Stuart and du Gay, Paul (eds.) (1996) *Questions of Cultural Identity.* London, Thousand Oaks and New Delhi: Sage Publications

Halliday, Fred (1994) 'The Politics of Islamic Fundamentalism: Iran, Tunisia and the Challenge to the Secular State', in Ahmed and Donnan (eds.) *Islam, Globalization and Postmodernity*

Halliday, Fred and Alavi, Hamza (eds.) (1988) *State and Ideology in the Middle East and Pakistan.* London: Macmillan Education

Hamdan, Gamal (1980–4) *Shakhsiyyat Misr: Dirasa fi 'Abariyyat Al-Makan* (The Personality of Egypt: A Study in the Genius of Place). Cairo: Madbouli

Hammoudi, Abdellah (1993) *The Victim and its Masks: An Essay on Sacrifice and Masquerade in the Maghreb.* Chicago: University of Chicago Press

Hanna, Milad (1989) *The Seven Pillars of Egyptian Identity.* Cairo: Dar El-Kutub

Haraway, Donna (1988) 'Situated Knowledges: The Science Question in Feminism and the Privilege of the Partial Perspective', *Feminist Studies* 14: 575–99

Harding, Sandra (1991) *Whose Science? Whose Knowledge? Thinking from Women's Lives.* Ithaca: Cornell University Press

Harding, Sandra (ed.) (1987) *Feminism and Methodology.* Bloomington and Indianapolis: Indiana University Press

Harman, Chris (1992) 'The Return of the National Question', *International Socialism* 56: 3–61

Hartman, Heidi (1979) 'Capitalism, Patriarchy and Job Segregation', in Eisenstein (ed.), *Capitalist Patriarchy and the Case for Socialist Feminism*

Hastrup, Kirsten (1992) 'Writing Ethnography: State of the Art', in Okely and Callaway (eds.), *Anthropology and Autobiography*

Hatem, Mervat (1986) 'The Enduring Alliance of Nationalism and Patriarchy in Muslim Personal Status Laws: The Case of Modern Egypt', *Feminist Issues* 6 (1): 19–43

(1992) 'Economic and Political Liberation in Egypt and the Demise of State Feminism', *International Journal of Middle East Studies* 24: 231–51

(1993) 'Toward the Development of Post-Islamist and Post-nationalist Feminist Discourses in the Middle East', in Tucker (ed.), *Arab Women*

(1994) 'Egyptian Discourses on Gender and Political Liberalization: Do Secularist and Islamist Views Really Differ?', *Middle East Journal* 48 (4), Autumn: 661–76

Hawley, John C. (ed.) (1998) *The Postcolonial Crescent: Islam's Impact on Contemporary Literature*. Baltimore: Peter Lang Publications

Hekman, Susan (1997) 'Truth and Method: Feminist Standpoint Theory Revisited', *Signs: Journal of Women in Culture in Society* 22 (2): 341–65

Hill Collins, Patricia (1991) *Black Feminist Thought: Knowledge, Consciousness and the Politics of Empowerment*. Boston: Unwin Hyman

Hobsbawm, Eric (1990) *Nations and Nationalism since 1780*. Cambridge: Cambridge University Press

Hobsbawm, E. and Ranger, T. (1983) *The Invention of Tradition*. Cambridge: Cambridge University Press

hooks, bell (1990) *Yearning: Race, Gender and Cultural Politics*. Boston: South End Press

Hopwood, Derek (1991) *Egypt: Politics and Society 1945–1984*, 2nd edn. London: Allen & Unwin

Hourani, Albert (1962) *Arabic Thought in the Liberal Age, 1789–1939*, 1st edn. Cambridge: Cambridge University Press

(1983) *Arabic Thought in the Liberal Age, 1789–1939*, 2nd edn. Cambridge: Cambridge University Press

(1991) *A History of the Arab People*. London: Faber & Faber

Howard-Merriam, Kathleen (1990) 'Guaranteed Seats for Political Representation of Women: The Egyptian Example', *Women and Politics* 10 (1): 17–42

Huizer, Gerrit (1986) 'Women in Resistance and Research: Potential against Power?', in Dube et al. (eds.) *Visibility and Power*

Humphrey, C. (1995) 'Creating a Culture of Disillusionment: Consumption in Moscow, a Chronicle of Changing Times', in Miller (ed.), *Worlds Apart*

Hussain, 'Adel (1996) 'National Culture: An Islamic Perspective', paper presented at 'Egypt Today: State, Society and Regional Role', University of Manchester, 16–19 May

Hussein, Nasser (1990) 'Hyphenated Identity: Nationality Discourse, History, and the Anxiety of Criticism in Salman Rushdie's *Shame*', *Qui Parle?* Summer

Ibrahim, Barbara (1982) 'Family Strategies: A Perspective on Women's Entry to the Labor Force in Egypt', *International Journal of Sociology of the Family*, December

Ibrahim, Saad Eddin (1988) 'Egypt's Islamic Activism in the 1980's', *Third World Quarterly* 10 (2): 632–57

(1995) 'Civil Society and Prospects for Democratization in the Arab World', in Norton (ed.), *Civil Society in the Middle East*, I

(1996) 'Egyptian Law 32 on Egypt's Private Sector Organizations: A Critical Assessment', Ibn Khaldoun Working Paper no. 3. Cairo: Ibn Khaldoun Centre for Development Studies

Ibrahim, Saad Eddin (ed.) (1988) *Society and State in the Arab World*. Amman: Arab Thought Forum

(1993) *Al-Mujtama' Al-Madani* . . . (Civil Society and Democratic Transformation in the Arab Homeland: The Annual Report). Cairo: Markaz Ibn Khaldoun

Jackson, Michael (ed.) (1996) *Things as they Are: New Directions in Phenomenological Anthropology*. Bloomington and Indianapolis: Indiana University Press

Jankowski, J. P. (1986a) 'Nationalism in Twentieth Century Egypt', in M. Curtis (ed.), *The Middle East Reader*. New Brunswick: Transaction Books

(1986b) 'The Egyptian WAFD and Arab Nationalism, 1918–1944', *National and International Politics in the Middle East* 4 (34): 164–86

(1997) 'Arab Nationalism in "Nasserism" and Egyptian State Policy, 1952–1958', in Jankowski and Gershoni (eds.), *Rethinking Nationalism*

Jankowski, James and Gershoni, Israel (eds.) (1997) *Rethinking Nationalism in the Arab Middle East*. New York: Columbia University Press

Jayawardena, Kumari (1986) *Feminism and Nationalism in the Third World*. London and New York: Zed Books

(1995) *The White Woman's Other Burden: Western Women and South Asia during British Rule*. New York and London: Routledge

John, Mary E. (1996) *Discrepant Dislocations: Feminism, Theory and Postcolonial Histories*. Berkeley, Los Angeles and London: University of California Press

Joseph, Suad (1993) 'Gender and Civil Society', *MERIP* 183: 22–6

Kabbani, Rana (1986) *Europe's Myths of Orient*. London: Macmillan

Kandiyoti, Deniz (1991) 'Identity and its Discontents: Women and the Nation', *Millenium* 20 (3): 429–43

(1995) 'Reflections on the Politics of Gender in Muslim Societies: From Nairobi to Beijing', in Afkhami (ed.), *Faith and Freedom*

(1996) 'Contemporary Feminist Scholarship and Middle East Studies', in Kandiyoti (ed.), *Gendering the Middle East*

Kandiyoti, Deniz (ed.) (1991) *Women, Islam and the State*. Philadelphia: Temple University Press

(1996) *Gendering the Middle East: Emerging Perspectives*. London and New York: I. B. Tauris

Kaplan, Gisela (1992) *Contemporary Western European Feminism*. London: UCL Press, Allen & Unwin

Karam, Azza (1993) '"Fundamentalism", "Modernity" and Women's Groups in

Egypt: Activist Women's Realities'. Occasional Paper no. 20, December. Amsterdam: MERA

(1994) 'Gender in Egypt: Between Islamism, Feminism and the State, Perspectives of Some Women Activists', *Vena Journal: Gender, the Family and the State* 6 (10), June: 41–7

(1996) 'An Apostate, a Proposed New Marriage Contract and Egyptian Women: Where To Now?', *WAF – Women against Fundamentalism* 8: 29–31

(1998) *Women, Islamisms and the State: Contemporary Feminisms in Egypt.* London: Macmillan; New York: St Martin's Press

Karas, Shawky (1985) *The Copts since the Arab Invasion: Strangers in their Land.* Jersey City: American, Canadian and Australian Coptic Associations

Keddie, Nikki (1988) 'Ideology, Society and the State in Post-colonial Muslim Societies', in Halliday and Alavi (eds.), *State and Ideology in the Middle East and Pakistan*

(1997) 'Secularism and the State: Towards Clarity and Global Comparison', *New Left Review* 226, November/December: 21–40

Kedourie, Elie (1960) *Nationalism.* London: Hutchinson & Co.

(1992) *Democracy and Arab Political Culture.* Washington, D.C.: Washington Institute for Near East Policy

Kepel, Gilles (1985) *The Prophet and Pharaoh: Muslim Extremism in Egypt.* London: Al-Saqi Books

Khalifa, Ijlal (1973) *Al-Haraka Al-Nissa'iyya Al-Haditha* (The Modern Women's Movement). Cairo: Dar El-Kutub

Khalil, Samir (1989) *Republic of Fear: The Politics of Modern Iraq.* London: Hutchinson Press

Khater, Akram (1987) 'Egypt's Feminism', *The Middle East*, February: 17–18

Khater, Akram and Nelson, Cynthia (1988) 'Al-Haraka Al-Nissa'iya: The Women's Movement and Political Participation in Modern Egypt', *Women's Studies International Forum* 11 (5): 465–83

Khuri, Fuad (1980) *Tribe and State in Bahrain: The Transformation of Social and Political Authority in an Arab State.* Chicago: Chicago University Press

Kohn, Hans (1955) *Nationalism, its Meaning and History.* Princeton: Princeton University Press

Kramer, Martin (ed.) (1991) *Middle Eastern Lives: The Practice of Biography and Self-narrative.* Syracuse: Syracuse University Press

Laclau, Ernesto (1990) *New Reflections on the Revolution of our Time.* London: Verso

Larrain, Jorge (1994) *Ideology and Cultural Identity: Modernity and the Third World Presence.* Cambridge: Polity Press

Lash, Scott and Friedman, Jonathan (eds.) (1992) *Modernity and Identity.* Oxford and Cambridge, Mass.: Blackwell

Lazreg, Marnia (1988) 'Feminism and Difference: The Perils of Writing as a Woman in Algeria', *Feminist Studies* 14 (1): 81–107

(1994) *The Eloquence of Silence: Algerian Women in Question.* New York and London: Routledge

Lewis, Philip (1994) *Islamic Britain: Religion, Politics and Identity among British Muslims: Bradford in the 1990's.* London and New York: I. B. Tauris

Lewis, Reina (1996) *Gendering Orientalism: Race, Femininity and Representation*. London and New York: Routledge

Lindholm, Charles (1995) 'The New Middle Eastern Ethnography', *Journal of the Anthropological Institute* 1 (4): 805–20

Lindisfarne, Nancy (1997) 'Local Voices and Responsible Anthropology', in Stolcke (ed.), *Reassessing Anthropological Responsibility*

Longino, Helen (1993) 'Feminist Standpoint Theory and the Problems of Knowledge', *Signs: Journal of Women and Culture in Society* 19: 201–12

Ma 'an–Markaz Dirasat Al-Mar'a (1995) *Ma 'an*, October (in Arabic)

Macleod, Arlene Elowe (1991) *Accommodating Protest: Working Women, the New Veiling, and Change in Cairo*. New York: Columbia University Press

Maiello, Amedeo (1996) 'Ethnic Conflict in Post-colonial India', in Chambers and Curti (eds.), *The Post-colonial Question*

Mannheim, Karl (1952) 'The Problems of Generations', in Karl Mannheim, *Essays on the Sociology of Knowledge*. New York: Oxford University Press

Markaz Dirasat Al-Mar'a Al-Gedida (1993a) *Al-Mar'a wa Al-Unf* (Women and Violence), special issue of *Al-Mar'a Al-Gedida* (The New Woman), 5

(1993b) *Al-Mar'a wa Al-A'lam* (Women and the Media), special issue of *Al-Mar'a Al-Gedida* (The New Woman), 6

(1995) *Al-Mar'a wa Al-'Aml* (Women and Work), special issue of *Al-Mar'a Al-Gedida* (The New Woman), 7

Marsot, Afaf Lutfi al-Sayyid (1978) 'The Revolutionary Gentlewoman in Egypt', in Beck and Keddie (eds.), *Women in the Muslim World*

Marty, Martin E. and Appleby, R. Scott (1991) (eds.) *Fundamentalisms Observed*. Chicago and London: University of Chicago Press

Marx, Karl (1959) *Economic and Philosophical Manuscripts of 1844*. London: Lawrence & Wishart

(1962) 'The 18th Brumaire of Louis Bonaparte', in *Selected Works. Karl Marx and Frederick Engels*. Moscow: Foreign Languages Publishing House

Mayer, Ann Elizabeth (1995) 'Rhetorical Strategies and Official Policies on Women's Rights: The Merits and Drawbacks of the New World Hypocrisy', in Afkhami (ed.), *Faith and Freedom*

McClintock, A. (1992) 'The Myth of Progress: Pitfalls of the Term Post-colonialism', *Social Text* 31/32

McDermott, Anthony (1988) *Egypt from Nasser to Mubarak: A Flawed Revolution*. London, New York and Sydney: Croom Helm

Meijer, Roland (1995) 'The Quest for Modernity: Secular Liberal and Left-wing Political Thought in Egypt, 1945–58', unpublished Ph.D. dissertation, Institute for Near Eastern and Islamic Studies, University of Amsterdam

Merleau-Ponty, Maurice (1962) *Phenomenology of Perception* (trans. C. Smith). London: Routledge

Merton, Robert K. (1957) *Social Theory and Social Structure*. Glencoe, Ill.: Free Press

Messick, Brinley (1993) *The Calligraphic State: Textual Domination and History in a Muslim Society*. Berkeley: University of California Press

Mies, Maria, Bennholdt-Thomsen, Veronika and von Werlhof, Claudia (eds.) (1988) *Women: The Last Colony*. London and New York: Zed Books

Migdal, Joel S. (1988) *Strong Societies and Weak States: State–Society Relations and State Capabilities in the Third World.* Princeton: Princeton University Press

Miller, Daniel (1994) *Modernity – An Ethnographic Approach: Dualism and Mass Consumption in Trinidad.* Oxford and Providence: Berg

Miller, Daniel (ed.) (1995) *Worlds Apart: Modernity through the Prism of the Local.* London and New York: Routledge

Mitchell, Timothy (1988) *Colonising Egypt.* Cambridge: Cambridge University Press

—— (1991) 'America's Egypt: Discourse and Development Industry', *MERIP* 169, March–April: 18–33

Mitchell, Timothy and Abu-Lughod, Lila (1993) 'Questions of Modernity', *Items* 47 (4): 79–83

Moghadam, Valentine M. (1993) *Modernizing Women: Gender and Social Change in the Middle East.* Boulder and London: Lynne Rienner Publishers

—— (1994) 'Reform, Revolution and Reaction: The Trajectory of the "Woman Question" in Afghanistan', in Moghadam (ed.), *Gender and National Identity*

Moghadam, Valentine (ed.) (1994a) *Gender and National Identity: Women and Politics in Muslim Societies.* London and New York: Zed Books; Karachi: Oxford University Press

—— (1994b) *Identity Politics and Women: Cultural Reassertions and Feminisms in International Perspective.* Boulder, San Francisco and Oxford: Westview Press

Mohanty, Chandra Talpade (1988) 'Under Western Eyes: Feminist Scholarship and Colonial Discourses', *Feminist Review* 30, Autumn: 65–88

Mohanty, Chandra Talpade, Russo, Ann and Torres, Lourdes (1991) *Third World Women and the Politics of Feminism.* Bloomington and Indianapolis: Indiana University Press

Molyneux, Maxine (1998) 'Analysing Women's Movements', *Development and Change* 29: 219–45

Moore, Henrietta (1988) *Feminism and Anthropology.* Minneapolis: University of Minnesota Press

—— (1994) *A Passion for Difference.* Cambridge: Polity Press

Moore-Gilbert, Bart (1997) *Postcolonial Theory: Contexts, Practices, Politics.* London and New York: Verso

Morsy, Soheir, Nelson, Cynthia, Saad, Reem and Sholkamy, Hania (1991) 'Anthropology and the Call for Indigenization of Social Science in the Arab World', in E. L. Sullivan and J. S. Ismael (eds.), *Contemporary Studies of the Arab World.* Edmonton: University of Alberta Press

Munson, Henry (1988) *Islam and Revolution in the Middle East.* New Haven and London: Yale University Press

—— (1993) *Religion and Power in Morocco.* New Haven: Yale University Press

Myrdal, Gunter (1968) *Asian Drama: An Enquiry into the Poverty of Nations,* I–III. Harmondsworth: Penguin

Narayan, Uma (1997) *Dislocating Cultures: Identities, Traditions and Third World Feminism.* New York and London: Routledge

National NGO Committee for Population and Development (NCPD) (Gender Equity Subcommittee) (1995) *The Road from Cairo to Beijing.* Cairo: Dar El-Thaqqafa Press

Nederveen, Pieterse and Parekh, Bikhu (1995) *The Decolonization of Imagination: Culture, Knowledge and Power.* London and New York: Zed Books

Nelson, Cynthia (1984) 'Islamic Tradition and Women's Education: The Egyptian Experience', in Sandra Hacker et al. (eds.), *World Yearbook of Education: Women and Education.* New York: Nicholar Publishing

(1986) 'The Voices of Doria Shafik: Feminist Consciousness in Egypt, 1940–1960', *Feminist Issues*, Fall: 15–31

(1988) 'An Anthropologist's Dilemma: Fieldwork and Interpretive Inquiry', *Alif* 8: 53–65

(1992) 'Biography and Women's History: On Interpreting Doria Shafik', in Nikki Keddie and Beth Baron (eds.), *Women in Middle Eastern History: Shifting Boundaries in Sex and Gender.* New Haven and London: Yale University Press

(1996) *Doria Shafik: Egyptian Feminist – A Woman Apart.* Cairo: American University in Cairo Press

(1998) 'Feminist Expression as Self-identity and Cultural Critique: The Discourse of Doria Shafik', in Hawley (ed.), *The Postcolonial Crescent*

Nelson, C. and Grossberg, L. (eds.) (1988) *Marxism and the Interpretation of Culture.* Urbana: University of Illinois Press

NGOs' position paper on the draft Law of Associations (1998): 'Defending the Autonomy of Civil Associations' 27 May (http://chrla.org/ngolaw/position.htm)

Nicholson, Linda J. (ed.) (1990) *Feminism/Postmodernism.* New York and London: Routledge

Norton, Augustus Richard (1993) 'The Future of Civil Society in the Middle East', *Middle East Journal* 47 (2): 205–16

Norton, Augustus Richard (ed.) (1995) *Civil Society in the Middle East.* Leiden, New York and Cologne: E. J. Brill, 2 vols.

Oakley, Ann (1981) 'Interviewing Women: A Contradiction in Terms', in Helen Roberts (ed.), *Doing Feminist Research.* London: Routledge & Kegan Paul

Okely, Judith (1992) 'Anthropology and Autobiography: Participatory Experience and Embodied Knowledge', in Okely and Callaway (eds.), *Anthropology and Autobiography*

Okely, Judith and Callaway, Helen (eds.) (1992) *Anthropology and Autobiography.* London and New York: Routledge

Owen, Roger (1992) *State, Power and Politics in the Making of the Modern Middle East.* London: Routledge

Paidar, Parvin (1995) *Women and the Political Process in Twentieth-century Iran.* Cambridge Middle East Studies. Cambridge: Cambridge University Press

(1996) 'Feminism and Islam in Iran', in Kandiyoti (ed.), *Gendering the Middle East*

Papanek, Hanna (1994) 'The Ideal Woman and the Ideal Society: Control and Autonomy in the Construction of Identity', in Moghadam (ed.), *Identity Politics and Women*

Parker, Andrew, Russo, Mary, Sommer, Doris and Yaeger, Patricia (eds.) (1992) *Nationalisms and Sexualities.* New York and London: Routledge

Patai, Daphne (1991) 'US Academics and Third World Women: Is Ethical Research Possible?', in Gluck and Patai (eds.), *Women's Words*

Pateman, Carole (1989) *The Disorder of Women*. Cambridge: Polity

Peters, Julie and Wolper, Andrea (eds.) (1995) *Women's Rights, Human Rights: International Feminist Perspectives*. New York and London: Routledge

Philipp, Thomas (1978) 'Feminism and Nationalist Politics in Egypt', in Beck and Keddie (eds.), *Women in the Muslim World*

——— (1988) 'Nation State and Religious Community in Egypt – the Continuing Debate', *Die Welt des Islam* 28: 378–91

Pipes, Daniel (1983) *In the Path of God: Islam and Political Power*. New York: Basic Books

——— (1992) 'Fundamental Questions about Muslims', *Wall Street Journal*, 30 October

Piscatori, James P. (1986) *Islam in a World of Nation-States*. Cambridge and New York: Cambridge University Press. Published in Association with the Royal Institute of International Affairs

Prakash, Gyan (1990) 'Writing Post-orientalist Histories of the Third World: Perspectives from Indian Historiography', *Comparative Studies in Society and History* 32 (2): 383–408

——— (1995) 'Introduction: After Colonialism', in Prakash (ed.), *After Colonialism*

Prakash, Gyan (ed.) (1995) *After Colonialism: Imperial Histories and Postcolonial Displacements*. Princeton: Princeton University Press

Pringle, Rosemary and Watson, Sophie (1992) ' 'Women's Interests' and the Post-structuralist State', in Barrett and Philips (eds.), *Destabilizing Theory*

Rabinow, Paul (1992) 'A Modern Tour in Brazil', in Lash and Friedman (eds.), *Modernity and Identity*

Radhakrishnan, R. (1992) 'Nationalism, Gender, and the Narrative of Identity', in Parker et al. (eds.), *Nationalisms and Sexualities*

Radwan, Zeinab (1982) *Bahth Zahirat Al-Hijab bain Al-Jami'iyat* (A Study of the Phenomenon of the Veil among Female Students). Cairo: National Centre for Sociological and Criminological Research

Rai, Shirin (1996) 'Women and the State in the Third World', in Rai and Lievesley (eds.), *Women and the State*

Rai, Shirin M. and Lievesley, Geraldine (1996) 'Introduction', in Ray and Lievesley (eds.), *Women and the State*

Rai, Shirin M. and Lievesley, Geraldine (eds.) (1996) *Women and the State: International Perspectives*. London: Taylor & Francis

Rattansi, Ali (1997) 'Postcolonialism and its Discontents', *Economy and Society* 26 (4), November: 480–500

Reinharz, Shulamit (1992) *Feminist Methods in Social Research*. New York and Oxford: Oxford University Press

Robins, Kevin (1996) 'Interrupting Identities: Turkey/Europe', in Hall and du Gay (eds.), *Questions of Cultural Identity*

Rossiter, Ann (1992) ' "Between the Devil and the Deep Blue Sea": Irish Women, Catholicism and Colonialism', in Saghal and Yuval-Davis (eds.), *Refusing Holy Orders*

Rowlands, C. (1995) 'Inconsistent Temporalities in a Nation-state', in Miller (ed.), *Worlds Apart*

Rugh, Andrea (1979) 'Coping with Poverty in a Cairo Community', *Cairo Papers in Social Science*, 2 (1). Cairo: Social Research Center, American University in Cairo

(1985) *Family in Contemporary Egypt*. Cairo: American University in Cairo Press

Saad, Reem (1988) 'Social History of an Agrarian Reform Community', *Cairo Papers in Social Science*, 11 (4) (monograph)

(1997) ''Ceci n'est pas la femme égyptienne!': L'Egypte entre représentations occidentales et discours nationaliste', *Egypte/Monde Arabe* 30–1

(1998) 'Shame, Reputation and Egypt's Lovers: A Controversy over the Nation's Image', *Visual Anthropology* 10 (2–4)

Sacks, Karen Brodkin (1989) 'What's a Life Story got to do with it?', in Personal Narratives Group (eds.), *Interpreting Women's Lives: Feminist Theory and Personal Narratives*. Bloomington and Indianapolis: Indiana University Press

Sadowski, Yahya (1997) 'The New Orientalism and the Democracy Debate', in Beinin and Stork (eds.), *Political Islam*

Saghal, Gita (1992) 'Secular Spaces: The Experience of Asian Women Organizing', in Saghal and Yuval-Davis (eds.), *Refusing Holy Orders*

Saghal, Gita and Yuval-Davis, Nira (1992) 'Introduction: Fundamentalism, Multiculturalism and Women in Britain', in Saghal and Yuval-Davis (eds.), *Refusing Holy Orders*

Saghal, Gita and Yuval-Davis, Nira (eds.) (1992) *Refusing Holy Orders: Women and Fundamentalism in Britain*. London: Virago Press

Sagiv, David (1992) 'Judge Ashmawi and Militant Islam in Egypt', *Middle Eastern Studies* 28 (2), July: 531–46

Said, Edward (1978) *Orientalism*. New York: Random Books

(1993) *Culture and Imperialism*. London: Vintage

Sangari, Kumkum and Vaid, Sudesh (eds.) (1990) *Recasting Women: Essays in Indian Colonial History*. New Brunswick: Rutgers University Press

Sayigh, Rosemary (1996) 'Researching Gender in a Palestinian Camp: Political, Theoretical and Methodological Questions', in Kandiyoti (ed.), *Gendering the Middle East*

Sayyid, Bobby S. (1997) *A Fundamental Fear: Eurocentrism and the Emergence of Islamism*. London and New York: Zed Books

Schick, Irvin Cemil (1990) 'Representing Middle Eastern Women: Feminism and Colonial Discourse', *Feminist Studies* 16 (2): 345–79

Schlesinger, P. (1987) 'On National Identity: Some Conceptions and Misconceptions Criticized', *Social Science Information* 26 (2): 219–64

Schutz, Alfred and Luckmann, Thomas (1989) *The Structures of the Life-World*, II (trans. R. M. Zaner and D. J. Parent). Evanston: Northwestern University Press

Scott, Joan. W (1992) 'Experience', in Butler and Scott (eds.), *Feminists Theorize the Political*

Sedgwick, Eve Kosofsky (1992) 'Nationalism and Sexualities in the Age of Wilde', in Parker et al. (eds.), *Nationalisms and Sexualities*

Seif El-Dawla, Aida (1996) 'Women's Rights in Egypt', *WAF – Women against Fundamentalism* 8: 25–8

Seif El-Dawla, Aida and Ibrahim, Somaya (1995) 'Ägyptische Frauenorganizationen auf dem Weg von Kairo nach Peking: Historischer Überblick', *Feministische Studien*, 13. Jahrgang, May, 1: 113–18

Sen, Gita and Groven, Caren (1988) *Development, Crises and Alternative Visions: Third World Women's Perspectives*. London: Earthscan Publishers

Shafik, Doria (with Abdou, Ibrahim) (1955) *Al-Mar'a Al-Misriyah min Al-Faraunah ila Al-Yawm* (The Egyptian Woman from the Pharaohs until Today). Cairo: Matba'at Misr

Shohat, Ella (1992) 'Notes on the Postcolonial', *Social Text* 31/32

Sholkamy, Hania (1996) *Women's Health Perceptions: A Necessary Approach to Understanding Health and Well-Being*. Monograph in Reproductive Health no. 2, Reproductive Health Working Group. Cairo: Population Council, Regional Office for West Asia and North Africa

——— (1999) 'The Un-addressed Problems of Qualitative Researchers in Egypt', in *Emerging Voices – Cairo Papers in Social Science*. Cairo: American University in Cairo

Shukrallah, Hala (1994) 'The Impact of the Islamic Movement in Egypt', *Feminist Review* 47: 15–32

Sid-Ahmed, Mohammed (1982) 'The Masses Speak the Language of Religion to Express themselves Politically', interview with Mohammed Sid-Ahmed in *MERIP Reports*, January: 18–23

——— (1998) article in *Al-Ahram Weekly*, 28 September

Singerman, Diane (1995) *Avenues of Participation: Family, Politics and Networks in Urban Quarters of Cairo*. Princeton: Princeton University Press

Smith, Antony D. (1971) *Theories of Nationalism*. New York, Evanston, San Francisco and London: Harper Torchbooks

——— (1976) *Nationalist Movements*. London and Basingstoke: Macmillan

Smith, Dorothy (1987) *The Everyday World as Problematic: A Feminist Sociology*. Boston: Northeastern University Press

Spivak, Gayatri (1987) *In Other Worlds: Essays in Cultural Politics*. New York: Methuen

——— (1988) 'Can the Subaltern Speak?', in Nelson and Grossberg (eds.), *Marxism and the Interpretation of Culture*

Stolcke, Verena (ed.) (1997) *Reassessing Anthropological Responsibility*. London and New York: Routledge

Stowasser, Barbara Freyer (ed.) (1987) *The Islamic Impulse*. London and Sydney: Croom Helm (in association with the Center for Contemporary Arab Studies, Georgetown University, Washington, D.C.)

Strathern, Marilyn (1987a) 'An Awkward Relationship: The Case of Feminism and Anthropology', *Signs: Journal of Women in Culture and Society* 12 (2): 276–92

——— (1987b) 'Out of Context: The Persuasive Fictions of Anthropology', *Current Anthropology* 28 (3): 251–82

Sullivan, Denis J. (1994) *Private Voluntary Organizations in Egypt: Islamic Development, Private Initiative, and State Control*. Gainesville: University Press of Florida

Sullivan, Earl (1987) *Women in Egyptian Public Life*. Cairo: American University in Cairo Press

Tadros, Marlyn (1998) *Rightless Women, Heartless Men: Egyptian Women and*

Domestic Violence. Cairo: Legal Research and Resource Center for Human Rights

Tapper, Richard and Tapper, Nancy (1987) '"Thank God we're Secular!" Aspects of Fundamentalism in a Turkish Town', in Lionel Caplan (ed.), *Studies in Religious Fundamentalism*. London: Macmillan

Tavakoli-Targhi, Mohamad (1994) 'Women of the West Imagined: The *Farangi* Other and the Emergence of the Woman Question in Iran', in Moghadam (ed.), *Identity Politics and Women*

Tignor, Robert (1966) *Colonial Modernization and British Rule in Egypt, 1882–1914*. Princeton: Princeton University Press

Toubia, Nahid (ed.) (1988) *Women of the Arab World: The Coming Challenge*. London and New York: Zed Books

Trinh T, Min-ha (1991) *When the Moon Waxes Red*. New York: Routledge

Tripp, Charles (ed.) (1993) *Contemporary Egypt: Through Egyptian Eyes*. London and New York: Routledge

Tucker, Judith (ed.) (1993) *Arab Women: Old Boundaries – New Frontiers*. Bloomington and Indianapolis: Indiana University Press

Turner, Bryan (1994) *Orientalism, Postmodernism and Globalism*. London and New York: Routledge

Vatikiotis, P. J. (1983) 'Religion and the State', in Warburg and Kupferschmidt (eds.), *Islam, Nationalism and Radicalism*

—— (1987) *Islam and the State*. London: Croom Helm

—— (1991) *The History of Modern Egypt: From Muhammad Ali to Mubarak*, 4th edn. London: Weidenfeld & Nicolson

Vickers, Jeanne (1991) *Women and the World Economic Crisis*. London and New York: Zed Books

Visweswaran, Kamala (1994) *Fictions of Feminist Ethnography*. Minneapolis and London: University of Minnesota Press

Warburg, G. R. and Kupferschmidt, U. M. (eds.) (1983) *Islam, Nationalism and Radicalism in Egypt and the Sudan*. New York: Praeger

Wassef, Nadia (1998). *Da Min Zaman: Munadharat Al-Madi wa Al-Muhadar hawl Al-Tashawiyya Al-Jins lil-Inath fi Misr* (Da Min Zaman: Past and Present Discourse on Female Genital Mutilation). NCPD, FGM Task Force and Friedrich Ebert Stiftung

—— (forthcoming) 'Female Genital Mutilation: An Ongoing Violation of Egyptian Women's Reproductive Health and Rights', in *Beyond Bejing, towards the Year 2000: Political Strategies of Women's Organizations in Selected Mediterranean Countries*. Proceedings of the Regional Seminar (9–11 June 1998)

Waterbury, John (1985) 'The "Soft" State and the Open Door: Egypt's Experience with Economic Liberalization, 1974–1984', *Comparative Politics* 18 (1): 65–83

Watson, Helen (1992) *Women in the City of the Dead*. London: Hurst & Co.

Weber, Max (1930) *The Protestant Ethic and the Spirit of Capitalism* (trans. T. Parsons). London: George Allen & Unwin

—— (1949) *The Methodology of the Social Sciences* (ed. and trans. E. Shils and F. Finsh). New York: Free Press

Wiebke, W. (1981) *Women in Islam – From Medieval to Modern Times*. Princeton and New York: Markus Wiener Publishing

Wikan, Uni (1980) *Life among the Poor in Cairo* (trans. Ann Henning). London: Tavistock Publications

Wright, Marcia (1986) '"Women in Peril": Reconsiderations of Biography, Autobiography and Life Stories of Some African Women with Special Reference to Marriage', paper presented at conference on Autobiographies, Biographies and Life Histories of Women: Interdisciplinary Perspectives, University of Minnesota, 23 May

Young, Iris Marion (1990) *Justice and the Politics of Difference*. Princeton: Princeton University Press

Yuval-Davis, Nira (1991) 'The Citizenship Debate: Women, the State and Ethnic Processes', *Feminist Review* 39: 58–68

(1992) 'Jewish Fundamentalism and Women's Empowerment', in Saghal and Yuval-Davis (eds.), *Refusing Holy Orders*

(1997) *Gender and Nation*. London, Thousand Oaks and New Delhi: Sage Publications

Yuval-Davis, Nira and Anthias, Floya (1989) 'Introduction', in Yuval-Davis and Anthias (eds.), *Woman – Nation – State*

Yuval-Davis, Nira and Anthias, Floya (eds.) (1989) *Woman – Nation – State*. Basingstoke and London: Macmillan

Zakariyya, Fu'ad (1989) *Al-Sahwa Al-Islamiyya Fi Mizan Al-'Aql* (The Islamic Revival from a Rational Perspective). Cairo: Dar al-Fikr

Zaki, Moheb (1995) *Civil Society and Democratization in Egypt, 1981–1994*. Cairo: Dar El-Kutub

Zubaida, Sami (1988) 'Islam, Cultural Nationalism and the Left', *Review of Middle East Studies* 4: 7

(1989) 'Nations: Old and New. Comments on Antony D. Smith's "The Myth of the 'Modern Nation' and the Myths of Nations"', paper presented at the Anthropology Seminar Series, University College London

(1992) 'Islam, the State and Democracy: Contrasting Conceptions of Society in Egypt', *MERIP*, November–December: 2–10

(1993) *Islam, the People and the State: Political Ideas and Movements in the Middle East*, 2nd edn. London: I. B. Tauris

(1994) 'Human Rights and Cultural Difference: Middle Eastern Perspectives', *New Perspectives on Turkey* 10, Spring: 1–12

Zuhur, Sherifa (1992) *Revealing Reveiling: Islamist Gender Ideology in Contemporary Egypt*. Albany: State University of New York Press

Zulificar, Mona (1993) *The Egyptian Woman in a Changing World*. Cairo: New Civic Forum

(1995a) *Women in Development: A Legal Study*. Cairo: UNICEF

(1995b) 'Wad'e Al-Mar'a Al-Misriyya Fi Daw'ah Al-Ittifaqiyya Al-Dawliyya lil Qada' 'ala Kafat Ashkal Al-Tamyeez did al-Mar'a' (The Position of Egyptian Women in Light of the International Convention for the Elimination of All Forms of Discrimination against Women), in Abdallah (ed.), *Al-Wa'y Al-Qanuni*

Zureik, Elia (1981) 'Theoretical Considerations for a Sociological Study of the Arab State', *Arab Studies Quarterly* 3 (3), Autumn: 229–57

Index

Other books in the series